The Essential Literacy Workshop Book
10 Complete Early Childhood Training Modules
By Holly Seplocha, Judy Jablon, and Janis Strasser

Acknowledgments

This project was inspired by our prior classroom teaching experiences; our work training thousands of early childhood teachers, mentors, supervisors, and administrators; and our university graduate and undergraduate teaching. We chose to focus on literacy as it permeates all classroom teaching and experiences.

We owe special thanks to Ellen Frede and Ellen Wolock of the New Jersey Department of Education, Office of Early Childhood Education, for inspiring the foundational work in literacy for the preschool and kindergarten children in New Jersey's poorest school districts.

We are indebted to Isabel Baker and her staff at The Book Vine who provided assistance in developing our recommended booklist.

As authors and teacher educators, we gratefully acknowledge the input and suggestions of New Jersey's Abbott early childhood supervisors, master teachers, and participating preschool and kindergarten teachers, and the input and ideas from the New Jersey Early Learning Assessment System (ELAS) trainers from New Jersey City University, Rutgers University, William Paterson University, and the staff of the New Jersey Department of Education, Office of Early Childhood Education.

We also would like to recognize and thank Mary DeBlasio and the Early Learning Improvement Consortium (ELIC) staff of William Paterson University, Cindy Gennarelli, Nancy Janow, and Charlotte Stetson for their invaluable help. We extend appreciation to the children and families who shared their writing samples. And, of course, a special thanks to our supportive spouses, Robert, Andrew, and Robby.

We cannot end without thanking Kathy Charner and the staff at Gryphon House who helped us share our ideas with other educators.

A Gryphon House Guide
for Professional Development

The Essential
Literacy
WORKSHOP
BOOK

10 Complete
Early Childhood
Training Modules

e CD-ROM includes:
owerPoint presentations
andouts for participants
verheads

Holly Seplocha
Judy Jablon
Janis Strasser

Copyright

© 2007 Holly Seplocha, Judy Jablon, and Janis Strasser
Printed in the United States of America.

Published by Gryphon House, Inc.
10726 Tucker Street, Beltsville, MD 20705
301.595.9500; 301.595.0051 (fax); 800.638.0928 (toll-free)

Visit us on the web at www.ghbooks.com

Library of Congress Cataloging-in-Publication Data

Seplocha, Holly.
  The essential literacy workshop book / Holly Seplocha, Judy R. Jablon, Janis Strasser.
       p. cm.
  ISBN-13: 978-0-87659-059-1
  1. Early childhood teachers--In-service training--United States. 2. Language arts (Early childhood)--United States. I. Jablon, Judy R. II. Strasser, Janis. III. Title.
  LB1775.6.S46 2007
  372.6--dc22

                              2006102861

Green Press Initiative

Gryphon House is a member of the Green Press Initiative, a nonprofit program dedicated to supporting publishers in their efforts to reduce their use of fiber sourced forests. For further information visit www.greenpressinitiative.org.

Bulk Purchase

Gryphon House books are available for special premiums and sales promotions as well as for fundraising use. Special editions or book excerpts also can be created to specification. For details, contact the Director of Marketing at Gryphon House.

Table of Contents

Keys to Effective Training

The purpose of this introduction is to provide information and guidance to individuals who train early childhood teachers, whether center-based, school-based, or in higher education.

Regardless of the specific training ideas and strategies you use from the Workshop Sessions, your enthusiasm and commitment to developmentally appropriate practices and to helping teachers grow are key to effective training. Your passion for supporting all aspects of children's literacy development, your belief that effective engagement is critical to good teaching, and your patience with teachers as they struggle to figure out how to integrate literacy in all ways every day in their classrooms and to improve their teaching and learning will make or break the success of your training.

Remember…We are all in this on behalf of the children!

The Basics of Good Training

Many factors go into making workshops successful. First, be clear about the desired outcomes and essential messages you want participants to take away from the workshop. This book outlines specific outcomes for every workshop, as well as essential messages. Read through each module carefully and take ownership of the essential messages for each workshop.

Second, it is important to be knowledgeable. The content of these workshops is "best practices" in early childhood, with a focus on early literacy. This book provides detailed information about content as well as specific resources for each workshop.

Finally, knowing how to shape a workshop determines how much participants will learn from what you are teaching. When planning your workshop, it is important to:
1. Know adult learners.
2. Establish a positive climate.
3. Promote engagement and positive group dynamics.

Know Adult Learners

Knowing the learner is a key principle in developmentally appropriate practice. In planning workshops for adults, tune into characteristics of adult learners, their different learning styles, and what motivates them to learn.

Characteristics: Research has identified the following characteristics of adult learners.

- Adult learners bring a wide range of personal and professional experiences to each new learning situation.
- Adult learners are goal-oriented; they want to solve problems relevant to their professional setting.
- Adult learners are a valuable resource to one another; sharing experiences should be a central part of workshops.
- Adult learners lead busy lives; their time must be respected.
- Adult learners often have fixed viewpoints and entrenched habits; it takes time, patience, and a supportive environment to unlearn behaviors.
- Adult learners are affected by the aging process, and age affects memory, recall, and energy level.
- Adult learners need to be self-directing; they want to make decisions about what and how they learn, who they sit with, and the extent to which they will take in new information.
- Adult learners need to be treated with dignity and respect; they do not want to be treated like children or asked to perform meaningless tasks.

Learning styles: Everybody takes in and processes information in different ways. Providing variety and choice in the workshop ensures that you respond to different learning styles. Three categories of learning styles are:

- **Visual:** Visual learners take in information best when it is written out, diagrammed, or charted. Visual learners like pictures and videos. They do better with written rather than verbal directions. PowerPoint presentations or overhead slides are key for visual learners.
- **Auditory:** Auditory learners take in information by hearing things that are spoken. They are likely to appreciate small- and large-group discussion, lectures, storytelling, and good speakers. Some like music, while others are distracted by environmental sounds. Speaking clearly and slowly with an even pace, as well as varying your tone as you speak assists auditory learners.
- **Kinesthetic:** Kinesthetic learners take in information through movement, touching, and feeling. They learn best by acting out scenarios, manipulating objects, and playing games. When these characteristics are respected and appreciated in workshops, participants are more likely to be motivated to participate actively. Many of the activities in the sessions will help kinesthetic learners act on the knowledge to understand the essential messages.

Motivators: Learning does not just happen in the head, it also happens in the heart. Factors that affect motivation in adult learners include the following:

- Adult learners want social relationships; they want to interact with others, to feel respected and appreciated by others, and to nurture friendships.
- Adult learners have external expectations; they want to fulfill the expectations or recommendations of someone with formal authority.
- Adult learners are interested in social welfare; they want to provide service to the community.

- Adult learners are interested in personal advancement; they want to achieve higher job status and greater job security.
- Adult learners want an escape/stimulation; they want to relieve boredom and experience a break in the routine of home or work.
- Adult learners have intellectual interests; they want to learn for the sake of learning.

Strategies: The following list of strategies can help you get to know participants and to show respect and appreciation for who they are as adult learners with diverse learning styles.

- Make positive connections with participants.
- Learn and use participants' names.
- Ask open-ended questions.
- Listen to participants.
- Learn about and from participants.
- Circulate among participants (during activities, during break, and after lunch) and make individual connections through informal conversations with them.
- Learn about participants' interests and strengths.
- Observe and respond to participants' affect and facial expressions.
- Ensure that the content is relevant to participants' needs.
- Adjust content on the spot.
- Foster meaningful discussions (encourage them to talk, make large-group discussions lively, and so on).
- Debrief participants in interesting ways.
- Energize the group (alter a negative or low mood).
- Model respect and appreciation.
- Invite many responses.
- Allow wait time. Pause (and count silently to 10 or 20) after you ask a question.
- Suggest that participants reflect on what they learned and jot down their thoughts.
- Make comments such as, "All ideas are welcome, valid, and appreciated."
- Ask for elaboration.
- Try to avoid vague replies such as, "Great idea" or "Not exactly."
- Chart participants' ideas to validate them and for future reference.
- Make links to comments by referring back to a participant's comment, for example, when it relates to comments you are making later in the presentation.
- Pay attention to the clues participants give you about their level of understanding.
- Ask questions such as, "Does this make sense?" "What do you think about what (Ann) just said?"
- Add comments such as, "I can tell from your nods that this resonates for many of you," or "Is everyone clear about this? Do you need to hear this again?"
- Say, "Please say more about what you mean" or "Help me understand" if you need help understanding a question or comment. Or you might say, "Tell me if I understand you correctly," and then paraphrase what he or she said.
- Ask for a "headline" if an idea is too wordy or vague.

Creating a positive climate has enormous benefits: participants relax, speak up, collaborate more productively with colleagues, and ultimately establish trusting relationships with you and others.

■ ■

Establish a Positive Climate

The *climate* is the mood or tone of the workshop. As mentioned earlier, social relationships are a key motivator for adult learners. The mood of the workshop affects participation. Creating a positive climate has enormous benefits: participants relax, speak up, collaborate more productively with colleagues, and ultimately establish trusting relationships with you and others. Many of the strategies defined on the previous page help to establish a positive climate for learning in the workshop. Seating arrangements and a pleasant environment can help to establish a positive climate for learning.

Seating arrangements: An interactive workshop allows participants to talk easily to each other in small groups and to share as a whole group. Participants can see audiovisual materials and hear you easily. Conference-style tables, round tables, or tables in a "U" shape foster comfortable discussion. Sometimes you have little control over the room arrangement. In this case, acknowledge this situation with participants and ask them if they have suggestions for increased comfort.

Creating a pleasant environment: Space to hang charts produced during the workshop is key. It is a way to convey the message that the learning taking place is important and valued. One suggestion for hanging charts is to pick a starting point and then continue to hang charts clockwise throughout the day. This way, when summarizing the day, you can begin with the first chart and review the charts from left to right.

Having common materials on tables, such as markers, Post-its, pens, and even candy in bins or baskets, sends a message that the group is a community of learners and that you have provided them with tools for learning. Some trainers drape swatches of fabric on tables for color. Others bring a vase of flowers. Creating a pleasant ambience affects the tone of the workshop.

Try to tune into the temperature and lighting in the room. If possible, open curtains or blinds for at least part of the time. A dark environment makes people sleepy. The temperature of the room is often out of your control, but if there is a thermostat, ask the participants to take charge of it.

Other ideas that contribute to creating a pleasant environment for learning include using music during arrival and at breaks, providing snacks, and making sure that your presentation table stays tidy throughout the day.

Having common materials on tables, such as markers, Post-its, pens, and even candy in bins or baskets, sends a message that the group is a community of learners and that you have provided them with tools for learning.

Promote Engagement and Positive Group Dynamics

Pay attention to details throughout the day, from the first moment participants arrive until they leave at the end of the workshop. Keep in mind the following to help ensure that things go smoothly.

- Set ground rules. Take a few minutes at the beginning of the day to establish shared expectations for behavior.
- Plan diverse learning activities. Make sure you incorporate a wide range of learning activities throughout the workshop so all participants are engaged regardless of their learning styles.
- Include energizers and movement opportunities. No one likes to sit all day, especially teachers! Use gallery walks, round-robin brainstorming, and walk-and-talks to get everyone up and moving (see Appendix E, Glossary of Training Terms). When participants' energy seems low, do a quick energizer such as stretching, singing a song, or taking a quick walk around the room.
- Make interesting charts. Use at least two colors on each chart if you want everyone to read the charts. Include and underline titles on all charts.
- Manage time and space. As facilitator, you are responsible for ensuring that the group begins and ends on time, that lunch and breaks occur when promised, and that everyone can see and be heard. You can enlist helpers among participants and use a timer.
- Wrap up the day. Be sure to end the day with closure. This does not mean just filling out the evaluation. Each workshop includes a closing activity that lasts about 10–15 minutes that is an opportunity to summarize key ideas. The impression at the end of the workshop will determine how participants return the next time.
- Handle questions well. Emphasize that questions are a positive thing. Sometimes they may appear negative but appearances are not necessarily accurate. The following are a few guidelines for responding to questions.
    - Prepare! Part of getting ready for a presentation is imagining the questions you might be asked and preparing useful responses.
    - It is okay if there are no questions at all! Allow a moment or two of silence. Then, if there are no questions, restate the key idea one final time.
    - Be a good listener. Stay calm, listen to the whole question, use good eye contact, and nod your understanding.
    - Allow yourself time to think before you reply. Do not feel that you have to answer right away—allow yourself a beat or two of silence.
    - Keep your answers direct and clear.
    - Once the question has been asked, present your answer to the whole group, not just to the questioner.
    - Diffuse hostility by acknowledging feelings. Then answer the question directly.
    - Repeat the question to make sure you understood it and to allow the whole group to hear it.
    - Acknowledge statements, then redirect back to the questions. "Thank you for bringing that up. Are there any other questions?"

- Do not be led off topic. Put off-topic questions or issues in the "parking lot" (see Appendix E, Glossary of Training Terms). For example, you might say, "That's a really interesting area that would benefit from more discussion time. Please put it in the parking lot (write it on a separate piece of chart paper labeled the "Parking Lot."). If we have time, we can get back to it. Right now, I would like to see if there are any more questions about…"
- Close the session by going back to the key idea(s). Do not let the last thing they hear be someone else's question.
- If you do not know the answer to a question, state comfortably that you will find out the answer for the questioner. No one is an expert on everything.

Planning Training

The primary purpose of staff development is to enhance teachers' skills to support children's learning.

This book offers 10 workshops addressing various components of literacy that provide early childhood teachers with numerous techniques and ideas to enhance literacy learning in the classroom. Workshops are also appropriate for use with paraprofessionals, college students, and pre-service classroom staff. Content and strategies are appropriate for classroom staff working in a childcare center, preschool, or kindergarten. One workshop is specifically for kindergarten teachers, recognizing the increased emphasis on literacy and the use of literacy centers or language arts blocks in kindergarten. Begin the sequence of topics selected with Workshop 1: Fostering Language Development. This forms the basis for understanding how children grow in language and the role of the teacher in facilitating this development.

Each workshop is designed for a 3-hour format and includes various active learning and small group activities. You may implement a portion of a session in a shorter time frame by holding back some content and its related activity for a later session. The sessions can be adapted easily to accommodate 1 hour, 1.5 hour, 2 hour, or 2.5 hour frameworks. This allows you to select the necessary depth based on need and time constraints and to combine topics based on length of session. Workshops can also be split or extended. In addition, activities can be split between sessions or added to others. (Suggested agendas for shorter workshops are in Appendix F, Sample Agendas for Each Workshop with Shorter Time Frames, pages 318-330.)

We do not recommend a one-shot approach to training but rather encourage a sustained effort over time.

Because schools and districts vary in formats and time for professional development, keep the following in mind.
- Plan to begin training early (summer whenever possible, and in-service training prior to the start of the school year).
- Space training over the school year to allow teachers time to implement and use what they are learning.

- Have no more than 40 participants in any workshop to allow for adequate interaction, participation, and processing. Whenever possible, limit group size to 20–25.
- Have two trainers for groups of more than 25 or for full-day workshops if you are combining two workshop sessions in one day. Two trainers are preferred when possible.
- Arrange for space for training and establish a calendar of training dates.
- Review the training topics and agendas for each of the 10 literacy topics. This book provides information, suggested materials, and activities for a total of 30 hours of training on literacy.
- Select appropriate topics and duration based on prior training and needs with knowledge of and input from participants. For example, if all of the children are English speaking, do not select the Supporting English Language Learners session. If the group is kindergarten teachers, select the session titled Using Literacy Centers in Kindergarten.

Teachers benefit from ongoing support and follow-up to implement effective literacy practices and integrate their new learning into their teaching. They need time to reflect and discuss their observations and documentation, successes and questions from trying new ideas, and to hear and learn from each other. Follow-up support and feedback is needed to ensure that misconceptions are uncovered and to help teachers consolidate their understandings and application to practice.

Prior to Implementing a Workshop

1. Read the entire text for the workshop several times to familiarize yourself with the content and activities.
2. Read through appropriate chapters in the reference books mentioned to give you more solid background information.
3. Gather materials necessary for the workshop activities.
4. Make necessary additions to the agenda, which can be found at the beginning of each handout section and on the accompanying CD. Include your name, date, school, or district information.
5. Print and make copies of the agenda for the participants.
6. Pull necessary handouts for the workshop based on the time allotted and activities selected.
7. If you do not have access to PowerPoint for the workshop, copy overhead sheets onto transparencies. If the workshop is to be a shorter time frame, print only handouts and overheads needed for the topics and activities you plan to use.
8. Read through the text for the workshop again and make any personal notes necessary for the presentation.
9. Gather any materials needed for creating a pleasant environment.

How This Book Is Organized

At the beginning of each of the 10 workshops you will find information on how to organize each workshop and what to say and do. In addition, there are reproducible masters of overheads and handouts. Files for handouts for each workshop are also on the accompanying CD. Hard copies of PowerPoint slides are presented in the appendix and are available on the accompanying CD. The following information is included for each workshop.

Title of the session

Suggested time frame: All workshops are formatted for a three-hour workshop. Times are provided for each section of the training to assist you in organizing the session. The times will help you know when to schedule a 15-minute break, or to how to reduce or extend the session based on time available.

Handout list: A list of the handouts is provided. Make copies for each participant. Electronic files of the handouts are included on the accompanying CD.

Workshop objectives: Expected participant outcomes.

Workshop materials: Items necessary to present the workshop.

Supplemental resources: This includes resources for the trainer who may need to refresh his or her background content knowledge on the topic prior to the workshop or for those trainers who would like to enhance their own understanding of the topic. They may also be considered suggestions for supports to enhance the workshop.

Essential messages: These are the big ideas of the session, the key points to reiterate and focus on during your presentation.

Opening activity: This is an icebreaker or warm-up activity to begin the session. Opening activities have been designed to motivate and frame the topic for the session.

Welcome and logistics: Introduce yourself, distribute the agenda, review objectives, and discuss logistics (such as break times, where bathrooms are, and so on). Review ground rules.
- Be respectful of each other: be active listeners, turn cell phone off or on vibrate, refrain from sidebar conversations.
- Be responsible: stay on task, return on time from breaks, ask questions.

Introducing the topic: A mini-lecture and whole-group discussion. This provides the theory and key ideas of the sessions. To assist you, information from overheads/ PowerPoint slides are in bold print; annotations and script for you is not in bold print.

Activity: Small-group, active learning tasks. Decide how you want to divide the group into smaller groups and vary how you do this for each activity. Benefits of dividing participants into groups include promoting movement and fostering discussion with different people. Workshop participants tend to sit with co-workers. Sitting with colleagues or friends for one activity is fine, but when the workshop includes multiple activities it is important to vary the groupings. Use a variety of strategies to divide the large group into smaller work groups ranging in size from partners (twos), to triads (threes), to groups of four to six participants, depending on the activity.

To form groups, you can have participants count off by twos, threes, fours, or fives, depending on the number of groups you plan to form. You might group them alphabetically by first name (for example, participants with names beginning with A and B move to Table 1; C, D, and E move to Table 2…), by clothing colors ("If you are wearing red, go to Table 1, if you are wearing orange or pink, move to Table 2…"), and so on. Other ways to form groups include by birth month, shoe size, or astrological sign. You might use items to help form groups such as shapes, colored paper clips, colored sticky notes, colored M&Ms, stickers on name tags, or playing cards. These materials can be distributed at the beginning of the session when participants arrive and sign in (for example, attach different colored paper clips to their agenda and then when groups need to be formed ask the ones with blue paper clips to move to Table 1, the red paper clips to Table 2…), or immediately prior to dividing the participants into a group (for example, pass around a basket of various shapes and ask participants to select a shape, then have the triangles move to Table 1, the ovals to Table 2…).

Discussion: A whole-group time to process the activity task and their reflections and learning. Discussion questions and trainer comments are noted. This is also a time to solicit questions and comments from participants to ensure understanding.

Activities and discussions are repeated depending on the planned duration of each.

Closure: How to wrap up and summarize the session.

Workshop materials: Each workshop has the following items in this order: assignment or activity cards, if used (workshops 1, 4, 5, 7, 8); overheads; and handouts.

Appendix: This book has seven appendices:

Appendix A: Recommended Children's Literature to Support Literacy. Books are organized by topic or the literacy skill that particular book enhances. When using children's books for participant activities in any session, select books included on this list appropriate for the topic or those suggested in the trainer's guide. You do not need to buy the books. When books are needed, ask a few classroom teachers to bring five books from the list to the training session. Many are also available in public libraries. For early childhood directors and principals, this list may also be useful in building good classroom libraries.

*Children
have real
understanding
only of that
which they
invent
themselves,
and each time
that we try
to teach them
something
too quickly,
we keep
them from
re-inventing it
themselves.
—Jean Piaget
(1896–1980).*

Appendix B: Resources for Literacy and Language Development. Full citations for all resources are organized alphabetically by author. We have included some newer references to enhance your knowledge. This list may be useful to develop or add to a good staff resource library.

Appendix C: Resources for Training and Presenting Workshops. This list provides additional books, articles, and websites focused on enhancing your skills as a trainer.

Appendix D: Glossary of Literacy Terms. These may be copied and distributed to workshop participants as appropriate. They are also provided as a reference to ensure shared meaning of terms.

Appendix E: Glossary of Training Terms. This provides a detailed explanation about the training words (gallery walk and carousel brainstorming) that are used in the workshop directions. Review this glossary to ensure that you understand how to use the strategies.

Appendix F: Sample Agendas with Shorter Time Frames. This includes suggested agendas for each workshop to accommodate a shorter time frame. Use these agendas as is or modify them according to your needs.

Appendix G: PowerPoint Presentations for Workshops. Hard copies of each PowerPoint presentation are included in this section.

Effective training requires organization and preparation. This book is designed to provide the trainer with a common framework and materials to train teachers in supporting children's language and literacy development. Trainers have flexibility in selecting activities and tasks for many of the sessions and in selecting from among the literacy topics to fit the needs of participants. Trainers may also develop their own small-group activities as long as the new activity is consistent with the objectives and essential messages for the workshop.

GOOD LUCK!

Fostering Language Development

Workshop Objectives

In this workshop, participants will:

- gain a deeper understanding of children's language development and its relationship to their thinking;
- learn more ways to encourage conversation and support children's vocabulary development;
- acquire strategies for developing children's listening and speaking skills throughout the day; and
- examine ways to promote children's language and thinking through good literature.

Workshop Materials

- Overhead projector and Overheads 1.1–1.4 or computer and PowerPoint Workshop 1 (on accompanying CD)
- Handouts 1.1–1.4, one copy for each participant
- Chart paper, markers, tape
- Large Post-its (4" x 6" or 5" x 8") for the activity *Talk in the Classroom*
- Index cards and pens for Introducing the Topic: Fostering Language Development and for the activity *Using Interesting Vocabulary Throughout the Day*
- One or two copies of the Vocabulary Assignment Cards (see page 27) cut out
- Several children's books from the recommended book list. This is an opportunity to introduce teachers to new, quality books. (See Recommended Children's Literature to Support Literacy in Appendix A on page 301 for suggestions.) Each group of 4–6 people will need at least two books.

Supplemental Resources

Owocki, G. 1999. *Literacy through play*. Portsmouth, NH: Heinemann (Chapter 3).

Schickedanz, J.A. 1999. *Much more than the ABCs: The early stages of reading and writing*. Washington DC: National Association for the Education of Young Children (Chapter 3).

Suggested Time Frame
3-hour workshop

Handout List
1.1
Agenda

1.2
Stages of Language Development

1.3
Fostering Language Development

1.4
Vocabulary Development

Trainers' Guide to Workshop 1

Essential Messages for This Workshop: Fostering Language Development

- Language development is critical to children's literacy learning.
- Listening carefully to children's language helps us understand their thinking.
- It is important to encourage children's conversations with adults and with other children throughout the day.
- Language development should be supported in the child's native language as well as in English.

▸▸ *Display Overhead 1.1 or PowerPoint Slide 1: Welcome to Today's Workshop as participants arrive.*

1. Opening Activity: Tuning into Children's Language and Thinking [20 minutes]

▸▸ *Choose from one of the examples below for preschool and kindergarten or use an example of your own.*

(Pre-K example) Begin by saying, "Young children are always experimenting with language. Their language gives us insight into their thinking. We have all been delighted by the inventive ways children express their ideas. For example, four-year-old Eli needed help screwing the cover on the peanut butter jar. He said, 'Mom, please spin this top on for me.' What does Eli show us that he knows and understands based on what he has said? What is the knowledge behind his words?"

Invite a few responses. You might add, "Eli's parents had not described closing the jar as spinning the top on. But Eli did not associate the word *close* with the jar. However, he associated the action of closing with turning or spinning. Not only did he get his message across, he was inventive with language. Rather than correcting him, admire what he said and extend his thinking. "You are right, Eli. To close the jar, we spin or turn the lid to get it tight."

(Kindergarten example) Begin by saying, "Young children are always experimenting with language. Their language gives us insight into their thinking. We have all been delighted by the inventive ways children express their ideas. For example, one fall day on the playground, Brooke ran over to her teacher and said, "Look, Mrs. Rams, the birds are flying fast away home for the winter." What does Brooke show us that she knows and understands based on what she has said? What is the knowledge behind her words?"

■ ■

Invite a few responses. You might add, "Brooke seems to understand that some birds migrate, but she does not know the term. However, she communicated what she knows. If we correct her, we limit her curiosity. Instead, we can admire and extend her thinking by saying, "You are right, Brooke. The birds are migrating south for the winter. As it gets cold up north, many birds migrate south before the snow comes."

Say to the participants, "Recall something delightful you have heard a child say and jot it down."

After a couple of minutes, say, "Form groups of three to share your recollections. After each person has shared a memory, admire the children's language. Reflect on what they know and understand and what their words reveal about their thinking."

Provide 5–7 minutes for sharing and discussion. Listen to a few recollections, both what the child said and the thinking behind it. As you make the transition to the formal introduction of the workshop, say, "Today's session focuses on the importance of language development."

Listening carefully to children's language helps us understand their thinking.

2. Welcome and Logistics [5 minutes]

▶▶ *Distribute* Handout 1.1: Agenda. *Review the agenda and workshop objectives.*

3. Introducing the Topic: Fostering Language Development [35–40 minutes]

▶▶ *Show* Overhead 1.2 or PowerPoint Slide 2: Fostering Language Development.

Ask, "Why is children's language development important in early childhood classrooms?" Hear some ideas, adding to or extending the ideas with the following points:

Learning language is a thinking process. As you observed in the opening activity, listening to children's language gives us insights into how children make sense of the rules of language. As they develop language, they solve problems, form hypotheses, and interact with others who use language. When we admire the thinking children use and build on it, we motivate them to use more language.

19

Language development is the first step toward literacy. Language development makes reading and writing possible. To read, we use language abilities to decode and comprehend text (Ruddell and Ruddell 1995). We need vocabulary for comprehension. Readers look for familiar patterns and sequences to help them understand text.

▸▸ *Show* Overhead 1.3 or PowerPoint Slide 3: How Children Acquire Language.

Language learning is innate for humans. Children are "hard wired" to learn and use language. Before children begin to speak, they understand and respond to both verbal and nonverbal language.

The environment and interactions have a significant impact on children's language development. Children learn the specific variety of language (dialect) spoken by the important people around them (Genishi 2002). From infancy, adults provide a language model for children, encouraging them as they begin to make sounds. Adults work at interpreting what the child is saying and coax, reinforce, and expand the child's language. For example, the infant says, "Ma, ma, ma," and the mother smiles and says, "Yes, you are saying 'mommy.' Say it again." Or, the toddler says, "Ball," and the parent says, "Yes, that is a big, red, beautiful ball." When a child's babbling and talking is not encouraged but instead is perceived as annoying, the child stops. The variety and quantity of language that children experience matters (Neuman, Copple, and Bredekamp 2000).

Children learn by "creating" language. Children are active participants in learning language. Through social interactions, they begin to learn the rules of language: phonology (the sounds of speech in language), syntax (grammar—how words work together in phrases, clauses, and sentences), and semantics (the vocabulary that gives language meaning). In the opening activity, many of the stories shared showed children forming hypotheses about how language works and what words mean. For example, as children learn to add the "s" sound to more than one of something (or plural), they say things like "peoples," "childrens," or "fishes." Or, as they begin to use "ed" for past tense, they are likely to say "broked" or "swimmed." These "errors" show that children are thinking. Rather than correct the children, we can accept and appreciate their hard work and thinking. And to expand their learning, we can respond in natural conversation using the correct form and at some point along the line, they will catch on.

Children learn language through play. Children show us their pleasure in language as they play with sounds and rhymes, make up words, and tell jokes and riddles. The more we encourage them and share their delight, the more we foster their language development. Through sociodramatic play, children learn and practice the functions of language; for example, how we use language to accomplish the tasks of daily living, to do our jobs, to satisfy curiosity, to gain and share information, to make connections with others, to express images and imagination, to remember, and to bring pleasure to our lives (Owocki 2001). A great deal of language learning and thinking occurs during the dialogue children have with each other in dramatic play settings. Often they communicate more easily (and more in quantity) with each other, both verbally and nonverbally, than they do with adults.

It is important to encourage children to use and develop their native language. All young children need encouragement to continue to develop language. Whatever language or dialect a child speaks, it is rule-governed and systematic and, therefore, helps the child develop more language.

> ▸▸ *Give each participant a pen and an index card.*

Ask the participants to jot down a phrase, comment, word, sound, or statement typical of a child they know between the ages of birth and six years old. Be sure they write the child's age.

> ▸▸ *Distribute* Handout 1.2: Stages of Language Development.

As you review each stage, invite participants to share examples of things they wrote for children of that age group.

Lead into the next activity by asking teachers to think about when and how they can promote talk in the classroom to ensure that children's language grows at the best rate of development.

---

4. Activity: Talk in the Classroom [20 minutes]

> ▸▸ *Prepare for this activity by putting large Post-its (5" x 8") and markers on each table.*

Label three charts: Whole Group, Small Group, and One-on-One. Do not hang the charts yet. Divide the participants into groups of 4–6.

Introduce the activity by saying, "Children learn language by using it. The classroom must be a place to nurture talk and conversation. Your job is to provide children with interesting things to talk about and many, many opportunities to talk. Let's think about all the times during the day when children are encouraged to talk."

Give the participants the following directions, "Picture your classrooms and think about all the different times and situations when children talk during the day. Working in your groups, take 5 minutes to come up with as many ideas as you can. Record each idea in large print on a separate Post-it." You might want to model one or two with the whole group. Ask them for ideas and record them in large print on Post-its.

The classroom must be a place to nurture talk and conversation.

21

> ➤➤ *While the groups are working, post the three charts.*

After 5 minutes, ask the groups to stop. Say, "You have generated many different times of the day that children talk. Please take 2 minutes to sort them into categories: whole group discussions, small group interactions, or one-on-one conversations." Invite participants to post their ideas on the appropriate chart.

5. Discussion [10 minutes]

Ask participants, "What do you notice about our charts?" Ideas might include: many are whole group discussions, there is an even distribution among all three categories, there are fewer one-on-one conversations, and most one-on-one conversations are between adults and children and not between children.

Highlight the importance of one-on-one conversations with children. These interactions are perfect opportunities for teachers to scaffold language by asking open-ended questions that take into account individual children's interests and language development. Point out that studies (Bowman, Donovan, and Burns 2000) show that there is limited one-on-one interaction between young children and their teachers.

Ask, "Why is it important to vary the settings we provide for children to talk?" Ideas to elicit include children's comfort, temperament, personal style, culture, and experience. Point out that when we provide many different opportunities for children to talk, they are more likely to do so.

Provide a few minutes for participants to reflect on their personal strengths and weaknesses in how they foster talk in the classroom. This can be a written reflection or a group discussion.

> ➤➤ *Distribute* Handout 1.3: Fostering Language Development.

Let the participants use the remaining time to review the handout, identifying two things they do extremely well and two things they would improve.

6. Activity: Using Interesting Vocabulary Throughout the Day [25 minutes]

> ➤➤ *Tape a piece of chart paper to the wall and put more chart paper and pens on the tables.*

Put one of the Vocabulary Assignment Cards onto each table. Each group will need a card; you can assign two groups to the same setting on a card. Consider having participants form new groups of 4–6 people. If you decide to form different groups than the ones for the activity *Talk in the Classroom*, do it before giving directions.

To introduce this activity, ask the participants to think about the words they use with children. Write the word *happy* on a chart. Ask, "What are some ways we might use language to convey the word *happy*?" Their ideas might include synonyms or phrases such as glad, content, pleased, cheerful, in high spirits, ecstatic, delighted, on cloud nine, and jovial.

▶▶ *Record their ideas on the chart paper.*

Then say, "Vocabulary is an essential part of learning to read fluently as well as learning complex concepts. To help children build rich vocabularies, we must use fanciful language with them. Hart and Risley (1999) found that children from professional families know about 20,000 words by age 6. (Note to trainer: If the participants work with lower-income children also add: "Children from families on welfare know about 4,000 words by age 6.") As children's vocabulary is linked to future reading ability and reading comprehension, it is important that we use rich vocabulary and introduce new words to children."

"Let's spend some time thinking about how to ensure that children leave our classrooms with 20,000 words or more!"

▶▶ *Ask each group to look at their Assignment Card.*

Give the participants the following directions, "With your group, brainstorm at least 10 interesting and fanciful words that you can use when talking with children in the setting on your assignment card. Feel free to make your list as long as 20 words!" Record the words on your chart.

Note: Most groups benefit from modeling. Use one of the Assignment Cards and brainstorm as a whole group, recording ideas on the chart.

Provide 10–15 minutes for them to work in groups. When they are finished, ask them to post their charts. Do a gallery walk (see Appendix E, page 316 for how to do a gallery walk) for 3–5 minutes to give participants time to read the charts as they walk around and suggest that participants write down three words they will use with children the next day. If possible, offer to type and distribute all the charts.

7. Discussion [5 minutes]

Invite a few participants to share the words they hope to use the next day. Ask, "As you worked on this task, what were some of the challenges?" Invite responses. "What are you excited about?"

▸▸ *Distribute* Handout 1.4: Vocabulary Development *as a reference.*

8. Activity: Using Fanciful Language [20 minutes]

▸▸ *Hand out index cards and pens.*

Participants remain in the same groups of 4–6 for this activity. Introduce the activity by saying, "Research (National Reading Panel 2000, Owocki 2001, Schickedanz 1999) also shows that the quality of adult-child conversation is as important as the quantity or amount of conversation for children's cognitive and literacy development. Let's practice using these rich vocabulary words in conversations."

▸▸ *Use* Overhead 1.4 or PowerPoint Slide 4: Using Fanciful Language *to give directions for the role-play.*

Note: The PowerPoint slides are arranged so you can go step by step. If you use the overhead, uncover each step as you go.

Say, "The first step of this task is to create a brief description (also called a vignette) of what might take place at a center or the setting from the Vocabulary Assignment Card you used in the activity *Using Interesting Vocabulary Throughout the Day.* Imagine this: You are in your classroom observing children either at a center or during a routine. What would you see a child doing or saying? Describe what the child might be doing and saying at the center or during the routine. For example, at snack time, you might observe Rashan eating celery and peanut butter for snack. He picks up the celery, licks the peanut butter off the top, and then takes a bite of the celery. Does everyone understand what I mean by a vignette? Take three minutes to come up with a vignette and record it on an index card." After they have finished, ask them to pass their vignettes to another group.

Say, "Read aloud the new vignette you received. Then, read the vocabulary chart from our last activity that relates to the vignette."

Allow a minute or two for each group to read its vignette. Say, "For the last part of this activity, role-play with a partner a conversation between a teacher and a child using some of the new fanciful vocabulary words. One partner will be the teacher and the other partner will be the child. The situation for the role-play is the vignette you have just read. Each pair is to role-play the same vignette as others in your group." After a few minutes, ask them to switch roles.

9. Discussion [3–5 minutes]

Invite comments and questions.

10. Activity: Interesting Words in Read-Aloud Books [15–20 minutes]

▸▸ *Create new groups of 4–6 participants (page 15 provides a variety of suggestions of how to divide into groups). Distribute two books to each group to prepare for this activity. (Appendix A (page 301) provides a comprehensive list of books from which to select.)*

Say, "Read-aloud books provide a wonderful opportunity for children to hear rich and fanciful vocabulary as well as to engage in meaningful conversations. Read aloud the books on your table. Identify rich vocabulary words. Think about interesting conversations you can have with children about the books."

11. Discussion [5–10 minutes]

Ask each group to give a brief synopsis of the book and one reason why the book supports children's language development. Summarize this activity by sharing this fact: "Children who engage in daily discussions about books are more likely to become critical readers and learners" (Neuman and Roskos 1998).

■ ■

12. Closure [5–10 minutes]

Ask the participants to jot down the three words they are excited about bringing to their classroom and one new idea or insight they will apply in their work starting tomorrow.

Provide time for the participants to think and write. Invite them to share a few ideas. Leave them with this message: "Use lots of expressive vocabulary, invite lots of conversations, and make language an exciting part of your classroom!"

Vocabulary Assignment Cards

Note to trainer: Cut these out and distribute one to each group. You can assign two groups to the same setting, if necessary.

Invention Center	**Science Center**
Cooking	**Library**
Blocks	**Dramatic Play**
Snack or Lunch	**Art Area**
Weather and Calendar	**Arrival and Departure**

OVERHEAD 1.1

WELCOME TO TODAY'S WORKSHOP

Fostering Language Development

Fostering Language Development

Learning language is a thinking process.

◆ Children work at figuring out the rules of language.

◆ Appreciating how children are hypothesizing about language motivates them to keep learning language.

Language development is the first step toward literacy.

◆ Language development makes reading and writing possible.

◆ Children need vocabulary to comprehend written language.

◆ Knowing the patterns and sequences of language supports comprehension.

Literacy
The Essential
WORKSHOP
BOOK

WORKSHOP 1

How Children Acquire Language

■ **Language learning is innate for humans.**

■ **The environment and interactions have a significant impact on children's language development.**

■ **Children learn by "creating" language.**

■ **Children learn language through play.**

■ **It is important to encourage children to use and develop their native language.**

Using Fanciful Language

Step 1: Write a vignette (with your group)

Write a two- to three-sentence vignette describing what a child is doing (and possibly saying) at the center or during the routine indicated on your Vocabulary Assignment Card. Record it on an index card.

Step 2: Exchange vignettes

Pass your group's vignette to another group.

Read and discuss the vignette you receive.

Review the vocabulary chart that relates to the center discussed in the vignette.

Step 3: Role-play a conversation between a teacher and a child

With a partner, take turns role-playing a conversation based on your vignette. (One person is the teacher, the other is the child.)

The partner playing the role of the teacher should use new and fanciful vocabulary words from the chart in the conversation.

Switch roles.

HANDOUT 1.1

AGENDA

Fostering Language Development

Date: _____

Trainer: _____

Contact Information: _____

OBJECTIVES

In this workshop, participants will:

- gain a deeper understanding of children's language development and its relationship to their thinking;
- learn more ways to encourage conversation and support children's vocabulary development;
- acquire strategies for developing children's listening and speaking skills throughout the day; and
- examine ways to promote children's language and thinking through good literature.

1. Opening Activity: Tuning into Children's Language and Thinking [20 minutes]

2. Welcome and Logistics [5 minutes]

3. Introducing the Topic: Fostering Language Development [35–40 minutes]

4. Activity: Talk in the Classroom [20 minutes]

5. Discussion [10 minutes]

6. Activity: Using Interesting Vocabulary Throughout the Day [25 minutes]

7. Discussion [5 minutes]

8. Activity: Using Fanciful Language [20 minutes]

9. Discussion [3–5 minutes]

10. Activity: Interesting Words in Read-Aloud Books [15–20 minutes]

11. Discussion [5–10 minutes]

12. Closure [5–10 minutes]

Stages of Language Development

Children birth—one year old

- babble, play with sounds, and combine sounds
- include intonation in their vocalization by six months
- respond to their name and understand angry and friendly tones
- comprehend much more language than they can produce and begin to say words (*mommy, daddy, bye-bye, no*) by about eight months

Children 1–2 years old

- use one or more words with meaning
- utter sounds with adult intonation as if speaking in sentences
- begin to combine words, such as "toy fall"
- usually have an emerging vocabulary around 18 months
- use mostly nouns

Children 2–3 years old

- experience a dramatic growth in language
- name objects common to their surroundings
- use pronouns (*I, me, you*) but not always correctly by age two; use the pronouns correctly by age three
- have increasingly larger vocabularies
- speak with two- to three-word sentences
- play with words, repeating words, making up nonsense words, and so on

Children 3–4 years old

- demonstrate increasing accuracy of sentence structure and vocabulary
- add syntax such as plurals, regular verbs, and past tense (but often with "errors" such as "broked" or "fishes")

Children 5–6 years old

- use language that sounds more and more like language used by adults
- increase their vocabulary typically to about 2,500 words
- sometimes have difficulty pronouncing certain sounds (such as "sh," as in "shoe" or "cash" and "th" as in "the" or "think")

Gryphon House, Inc. grants permission for this page to be photocopied by professionals using *The Essential Literacy Workshop Book*.

Fostering Language Development

To foster children's language development:

- Create an atmosphere in which children hear and use lots of language.
- Connect language with pleasure and enjoyable times (avoid creating stress around speaking).
- Provide opportunities for children to discriminate and classify sounds (poems, chants, songs, and rhymes).
- Expose children to lots of new and rich vocabulary.
- Use thematic units to introduce new vocabulary.
- Use books to introduce new vocabulary.
- Expose children to wordless books that invite them to invent their own stories from the pictures.
- Use riddles and jokes with children.
- Read poems with children.
- Encourage children to listen to others and to demonstrate their understanding.
- Welcome children's use of their native language.
- Provide children with opportunities to experience many different functions of language; encourage them to reflect on their feelings, express points of view, summarize events, solve problems, predict outcomes, and generate hypotheses.
- Connect language to math; invite children to describe size and amounts, make comparisons, define sets, and explain their thinking.
- Include many small group, one-on-one, and child-directed learning situations throughout the day.
- Promote language in social situations with adults and other children.
- Provide reinforcement for language use.
- Link language learning to learning centers.
- Use pictures in the classroom and encourage children to describe what they see in the pictures.
- Include materials in centers that spark new vocabulary and thinking.
- Encourage children to retell stories of books they have heard as well as stories from their personal experiences.
- Write and talk about class trips.
- Use the morning message in morning circle to encourage vocabulary. Morning messages can be phrases you invite children to complete such as, "This weekend I ….." or "Today is…." or "I like …."
- Create class stories.
- Summarize the day.

Vocabulary Development

Vocabulary refers to words that are necessary to communicate effectively.

There are two types of vocabulary:
- oral vocabulary—words used in speaking or recognized when listening; and
- reading vocabulary—words recognized or used in print.

Vocabulary plays an important part in learning to read. As beginning readers, children use words they have heard to make sense of words they see in print. For example, as a beginning reader comes to the word *apple* in a book, she begins to figure out the sounds represented by the letters. She recognizes that the sounds make up a very familiar word that she has heard and said many times. Beginning readers have more difficulty reading words that are not part of their oral vocabulary.

Vocabulary is also important to reading comprehension. Readers cannot understand what they are reading without knowing what most of the words mean. As children learn to read more advanced texts, they must learn the meaning of new words that are not part of their oral vocabulary.

To support children's vocabulary development:
- Engage children in meaningful, extended conversations every day.
- Encourage children to talk and think.
- Read aloud texts that include rich and challenging vocabulary.
- Read aloud from story books and informational books.
- Talk about books with children.
- Use new, interesting, and colorful words with children.
- Use a variety of words for common objects (for example, trash, garbage, and litter).
- Teach important, useful, and difficult words.
- Talk with children about synonyms and definitions.
- Expose children to age-appropriate dictionaries and other reference aids.
- Encourage curiosity about words.
- Help children see relationships between and among words, ideas, and objects.
- Highlight for children concept words, important words, and interesting words as they appear in books and everyday interactions.
- Help children link new words to familiar words, using new words frequently.

The Essential **Literacy** WORKSHOP BOOK

Beyond Open and Closed Questions

Workshop Objectives

In this workshop, participants will:

- develop an understanding of different ways teachers talk to children and the types of questions teachers ask;
- reflect on one's teaching practice, focusing on ways to extend language and encourage creative thinking; and
- acquire strategies for asking questions to support creativity and higher-level thinking.

Workshop Materials

- Overhead projector and Overheads 2.1–2.5 or computer and PowerPoint Workshop 2 (on accompanying CD)
- Handouts 2.1–2.6, one copy for each participant
- Chart paper, markers, tape
- 3″ x 5″ index cards or Post-it notes for the opening activity *Interesting Questions*
- Children's book, *The True Story of the 3 Little Pigs! by A. Wolf* by Jon Scieszka
- 12″ x 18″ construction paper in a variety of light colors, 5–6 sheets per participant
- Assorted colored markers for each table or group
- Sugar packets for each participant (to serve as a mnemonic after the session)

Supplemental Resources

Bagley, M. T. & Foley, J. P. 1996. *Suppose the wolf were an octopus: K to 2*. Unionville, NY: Royal Fireworks Press.

Trainers' Guide to Workshop 2

Essential Messages for This Workshop: Beyond Open and Closed Questions

- An important part of early childhood classroom practice is extending children's language and thinking throughout the day.
- Shape questions that invite many answers.
- Ask questions to help children contemplate and solve problems.
- Pose questions to extend children's thinking.

▸▸ *Display* Overhead 2.1 or PowerPoint Slide 1: Welcome to Today's Workshop *as participants arrive.*

---

1. Opening Activity: Interesting Questions
[10–15 minutes]

Begin by saying, "Young children are inquisitive by nature. As adults, we sometimes lose that exploratory nature and focus on what is or is not. We tend to be constrained by a limited or correct answer. For example, what is true is that most plants need water to grow. What is not true is that plants need milk to grow. However, I wonder what would happen if we watered plants with lemonade (which contains water). Would the plant turn yellow or die? Or would the plant extract the water and leave the lemon behind? I am going to give you a few minutes to think of a question that you have pondered. For example, I have always wondered why there are traffic jams when there is no accident."

▸▸ *Pass out index cards or Post-its and pens.*

Allow a few minutes for each person to write down a question. After everybody has finished, ask for a volunteer to share his or her question. Invite other participants to give answers. Ask several other volunteers to share their questions and invite others to offer possible answers.

Then ask, "How did this activity make you feel? Were you stimulated? We heard some very interesting questions and creative answers. While there may have been one correct or scientific answer to a question, were you able to think of a plausible or creative answer? What types of questions did you think about?" Pause after each question to allow responses from the group. Provide 5–7 minutes for sharing and discussion.

As you make the transition to the formal introduction of the workshop, say, "Most of your questions were open-ended questions. While there may actually be a right or wrong answer to some of them, you were very creative in coming up with responses to other people's questions. Did you notice that the more open-ended the question was, the more discussion it stimulated? Today's session focuses on the ways teachers talk to children and the types of questions we ask children."

Ask questions to help children contemplate and solve problems.

2. Welcome and Logistics [5 minutes]

▸▸ *Distribute Handout 2.1: Agenda. Review the agenda and workshop objectives.*

3. Introducing the Topic: How Teachers Talk to Children [15 minutes]

▸▸ *Show* Overhead 2.2 or PowerPoint Slide 2: How Teachers Talk to Children.

Say, "Teachers talk to children in a variety of ways. Researchers (Glickman, Gordon, and Ross-Gordon 1998) have identified four general areas of teacher talk." Extend the discussion with the examples below. Invite teachers to add their own examples.

Procedural—giving directions and managing behavior: Much of what teachers say is procedural information. Examples: "Come to the circle and sit on your bottom." "It is time to clean up." "Use your inside voice."

Informational—stating facts and answering questions: This is when teachers tell children things. Examples: "Today is Jordan's birthday." "The title of the book is *Bread, Bread, Bread*." "The author is the person who writes the book." "I see you are wearing red shoes today."

Praise or reprimand—acknowledging children's actions: This is when teachers speak in response to children's behavior, encompassing both positive talk and reprimands. Examples: "Good job!" "Sit down!" "Thank you for helping Jamal clean up the blocks." "Laura, keep your hands in your lap." "What a beautiful picture you made!"

Questions—inviting children to talk: There are two broad categories of questions: open and closed. Teachers ask children many questions throughout the day, but not nearly as many questions as they make statements. Many questions are closed, or lower-level, questions. We tend to ask children lower-level questions with a right or wrong orientation; in fact, we are very good at doing that. We do not need to learn how to ask closed questions.

Closed questions ask for information. Examples: "What color is the truck?" "Is that your hat?"

Open-ended questions stimulate thinking. Examples: "What do you remember about the story?" "What do you know about caterpillars?" "What do you think might happen if we mixed the blue paint with the red paint?" "What do you think happened to the water that was in the puddle?"

Summarize by saying, "Both open and closed questions have their place, but asking a variety of questions extends the language, creativity, and thinking skills of children."

4. Activity: Group Storytelling [10 minutes]

Ask for 10 volunteers who know the story of "The Three Little Pigs" to come forward. Arrange them in a standing row in front of the group. If there are fewer than 15 people in your workshop, the entire group can participate. Start with one person and go around the group. Say, "Because there are many versions of this story, we will do a group storytelling so we all have one version to work from."

Instruct the first person to begin the story with an opening sentence. Each person adds a sentence, continuing the sequence of what happened next. After the tenth person adds a sentence, have the same 10 volunteers add more sentences, as necessary, to complete the story. Note: It does not matter if the story is the "correct" version or a totally new version. The intention is to have a joint story for all the participants to hear.

Once the group storytelling is finished, refresh everyone's memory of this story by recapping the story in the sequence of how it was told.

5. Presentation of Taxonomy and Activity: Six Major Cognitive Operations [45 minutes]

Use Overheads 2.2–2.4 or PowerPoint Slides 3–4: Bloom's Taxonomy. Introduce the overhead by saying, "Benjamin Bloom (Bloom 1956) developed a taxonomy for examining the thinking process. It is hierarchical, from lower-level thinking to higher-level thinking."

▸▸ *Show the overheads or slides in order and extend with the following points.*

40

■ ■

Lower-Level Thinking Processes

L-1 Knowledge—Information gathering

These are questions that check the basic facts about people, places, or things.

Knowledge is basic recall; it tests memory. The child recalls or recognizes information. This is the lowest level of learning. Does the child remember what he or she has seen, heard, or read?

■ List the characters in the story.

■ What did Brown Bear see?

L-2 Comprehension—Confirming

These are questions that check understanding and memory of facts.

Comprehension is understanding or confirming facts; the child processes information and remembers. The child changes information and makes meaning. Can the child organize the facts of what he or she knows?

■ Tell me what happened to the little bird in the story.

■ Why did the straw house fall down?

■ Why did Goldilocks like the Baby Bear's chair best?

Higher-Level Thinking Processes

L-3 Application—Illuminating

Application questions test the ability to use knowledge in a practical, problem-solving manner.

In *Application,* the child uses knowledge to solve problems or to make generalizations. The child discovers relationships among facts, generalizations, definitions, values, or skills and applies that knowledge to solve problems. Can the child apply techniques and rules to solve problems that have correct answers?

■ If you were the hungry caterpillar, what would you have eaten?

■ If Goldilocks came into your house, what are some of the things she would have used?

L-4 Analysis—Pulling apart of pieces

These are questions that select, examine, and break apart information into its smaller, separate parts.

Analysis is pulling apart the pieces. The child solves a problem and can discuss his or her reasoning and thinking. Can the child identify motives and causes, make inferences, and find examples to support generalizations?

■ What parts of the story could not have happened?

■ How are Goldilocks and Little Red Riding Hood similar to each other?

L-5 Synthesis—Creating

Synthesis questions utilize the basic information in a new, original, or unique way.

Synthesis is creating a new way to put information together. The child solves problems that require creative thinking. Can the child make predictions, solve problems, or produce original communications, such as plays, stories, and posters?

■ Draw a picture to make up a new ending for the story.

■ How might the story have been different if the wolf had visited three fishes instead of three pigs?

L-6 Evaluation—Judging, predicting
Evaluation questions determine the value of information, including making judgments about the information.
Evaluation is about judging, predicting, and forming opinions. The child makes a judgment of good or bad or of right or wrong, according to standards set by the child. Can the child give opinions about issues, judge the validity of ideas, judge the merit of solutions to problems, or judge the quality of art and other products?

- Which wolf was worse, the wolf in "The Three Little Pigs" or the wolf in "Little Red Riding Hood"? Why?
- Do you think Goldilocks made a good decision by running away from the bears? Explain.

▸▸ *Distribute* Handout 2.2: Bloom's Taxonomy of Educational Objectives and Handout 2.3: Individual Activity: Six Major Cognitive Operations.

Instruct the participants to use "The Three Little Pigs" story that was told by the group earlier and develop at least one question for each level. Participants may work in pairs. Allow 10 minutes for the pairs to work.

▸▸ *When most pairs have finished, show* Overheads 2.3–2.4 or PowerPoint Slides 3-4.

Pause after each level to allow participants to share questions they wrote for that level. Invite several volunteers to share their questions to provide multiple examples of questions for that level.

After all of the levels are completed, discuss how easy it was to come up with lower-level questions, and how much harder it was to come up with higher-level questions.

Point out that it is always useful to create one or two questions to ask children about stories. Suggest that they may want to write questions inside the back cover of various books to have questions readily available.

▸▸ *Distribute* Handout 2.4: Applying Bloom's Taxonomy.

6. Activity: Creative Questioning [15–20 minutes]

▸▸ *Use* Overhead 2.5 or PowerPoint Slide 5: Creative Questioning *and extend as noted below.*

Begin this portion by saying, "While it is useful to use Bloom's Taxonomy to ensure that we challenge varying cognitive processes in children, what is most important is that we ask higher-level questions. Higher-level questions promote creative and critical thinking skills in children. They learn to think, not just to know something. They learn to go beyond recalling. They learn to create meaning, not just remember." Throughout the presentation, ask participants to provide examples of questions.

Ask open-ended questions: Open-ended questions have multiple answers. They stimulate thinking and encourage longer answers and thought. Open-ended questions also allow children to feel successful because there is not one right answer. For example:
- What are the people in the picture doing?
- What does it look like?
- What do you like to play with outside?
- What are some ways we use water?

Ask children to use their senses: Stretch young children's creative thinking by asking them to focus on one of their senses.
- Have children close their eyes and guess what you place in their hands (a ball, a piece of sandpaper, a small rock).
- Have children close their eyes and guess what they hear. Shake keys, jingle coins, open a can of soda, tear a piece of paper, and so on.

Ask children about changes: One way to help children think more creatively is to ask them to change things to make them the way they would like them to be. For example:
- What would taste better if it were sweeter?
- What would be nicer if it were smaller?
- What would be more fun if it were faster?
- What would be better if it were quieter?

Ask questions with many answers: Questions with multiple answers encourage children to use creative and analytical thinking skills.
- What do you notice about this tree?
- What do we need to set up a restaurant in our classroom?
- What could you use to make a flower?
- What else can you tell me about your dog?

Ask "What would happen if…" questions: These questions are fun to ask and allow the children to use their imaginations and higher-order thinking skills.
- What would happen if all the trees in the world were blue?
- What would happen if all the cars were gone?
- What would happen if everybody wore the same clothes?
- What would happen if you could fly?

■ ■

Ask "In how many different ways…" questions: These questions also extend a child's creative thinking.

■ In how many different ways could a spoon be used?
■ In how many different ways could a button be used?
■ In how many different ways could a string be used?

7. Activity: Creating Prompts for Centers
[15–20 minutes]

▸▸ *Distribute* Handout 2.6: Comments and Questions That Help You Learn About and Extend Children's Thinking.

Provide a few minutes for the individuals to review the information on the handout. Ask for comments or questions.

Divide the group into smaller groups of 5–6 people. Give each group a sheet of chart paper and markers. Assign each group to a different learning center. If the group is large, you can also assign a routine such as lunch, cleanup, snack, morning arrival, and so on, or assign the same center to two groups. Have each group brainstorm and record open-ended questions or opening phrases that would be appropriate to use in that center or with that routine. Allow 10–15 minutes for groups to chart their ideas.

8. Discussion [15–20 minutes]

Ask each group to present their questions and opening phrases and then post their chart on the walls. Ask questions such as the following: "Were some centers harder to develop questions for?" "Which centers were easier?" "What do the questions or statements have in common?"

Explain that teachers should:
■ Ask questions responsively; do not ask a string of questions.
■ Use questions to stimulate the child's dialogue and thinking.
■ Ask questions to help children contemplate, describe, and be more aware of their thought processes.
■ Pose questions related to what the child is doing.
■ Ask questions about the child's thought processes. "How many eyes does the fish have?" demands a factual answer. Asking, "How can you tell?" in response to a child's observation that the fish has one eye encourages the child to describe how he or she arrived at the conclusion. Only the child has the answer, so it is worth asking

the question. Other examples: "How do you know that?" "What do you think made that happen?" "How did you get the ball to…?" "What do you think would happen if…?"

- Use statements and expansions instead of questions to effectively facilitate children's language development. "I wonder how you could get that block to balance."

Highlight the importance of one-on-one conversations with children.

9. Closure [20–25 minutes]

▸▸ *Distribute construction paper to each group along with markers. Each person should have five or six sheets.*

Instruct the participants to review the charts on the wall, and to pick out five or six of their favorite questions or opening phrases. Ask them to print these in large letters on the paper provided, with one phrase or question on each piece of paper. These are for the teachers to bring back to their classrooms to serve as prompts to remind them to ask creative high-level questions. They should post the sheets high enough on their classroom walls so they can be seen from different locations in the room.

To summarize the workshop, say, "Today we looked at the different types of questions we ask children and how to use strategies for asking questions to encourage children's language development and foster creative thinking."

Ask, "What are some ways you can use these strategies to learn about children? How can children's responses inform you about their development?" Invite responses and rephrase the responses.

Ask, "What are some ways you can use these strategies in your data collection?" Invite participants' responses and extend their ideas. For example: When discussing a child's work sample, ask a higher-level question such as, "How did you get your block building to stay so straight?" After reading *The Grouchy Ladybug* out loud and discussing the story, ask a thinking question such as, "What is something that makes you grouchy?" noting what you asked and what the child said and did in your notes about this child. Or write an anecdote about a child's response to your interaction in their dramatic play when you asked, "What would happen if there was no food to feed the baby? What could you do?"

In closing, say, "We started earlier today with the story of "The Three Little Pigs." Now I am going to share with you Jon Scieszka's *The True Story of the 3 Little Pigs! by A. Wolf.*" Read the story aloud to the group, modeling good story reading skills (speak clearly; project your voice; vary your phrasing, pace, and volume for effect; read with feeling; hold the book facing the audience so all can see; identify the author and illustrator; and so on). At the end, note that you wanted to share the story with them because you hope

45

they will encourage language development and creative thinking in their children, as this author must have been similarly encouraged. Distribute a sugar packet to each teacher. Encourage them to hang the sugar packet on their classroom wall or to place it on their desk to remind them of this story when they see it, and to remind them to extend children's language through open-ended questions.

WELCOME TO TODAY'S WORKSHOP

Beyond Open and Closed Questions

W O R K S H O P 2

How Teachers Talk to Children

Procedural

giving directions and managing behavior

Informational

stating facts and answering questions

Praise or reprimand

acknowledging children's actions

Questions

inviting children to talk
- ◆ closed questions
- ◆ open-ended questions

(Glickman, Gordon, & Ross-Gordon 1998)

Bloom's Taxonomy of Educational Objectives

Six Major Cognitive Operations

Lower-Level Thinking Processes

L-1 Knowledge—Information gathering

These are questions that check the basic facts about people, places, or things.

L-2 Comprehension—Confirming

These are questions that check understanding and memory of facts.

(Bloom 1956)

W
O
R
K
S
H
O
P

2

Higher-Level Thinking Processes

L-3 Application—Illuminating
Application questions test the ability to use knowledge in a practical, problem-solving manner.

L-4 Analysis—Pulling apart of pieces
These are questions that select, examine, and break apart information into its smaller, separate parts.

Higher-Level Thinking Processes

L-5 Synthesis—Creating
Synthesis questions utilize the basic information in a new, original, or unique way.

L-6 Evaluation—Judging, predicting
Evaluation questions determine the value of information, including making judgments about the information.

Creative Questioning

Ask open-ended questions.

Ask children to use their senses.

Ask children about changes.

Ask questions with many answers.

Ask "What would happen if..." questions.

Ask "In how many different ways..." questions.

The Essential Literacy WORKSHOP BOOK

HANDOUT 2.1

AGENDA

Beyond Open and Closed Questions

Date:

Trainer:

Contact Information:

OBJECTIVES

In this workshop, participants will:
- develop an understanding of different ways teachers talk to children and the types of questions teachers ask;
- reflect on one's teaching practice, focusing on ways to extend language and encourage creative thinking; and
- acquire strategies for asking questions to support creativity and higher-level thinking.

1. Opening Activity: Interesting Questions [10–15 minutes)

2. Welcome and Logistics [5 minutes]

3. Introducing the Topic: How Teachers Talk to Children [15 minutes]

4. Activity: Group Storytelling [10 minutes]

5. Presentation of Taxonomy and Activity: Six Major Cognitive Operations [45 minutes]

6. Activity: Creative Questioning [15–20 minutes]

7. Activity: Creating Prompts for Centers [15–20 minutes]

8. Discussion [15–20 minutes]

9. Closure [20–25 minutes]

Bloom's Taxonomy of Educational Objectives

(Bloom 1956)

Knowledge: Does the child remember what he or she has seen or read?
Examples:
- What did the polar bear see?
- What was the teddy bear's name?

Comprehension: Can the child organize what he or she knows?
Examples:
- Tell me what happened to Max in the story.
- What is a Wild Thing?

Application: Can the child apply techniques and rules to solve problems that have correct answers?
Examples:
- What can you find in our room that has the shape of a circle?
- Show me how to build a tower so it does not fall down.

Analysis: Can the child identify motives and causes, make inferences, and find examples to support generalizations?
Examples:
- Why did you make your block building long?
- Why did the caterpillar eat so much food?

Synthesis: Can the child make predictions, solve problems, or produce original communications, such as plays, stories, and posters?
Examples:
- Make a design for the pattern you would like to follow for making a bead necklace.
- What can the man do to get his caps back from the monkeys?

Evaluation: Can the child give opinions about issues, judge the validity of ideas, judge the merit of solutions to problems, or judge the quality of art and other products?
Examples:
- Was Little Red Riding Hood's mother right to let her go off into the woods?
- There are six children who want to ride bikes and only four bikes. What is a fair way to decide who should get to ride?

The Essential Literacy WORKSHOP BOOK

Individual Activity: Six Major Cognitive Operations

Using the story discussed, brainstorm questions for each category.

LOWER-LEVEL THINKING PROCESSES

L-1 Knowledge—Information gathering, remembering
These are questions that check the basic facts about people, places, or things.

L-2 Comprehension—Confirming, understanding
These are questions that check understanding and memory of facts.

HIGHER-LEVEL THINKING PROCESSES

L-3 Application—Illuminating, using
Application questions test the ability to use knowledge in a practical, problem-solving manner.

L-4 Analysis—Pulling apart the pieces
These are questions that select, examine, and break apart information into its smaller, separate parts.

L-5 Synthesis—Creating; Putting together
Synthesis questions utilize the basic information in a new, original, or unique way.

L-6 Evaluation—Judging, predicting
Evaluation questions determine the value of information, including making judgments about the information.

WORKSHOP 2

The Essential
Literacy
WORKSHOP
BOOK

Applying Bloom's Taxonomy to "Goldilocks and the Three Bears"

Knowledge
- List the characters in the story.
- What were the bears eating?

Comprehension
- Retell the story in your own words.
- Why did Goldilocks like the Baby Bear's chair best?

Application
- If Goldilocks came into your house, what are some of the things she might use?
- Relate the story from the view of Baby Bear.

Analysis
- What parts of the story could not have happened?
- Compare Goldilocks' experience with that of Little Red Riding Hood's.

Synthesis
- Combine art and drama to make up a new ending for the story.
- How might the story have been different if Goldilocks had visited three fish?

Evaluation
- Do you think Goldilocks was good or bad? Why?
- Did Goldilocks make a good decision by running away from the bears? Explain.

Creative Questioning

Ask open-ended questions: Open-ended questions are questions that have multiple answers. They stimulate thinking and encourage longer answers and thought. Open-ended questions allow children to feel successful because there is not one right answer. For example:

- What are the people in the picture doing?
- What does it look like?
- What do you like to play with outside?
- What are some ways we use water?

Ask children to use their senses: Stretch young children's creative thinking by asking them to focus on one of their senses.

- Have children close their eyes and guess what you place in their hands (a ball, a piece of sandpaper, a small rock).
- Have children close their eyes and guess what they hear. Shake keys, jingle coins, open a can of soda, tear a piece of paper, and so on.

Ask children about changes: One way to help children think more creatively is to ask them to change things to make them the way they would like them to be. For example:

- What would taste better if it were sweeter?
- What would be nicer if it were smaller?
- What would be more fun if it were faster?
- What would be better if it were quieter?

Ask questions with many answers: Questions with multiple answers encourage children to use creative and analytical thinking skills.

- What do you notice about this tree?
- What do we need to set up a restaurant in our classroom?
- What could you use to make a flower?
- What else can you tell me about your dog?

Ask "What would happen if..." questions: These questions are fun to ask and allow the children to use their imaginations and higher-order thinking skills.

- What would happen if all the trees in the world were blue?
- What would happen if all the cars were gone?
- What would happen if everybody wore the same clothes?
- What would happen if you could fly?

Ask "In how many different ways..." questions: These questions also extend a child's creative thinking.

- In how many different ways could a spoon be used?
- In how many different ways could a button be used?
- In how many different ways could a string be used?

The Essential
Literacy
WORKSHOP
BOOK

Gryphon House, Inc. grants permission for this page to be photocopied by professionals using *The Essential Literacy Workshop Book*.

Comments and Questions That Help You Learn About and Extend Children's Thinking

1. To initiate an interaction with a child, you might say, "I notice that..." or "I see that..." For example:
   - I notice that your block building is really tall.
   - I see that you worked at the easel for a long time. Would you like to tell me about your work?
   - I see a problem here. Can someone tell me what you think is happening?
   - When you poured water through the top of the water wheel, I see that the wheel turned around. Why do you think that happened?
   - I noticed that you put the blocks into two groups. I wonder how you decided to group the blocks this way.

2. When posing a question, it is best to phrase it in a way that invites many responses. For example, asking the question, "What do you notice about the guinea pig?" is very different from asking, "Did you notice the guinea pig's legs?" or "Can you point to the guinea pig's nose?"

   Examples of open-ended questions are:
   - What do you think might happen next in the story?
   - What do you remember about the story?
   - What do you know about caterpillars?
   - What do you wonder about caterpillars?
   - What do you think might happen if we mix the blue paint with the red paint?
   - What do you think happened to the water that was in the puddle?

3. Some questions are used to gather specific information. Questions such as, "What color is this truck?" or "What shape is this?" are informational questions. They are also referred to as "closed questions" because they typically have one answer. Questions that begin with *who, what, when,* and *where* are typically closed questions.

The Essential
Literacy
WORKSHOP
BOOK

Supporting English Language Learners

Workshop Objectives

In this workshop, participants will:

- gain a deeper understanding of the development of home language and acquisition of a second language;
- acquire strategies for supporting home language development and English language learning; and
- collect ideas for literacy materials, props, and ways to meet the needs of English language learners.

Workshop Materials

- Overhead projector and Overheads 3.1–3.15 or computer and PowerPoint Workshop 3 (on accompanying CD)
- Handouts 3.1–3.5, one copy for each participant
- Chart paper, markers, tape
- A poem or short book in a language other than English
- Children's book, *The Other Side* by Jacqueline Woodson

Supplemental Resources

Beavers, L., & D'Amico, J. 2005. *Children in immigrant families: U.S. and state-level findings from the 2000 Census.* A KIDS COUNT/PRB Report on Census 2000. Baltimore: The Annie E. Casey Foundation; Washington, DC: Population Reference Bureau.

Culturally and Linguistically Appropriate Services (http://clas.uiuc.edu/links.html) provides additional resources on the subject of English language learners.

David, J., & Onchonga, O., Drew, R., Grass, R., Stuchuk, R. & Burns, M.S. (2005). "Head Start embraces language diversity." *Young Children* 60 (6): 40-43.

NAEYC Position Statement: Responding to Linguistic and Cultural Diversity (available online at (http://www.naeyc.org/about/positions/PSDIV98.asp).

Ordonez-Jasis, R. & Ortiz, R. 2006. "Reading their worlds: Working with diverse families to enhance children's early literacy development." *Young Children* 61 (1), 42-48.

Tabors, P.O. 1997. *One child, two languages.* Baltimore: Paul H. Brookes Publishing Co. (Recommended for all trainers but particularly those with limited knowledge on this topic.)

Suggested Time Frame
3-hour workshop

Handout List

3.1
Agenda

3.2
What We Know from Research

3.3
Supporting English Language Learners

3.4
English Language Learning

3.5
Taking a Look Within

Trainers' Guide to Workshop 3

Note: Throughout this workshop we use ELL as the acronym for English language learners to mean children whose native language is not English.

Essential Messages for This Workshop: Supporting English Language Learners

■ Teachers need to provide children who are English language learners with opportunities for listening, speaking, reading, and writing in both English and their native language. Experiences and materials must be available in both languages.

■ Supporting children in communicating effectively in their own language helps develop their capacity to learn a second language. A strong foundation in the first language promotes literacy achievement in the second language.

■ The focus should be on maintaining and supporting primary language development while supporting English acquisition, not on replacing the first language with English.

■ Teachers need to modify how they present vocabulary, directions, storytelling, reading, and other oral language communication when working with children for whom English is not their native language.

■ Teachers must be aware of their own personal biases and attitudes, be culturally sensitive, and be willing to learn about and accept the range of differences among the children in their classroom.

▸▸ *Display* Overhead 3.1 or PowerPoint Slide 1: Welcome to Today's Workshop *as participants arrive.*

1. Opening Activity: Many Languages [15 minutes]

The opening activity is designed for groups of 5–6 people. Prior to arrival of the group, set up tables with 5–6 chairs at each table.

▸▸ *Give each group a piece of chart paper and markers.*

Open the session by saying, "Today we are going to focus on supporting English language learners. With your group, brainstorm a list of as many different languages as you can."

Allow 3–4 minutes, and then say, "For each language on your list, write one word in that language followed by its English translation."

Allow 3–4 minutes for them to work. Ask each group's recorder to count the number of languages on the list and to write the number and circle it at the top of the chart. Then ask the recorder to count how many words in other languages are on the list and record that number next to the number at the top. Ask each group to report their two numbers to the whole group. As they call out their numbers, record them on a flip chart in two columns, labeled "languages" and "words." When all the numbers have been recorded, read them horizontally (for example, 26 languages, 6 words; 16 languages, 7 words; and so on).

Pose the question, "What do these numbers tell us?" A typical response will be that we know the names of more languages than words in a language. Ask each group to read the languages from their list in which someone knew a word. Note the languages most frequently known by the groups.

Invite the groups to share some of the non-English words on their lists. Ask, "What do these words have in common?" Typically, they will be numbers, colors, food, items of clothing, and bathroom words.

Summarize the activity by pointing out that collectively we know a few words in a few languages and that these words are generally nouns and simple adjectives. Note that when young children begin to talk, they typically learn to say nouns (what something is called), then verbs to supply an action ("ball went"), and then simple adjectives to describe the noun ("red ball went"). This is the way language is acquired, regardless of the language or the age of the second language learner.

▶▶ *Show* Overheads 3.2 and 3.3 or PowerPoint Slides 2 and 3: Demographics *to provide basic demographic information.*

Demographics
- Over the past two decades, the percentage of school-age children speaking a language other than English at home has nearly doubled.
- By the year 2010, more than 30% of all school-age children will come from U.S. homes in which the primary language is not English.
- 2005 Annie E. Casey Kids Count Data reported that 19% of U.S. children speak a language other than English at home. Note: By 2050, Hispanic and African-American children under age 5 will outnumber non-Hispanic whites in the United States.

- Over 300 languages are spoken by English language learners coming to U.S. schools, including:

Spanish	Portuguese	Mandarin	Korean
Hindi	Urdu	Japanese	Tagalog
Arabic	Russian	Gujarati	Haitian Creole
Polish	French	Hungarian	Vietnamese

Note: There are between 5,000 and 6,000 languages spoken in the world today. Spanish, Mandarin, Vietnamese, Arabic, Tagalog, and Russian are the most common, depending on where one is geographically.

2. Welcome and Logistics [5 minutes]

▸▸ *Distribute* Handout 3.1: Agenda. *Review the agenda and workshop objectives.*

3. Introducing the Topic: Foundations
[25–30 minutes]

Begin by saying, "One of the common and detrimental myths about young children who speak little or no English is that because they are young, they will learn a second language rapidly, and easily—without any targeted attention to their needs or efforts for ensuring an environment conducive to learning the new language" (Tabors, 1997).

Continue by adding, "If this were true, there would not be such a gap in achievement in our schools today."

▸▸ *Show* Overhead 3.4 or PowerPoint Slide 4: Literacy Achievement *and share the following data:*

Literacy Achievement

■ **38% of 4th graders in the United States scored below proficient reading level in 2005. Following are data from specific states:**

California = 50%	Nevada = 48%	Texas = 36%
Illinois = 38%	Florida = 35%	New York = 31%

■ **Compare the above percentages with the number of school-age children who speak a language other than English at home.**

California = 43%	Nevada = 28%	Texas = 31%
Illinois = 21%	Florida = 24%	New York = 26%

Invite comments from the group by asking questions such as, "What does this data tell you? What are the implications?"

▸▸ *Show* Overhead 3.5 or PowerPoint Slide 5: The Achievement Gap.

Say, "These are the results of the data."

■■

Achievement Gap

Children who speak a non-English language at home and children of Hispanic/Latino backgrounds are at significantly greater risk of reading difficulties and subsequent academic underachievement.
(Snow, Burns, & Griffin 1998)

Prompt comments with questions such as, "What do you think of this? Why is this so? Does this surprise you?"

▸▸ *Distribute* Handout 3.2: What We Know from Research *and annotate the part below as noted.*

What We Know from Research

■ **A solid foundation in English oral fluency is highly desirable prior to formal English literacy instruction for children who are not learning to read in their first language** (Snow, Burns & Griffin 1998). Children need a good vocabulary in English before they can be taught to read. Children's reading achievement is linked to vocabulary. For ELLs in preschool and kindergarten, we must first focus on developing oral fluency.

■ **A strong basis of vocabulary in the child's first language promotes literacy achievement in the second language.** Supporting children's first language helps them to become literate in the second language. As children learn the ins and outs of social language in their first language, they are learning about language and its use. This knowledge supports the acquisition of a second language as they learn vocabulary and ways to communicate in their first language and begin to make meaning of vocabulary and find ways to communicate in English.

Ask if any participants are or were ELLs and invite them to share their personal experiences in learning English.

▸▸ *Continue with* Overhead 3.6 or PowerPoint Slide 6: Language as a Foundation for Learning to Read. *Read the text.*

Language as a Foundation for Learning to Read

"Excellent literacy instruction in multilingual settings may be possible only if children's home languages are taken into account in designing instruction." National Reading Council, 1998

"Oral and written language experiences should be regarded as an additive process, ensuring that children maintain their home language while also learning to speak and read in English." International Reading Association, 1998

63

Ask, "Why do you think home language development is considered important?" Solicit responses.

▶▶ *Show* Overhead 3.7 or PowerPoint Slide 7: How Are These Children Being Taught? *and annotate as noted.*

How Are These Children Being Taught?
- **Decades of research documents academic and social benefits from having strong home language and cultural foundation (Garcia 1993; Tabors 1997; Espinosa & Burns 2003; NAEYC 1996; Ordonez-Jasis & Ortiz 2006).**

Say, "As we have just discussed, the evidence is clear and overwhelming."

- **However, many programs throughout the United States that serve English language learners focus on English learning and not maintenance of children's primary language. Attention to culture is often superficial and "touristy."**
  Note: Touristy refers to a tourist approach, which celebrates only holidays or a study of countries. It may stereotype a particular cultural group and neglect considering the here and now of children's own experiences in their homes and community. (See Workshop Session 9 for appropriate inclusion of Diversity into the environment.)

Ask, "Why do you suppose this is?" Invite a few comments.

▶▶ *Continue with* Overhead 3.8 or PowerPoint Slide 8: Why Support a Home Language? *and link text to the prior discussion.*

Why Support a Home Language?
- **All children are cognitively, linguistically, and emotionally connected to the language of their homes.**
- **Children are more likely to become readers and writers of English when they are already familiar with the vocabulary, grammar, and concepts (for example, colors, shapes, weather, time, family, and so on) in their primary language.**
- **Experiences with their own language allow children to develop phonemic awareness and other oral language skills, which predict later reading success.**
- **Many early literacy and other cognitive skills transfer from one language to another. Children literate in their first language will apply these skills to the second language.**

▶▶ *Continue by showing* Overhead 3.9 or PowerPoint Slide 9: How Can We Support ELLs in Our Classrooms?

■■■■■■■■■■■■■■■■■■■■■■■■■■■■■■■■■■■■■■■ ■

How Can We Support ELLs in Our Classrooms?

■ **Approach learning and language from a linguistic as well as a multicultural perspective.** Think about the ways your class supports diversity. Think also about ways to support children's home language while they are learning English.

■ **This perspective enables children to value and appreciate their cultural identity, to feel secure about their home language, and to respect the diversity of other children and adults.** In our rush to have children use English, we cannot overlook what research tells us. All children need to feel ethnic and cultural pride, to feel valued for who they are, and to feel safe in being themselves in the classroom (Espinosa & Burns, 2003; Bredekamp & Copple 1997).

Invite a few comments on participants' experiences and thoughts about inclusion of cultural diversity in their classroom environments and curriculum.

---

4. Activity: How Do English Language Learners Communicate? [20–25 minutes]

▶▶ *Divide the group into groups of 5–6 participants. Give each group two pieces of chart paper and markers.*

▶▶ *Show Overhead 3.10 or PowerPoint Slide 10: Bilingual Children. Invite a participant to read the information aloud and then proceed to the activity instructions.*

Bilingual Children

Children acquire language within a variety of cultural and linguistic settings and in the context of their homes and communities. (Tabors 1997; Hart & Risley 1999)

Ask the groups to select a recorder. Have them label their chart paper as follows: on the top of one chart, write "What have we noticed about the ways English language learners begin to communicate in English?" On the other, write "What have we noticed about the ways English language learners continue to communicate in their first language?" Brainstorm ideas based on their experiences.

To clarify, rephrase, and expand the directions for the participants, say, "Focus on listening, speaking, and writing. How do English language learners begin to understand, speak, and write English? How do they continue to understand and communicate orally and in writing in their home language?" Allow 10–15 minutes for groups to brainstorm. Invite each group to present its ideas.

65

■ ■

Note: If there are more than five groups, ask each group to present one idea from each of their two charts in a round-robin format (see Appendix E). Groups should present an idea not previously mentioned by another group.

5. Discussion [10 minutes]

▸▸ *Show* Overhead 3.11 or PowerPoint Slide 11: Language Development.

Link the information to the small-group ideas presented in the previous activity, *How Do English Language Learners Communicate?* **Note:** Overheads 3.11 and 3.12 or Powerpoint Slides 11 and 12 are intended to go fairly quickly and should serve as a vehicle to sum up and organize the small-group ideas presented.

Language Development
English language learners:
■ exhibit the same language milestones as children whose home language is English;
■ may acquire vocabulary at a slower rate and have limited total vocabularies in each language; and
■ have a combined vocabulary in both languages likely to equal or exceed that of the English language-only child.

All children develop language in direct relation to:
■ the number and variety of words spoken to a child, and
■ opportunities to use language to interact with adults and other children.

▸▸ *Show* Overhead 3.12 or PowerPoint Slide 12: Learning a Second Language: Developmental Sequence *and annotate as noted.*

Continue to link the information to the small-group ideas presented.

Learning a Second Language: Developmental Sequence (Tabors 1997)
There will be differences in the way children progress in learning a second language. English language learners:
1. **Use their home language:** When children come into an English-language preschool or kindergarten classroom and do not speak English, they have two choices: They can continue to speak their native language or they can remain silent. Some children will pursue the first option and speak their native language to ask questions and make comments. Some children will not speak at all.

2. **Go through a nonverbal period:** Sooner or later, children realize that only some people (or no one) can understand them. They will stop talking to those who do not understand them and will only attempt or initiate conversations with those who understand them. While children may not communicate verbally, most communicate nonverbally in varying ways, such as attention-seeking behavior, requesting help (by pointing to what they need or want or bringing the item to an adult for assistance), protesting, joking, imitating the behavior of other children (getting in line, following motions of a fingerplay).

English language learners exhibit the same language milestones as children whose home language is English.

Ask participants for examples of children's nonverbal communications.

3. **Use individual words and phrases in a new language, and some children will switch between languages:** Children realize that in order to communicate with some children and adults or to function in school, they need to learn a new language. Their initial communication is in content words (such as milk, blocks, or three) and frequently heard phrases (for example, "I'm mommy," "no," stop!" "okay," look it," "be careful"). Some children will use both English and their first language in the same sentence or phrase.

4. **Begin to develop productive use of the second language:** Children build their own sentences as they continue to construct knowledge about the new language. Typically, they make many mistakes as they adopt and adapt the English they hear and are learning.

6. Activity: Classroom Strategies [20–25 minutes]

Begin the activity by saying, "Now let's focus on some of the strategies and ways we can use to support English language learners in the classroom."

Because participants often sit with people they know, reorganize the whole group into smaller groups of five or six to mix participants (see page 15 for ways to divide the group).

▸▸ *Distribute copies of* Handout 3.3: Supporting English Language Learners *(a 2-page handout).*

Ask each person to take five minutes to jot down ideas for each of the boxes. After 5–7 minutes, invite participants to share with others in their group. Allow 8–10 minutes for sharing in small groups. Encourage participants to add ideas from other group members to their lists. **Note:** If there are more than 25 participants in the workshop, ask half of the participants to work on one handout and the other half to work on the other, but distribute both handouts to each person for later note-taking.

Ask each small group to share one idea for each box. Encourage participants to add new ideas to their own handouts.

7. Discussion [10–15 minutes]

▸▸ *Distribute* Handout 3.4: English Language Learning.

Provide a few minutes for participants to read and review the handouts. Call attention to strategies not previously mentioned by any of the small groups. Review the lists and encourage participants to share ways they use these strategies. Encourage participants to add strategies not included.

▸▸ *Show* Overhead 3.13 *or* PowerPoint Slide 13: Where to Start.

Where to Start
- **Gather information about the cultural and linguistic backgrounds of the children in your classroom.** Think about who the children are and what you know about their family life, perspectives, dreams, and beliefs.
- **Accomplish this through:**
  - **formal questionnaires;**
  - **informal discussions with family members;**
  - **telephone calls home; and**
  - **discussions with others (teachers, staff, community) from the same cultural and linguistic backgrounds.**

Invite the participants to offer other suggestions.

- **Reflect on your own culture, attitudes, and biases.**

8. Activity: Supporting Cultural Diversity
[35–40 minutes]

Begin this activity by saying, "For the next activity, we are going to explore our own cultural diversity."

■ ■

▸▸ *Read the children's book,* The Other Side *by Jacqueline Woodson.*

This story uses a fence as a metaphor for a barrier between people. Other options include *Pepito the Brave* by Scott Beck or *I Knew You Could* by Craig Dorfman. If you do not have a copy of the book, tell a story about a metaphorical fence or barrier you or someone you know experienced.

Ask participants to find someone in the room whom they do not know well and to form pairs or triads. Once the pairs or triads are formed, say, "Talk with your partner(s) about a fence or barrier from your own life."

Allow 10–12 minutes for partners to talk. Encourage two or three people to share their fence or barrier with the whole group.

▸▸ *Distribute* Handout 3.5: Taking a Look Within.

Instruct participants to complete the survey independently, writing down the first thing that comes to mind. Provide 8–10 minutes for individual work.

Divide the participants into groups of 5–6 by having each pair or triad from the prior activity join with one or two other pairs or triads. Ask participants to share their responses with their small group. Allow 15–20 minutes for small group sharing.

9. Discussion [15–20 minutes]

Call the whole group back together. For each item on the survey, encourage one or two participants to share their responses with the whole group. Discuss similarities and differences in responses.

Facilitate discussion by asking the following questions:
■ What did you learn from this activity?
■ Which parts were easier or harder to do or share with others?
■ How is this awareness of similarities and differences applicable to your work with children and families?
■ How do you learn or find out about the cultures of children and families in your class?

Brainstorm with the whole group on ways they support diversity in the classroom. Chart their responses. Encourage participants to move beyond holiday celebrations.

■ ■

Review the chart and ask if there are strategies on the list that may be leaning more towards supporting stereotyping. **Note:** Activities that may support stereotyping include those with a "tourist approach" (study of different countries, customs not based on children's present-day experiences, multicultural week or month). These types of activities should be discouraged.

Tell participants, "When your linguistic and cultural background and those of the children are different, it is especially important for you to spend time learning about the children's backgrounds, environments, and experiences. Be careful not to make assumptions. Racial and ethnic generalizations about particular groups may or may not apply to any child or family. It is important to collect and incorporate information relevant to the child and family. Different cultures place different value and norms on spoken and written language. Whether or not English language learners are in your classroom, good early childhood education programs support linguistic and cultural diversity, and advocate for the implementation of multicultural and anti-bias education."

10. Closure [10 minutes]

▸▸ *Ask participants to choose a partner and to share one new strategy they will try in the classroom.*

▸▸ *Show Overhead 3.14 or PowerPoint Slide 14: Remember… and invite volunteers to read each point aloud.*

R e m e m b e r …

■ **Teacher expectations significantly influence the quality of children's learning opportunities.**

■ **Teachers who have low expectations for children are not confident that they can teach those children, and as a result may attribute children's failures to lack of intellect and deficient home lives.**

■ **Teachers with strong self-confidence and feelings of efficacy in their teaching abilities have high expectations for all children.**

▸▸ *Show Overhead 3.15 or PowerPoint Slide 15 and allow a minute of quiet reflection.*

Instruction begins when you, the teacher, learn from the learner; put yourself in his place so that you may understand… what he learns and the way he understands it.
—Soren Kierkegaard (1813–1855)

▸▸ *Close by reading a favorite poem or short book in a language other than English. If you cannot read it, ask a participant who speaks the language to read it for the group. Book suggestions are included in Appendix A on page 306.*

OVERHEAD 3.1

WELCOME TO TODAY'S WORKSHOP

Supporting English Language Learners

Gryphon House, Inc. grants permission for this page to be photocopied by professionals using *The Essential Literacy Workshop Book.*

Demographics

Over the past two decades, the percentage of school-age children speaking a language other than English at home has nearly doubled.

By the year 2010, more than 30% of all school-age children will come from U.S. homes in which the primary language is not English.

2005 Annie E. Casey Kids Count Data reported that 19% of U.S. children speak a language other than English at home.

The Annie E. Casey Foundation KIDS COUNT State-Level Data Online (2005).

Literacy The Essential
WORKSHOP
BOOK

Over 300 languages are spoken by English language learners coming to school, including:

Spanish	**Portuguese**
Mandarin	**Hindi**
Urdu	**Japanese**
Arabic	**Russian**
Polish	**French**
Hungarian	**Gujarati**
Haitian Creole	**Korean**
Vietnamese	**Tagalog**

Literacy Achievement

- **38% of 4th graders in the United States scored below proficient reading level in 2005. Following are data from specific states:**

CA = 50%   NV = 48%   TX = 36%

IL = 38%   FL = 35%   NY = 31%

- **Compare the above percentages with the number of school-age children who speak a language other than English at home.**

CA = 43%   NV = 28%   TX = 31%

IL = 21%   FL = 24%   NY = 26%

The Annie E. Casey Foundation, KIDS COUNT State-Level Data Online www.kidscount.org

The Essential
Literacy
WORKSHOP
BOOK

W
O
R
K
S
H
O
P

3

Achievement Gap

Children who speak a non-English language at home and children of Hispanic/Latino backgrounds are at significantly greater risk of reading difficulties and subsequent academic underachievement.

(Snow, Burns & Griffin 1998)

The Essential
Literacy
WORKSHOP
BOOK

Language as a Foundation for Learning to Read

"Excellent literacy instruction in multilingual settings may be possible only if children's home languages are taken into account in designing instruction."

—National Reading Council, 1998

"Oral and written language experiences should be regarded as an additive process, ensuring that children maintain their home language while also learning to speak and read in English."

—International Reading Association, 1998

W
O
R
K
S
H
O
P

3

How Are These Children Being Taught?

Decades of research documents academic and social benefits from having strong home language and cultural foundation (Garcia 1993; Tabors 1997; Espinosa & Burns 2003; NAEYC 1996; Ordonez-Jasis & Ortiz 2006).

However, many programs throughout the United States that serve English language learners focus on English learning rather than on maintenance of children's primary language. Attention to culture is often superficial and "touristy."

Why Support a Home Language?

- **All children are cognitively, linguistically, and emotionally connected to the language of their homes.**

- **Children are more likely to become readers and writers of English when they are already familiar with the vocabulary, grammar, and concepts (for example, colors, shapes, weather, time, family, and so on) in their primary language.**

- **Experiences with their own language allow children to develop phonemic awareness and other oral language skills, which predict later reading success.**

- **Many early literacy and other cognitive skills transfer from one language to another. Children literate in their first language will apply these skills to the second language.**

The Essential
Literacy
WORKSHOP
BOOK

W
O
R
K
S
H
O
P

3

How Can We Support ELLs in Our Classrooms?

■ **Approach learning and language from a linguistic as well as a multicultural perspective.**

■ **This perspective enables children to value and appreciate their cultural identity, to feel secure about their home language, and to respect the diversity of other children and adults.**

Bilingual Children

Children acquire language within a variety of cultural and linguistic settings and in the context of their homes and communities.

(Tabors 1997; Hart & Risley 1999)

W
O
R
K
S
H
O
P

3

Language Development

English language learners:

◆ exhibit the same language milestones as children whose home language is English;

◆ may acquire vocabulary at a slower rate and have more limited total vocabularies in each language; and

◆ have a combined vocabulary in both languages likely to equal or exceed that of the English language-only child.

All children develop language in direct relation to:

◆ the number and variety of words spoken to a child; and

◆ opportunities to use language to interact with adults and other children.

The Essential
Literacy
WORKSHOP
BOOK

Learning a Second Language: Developmental Sequence

There will be differences in the way children progress in learning a second language.

English language learners:

1. Use their home language.

2. Go through a nonverbal period.

3. Use individual words and phrases in a new language, and some children will switch between languages.

4. Begin to develop productive use of the second language.

(Tabors 1997)

Literacy The Essential
WORKSHOP
BOOK

W
O
R
K
S
H
O
P

3

Where to Start

■ **Gather information about the cultural and linguistic backgrounds of the children in your classroom.**

■ **Accomplish this through:**

◆ formal questionnaires;

◆ informal discussions with family members;

◆ telephone calls home; and

◆ discussions with others (teachers, staff, community) from the same cultural and linguistic backgrounds.

■ **Reflect on your own culture, attitudes, and biases.**

Remember...

■ **Teacher expectations significantly influence the quality of children's learning opportunities.**

■ **Teachers who have low expectations for children are not confident that they can teach those children, and as a result may attribute children's failures to lack of intellect and deficient home lives.**

■ **Teachers with strong self-confidence and feelings of efficacy in their teaching abilities have high expectations for all children.**

W
O
R
K
S
H
O
P

3

Instruction begins when you, the teacher, learn from the learner; put yourself in his place so that you may understand... what he learns and the way he understands it.

—Soren Kierkegaard (1813-1855)

AGENDA

Supporting English Language Learners

Date: _____

Trainer: _____

Contact Information: _____

OBJECTIVES

In this workshop, participants will:

■ gain a deeper understanding of the development of home language and acquisition of a second language;

■ acquire strategies for supporting home language development and English language learning; and

■ collect ideas for literacy materials, props, and ways to meet the needs of English language learners.

1. Opening Activity: Many Languages [15 minutes]

2. Welcome and Logistics [5 minutes]

3. Introducing the Topic: Foundations [25–30 minutes]

4. Activity: How Do English Language Learners Communicate? [20–25 minutes]

5. Discussion [10 minutes]

6. Activity: Classroom Strategies [20–25 minutes]

7. Discussion [10–15 minutes]

8. Activity: Supporting Cultural Diversity [35–40 minutes]

9. Discussion [15–20 minutes]

10. Closure [10 minutes]

The Essential
Literacy
WORKSHOP
BOOK

What We Know from Research

(Snow, Burns, & Griffin 1998)

- **High quality language and literacy environments help children develop skills that most strongly predict later literacy achievement:**
  - **Vocabulary/Listening Comprehension:** Having a good vocabulary and understanding the meaning of words. Knowing vocabulary can help children use context clues as they begin to read.
  - **Extended discourse:** Ability to talk well.
  - **Phonological Awareness:** Understanding sounds and rhythms of speech, rhyming, and sound similarities.
  - **Print concepts (forms and functions):** Understanding that the printed word comes in many formats (lists, signs, menus) and serves different purposes—we use different forms for different functions (thank-you notes, order pad, phone book, informational, and so on).
  - **Letter identification:** Ability to recognize letters as letters (as opposed to numbers or other shapes) and to spot particular letters ("That is a "b," like in my name, Isabel").
- **A solid foundation in English oral fluency is highly desirable prior to formal English literacy instruction for children who are not learning to read in their first language** (Snow, Burns, & Griffin 1998): Children must have a good vocabulary in English before they can learn to read. Children's reading achievement is linked to vocabulary. For ELLs in preschool and kindergarten, we need to focus on developing oral fluency first.
- **A strong basis in the child's first language promotes literacy achievement in the second language:** Supporting a child's first language helps him or her become literate in his or her second language. For example, as a child learns the ins and outs of social language in his or her first language, he or she is learning about the use of language. This knowledge supports the acquisition of a second language as children learn what this language is.

Language as a Foundation for Learning to Read

"Excellent literacy instruction in multilingual settings may be possible only if children's home languages are taken into account in designing instruction."
—National Reading Council, 1998

"Oral and written language experiences should be regarded as an additive process, ensuring that children maintain their home language while also learning to speak and read in English."
—International Reading Association, 1998

The Essential
Literacy
WORKSHOP
BOOK

Supporting English Language Learners

Opportunity	What is currently in the classroom that supports ELLs?	What can I add or do to support ELLs?
Meals		
Cleanup		
Transitions		
Morning Circle		
Dramatic Play		

Gryphon House, Inc. grants permission for this page to be photocopied by professionals using *The Essential Literacy Workshop Book*.

**The Essential
Literacy
WORKSHOP
BOOK**

Supporting English Language Learners

Opportunity	What is currently in the classroom that supports ELLs?	What can I add or do to support ELLs?
Music & Movement		
Literacy Materials		
Gross Motor Time		
Greetings & Departures with Families		
Child-Related Displays & Print		

English Language Learning

Scaffolding English Language Acquistion

- Start with what the child knows and shows interest in.
- Introduce content in the child's primary language. Learn a few key words for your theme in the child's primary language. (**Note:** These websites can help: www.freetranslation.com and www.bubblefish.com.)
- Start slowly and create low demand. Ask for simple responses, for example, if the child wants milk or water, or to play with blocks or paint.
- Talk in English about the routine or activity in which the child is engaged. For example, say, "You are putting your coat on, coat on" or "That's red paint, red."
- Support communication with gestures, actions, facial expressions, pictures, and real-life objects. Ask the child what the word is in his or her primary language. Validate his or her words by repeating it in his or her language and then repeating the word in English.
- Embed all English instruction in context clues that connect words to objects, visuals, and movements. Demonstrate whenever possible.
- Use content themes that are based on topics of interest in which the child has background knowledge.
- Use repetition; simplify by using basic words and phrases (say, "O is like a circle" instead of "O is a circular shape"; or say, "in line" instead of "behind one another").
- Rephrase, expand, and extend. As children acquire more English vocabulary, add adjectives and adverbs to describe their actions and routines. ("That's the racing car" or "The sand is falling slowly.")
- Fine tune your language to the child's level of understanding.
- Provide challenges. As the children move from words into phrases and more productive language, challenge them to tell you more about a picture they have made or a building they are building.

Read-Aloud Adaptations

- Read aloud to small groups of children to engage them in the story.
- Select books carefully; use predictable books, information books, and stories that reflect the children's cultures and communities.
- Consider the book's length: talk about a book rather than read it, but keep it short. In talking about a book, use books with vivid pictures; instead of reading the text as written, tell what is happening by pointing to the pictures or shortening the text. You may also include props when telling the story. Make eye contact during pauses.
- Invite children to discuss personal experiences related to the book.
- Preview and review key concepts and key vocabulary using both languages whenever possible.
- Read the books again and again.
- Send home versions of the selected titles in the child's primary language.

Literacy The Essential
WORKSHOP
BOOK

HANDOUT 3.4

Supporting English Language Learning

- Speak clearly at a standard speed, pausing between phrases.
- Use simple, short sentences. Repeat routine phrases (for example, "criss cross applesauce").
- Allow children to practice following and giving instructions for routines ("Get your coat and stand in line"). Invite them to say the rule when appropriate ("Use your inside voices").
- Create a consistent and predictable routine that uses cooperation, working together, small-group interactions, and regular opportunities for English language learners to talk informally with English speakers.
- Organize small groups to include a mix of first- and second-language children for planned activities.
- Teach English-speaking children in the classroom to be word resources for English language learners.
- Take time to listen to each child. If he or she cannot find the word in English, help him or her with the word by offering a cue or a prompt.
- Demonstrate respect and interest in the diverse backgrounds of the children.

Supporting Home Language Learning

- Interact with children in their home language.
- Integrate a child's home language into everyday classroom routines and activities through songs, poems, dances, rhymes, chants, counting, and books.
- Create props and labels in the child's first language to represent familiar stories, songs, or poems.
- If you do not speak the languages spoken by the children, look for resources to learn their languages. Even learning a few words or phrases conveys respect, demonstrates that you value their language, and shows a desire to communicate with them. As the child learns the English word for an object, invite him or her to teach you the word in his or her language.
- Invite bilingual paraprofessionals, family members, and community members to visit your classroom to interact with children in their home language.
- Provide books and other printed materials in other languages. Recruit older children as volunteers to record books in other languages.
- Use environmental print, such as signs and labels in home languages.
- Encourage children and families to share and record stories in home languages.
- Look for computer programs that support home languages.
- Encourage parents to converse and read with their children using their own strongest language.

(Howes 2003; Tabors 1997)

Taking a Look Within

Understanding diversity begins with understanding how you see yourself, your place in the world, what makes you special, and your own uniqueness.

As a start, complete each statement below:

1. I wear my hair the way I do because

2. Growing up in my family, children were expected to

3. I often feel uneasy around people who

4. I am proud to be

5. When I hear people speaking another language, I think they are

6. If I had to choose between work and family, I would

7. I really feel like an outsider when

8. The most important thing in life is

9. My ethnicity or cultural background is special because

10. I am often attracted to people who (or whom)

Phonological and Phonemic Awareness

Workshop Objectives

In this workshop, participants will:
- gain understanding of phonological and phonemic awareness;
- acquire strategies for teaching phonological and phonemic awareness; and
- collect ideas for using chants, fingerplays, poetry, rhyming books, and songs to promote phonological and phonemic awareness.

Workshop Materials

- Overhead projector and Overheads 4.1–4.9 or computer and PowerPoint Workshop 4 (on accompanying CD)
- Handouts 4.1–4.6, one copy for each participant
- Chart pad, markers, tape
- Index cards for the opening activity *Name Play*
- 1 or 2 copies of Assignment Cards cut into three sections (assignment one, two, and three). (If you plan for six groups, you will need two sets of Assignment Cards.)
- Enough poetry books to provide each table with two or three books
- Cups and beans
- Paper plates
- Several children's books from the categories of alliteration, phonological, and rhymes (see Appendix A). If you are using tables, place two or three books on each table.
- A read-aloud book rich in alliteration or rhyme, such as Mary Ann Hoberman's *A House Is a House for Me,* for closure activity

Supplemental Resources

Adams, M. J., Foorman, B.R., Lundberg, I., & Beeler, T. 1997. *Phonemic awareness in young children: A classroom curriculum.* Baltimore, MD: Paul H. Brookes Publishing.

Ericson, L. & Juliebo, M. 1998. *The phonological awareness handbook for kindergarten and primary teachers.* Newark, DE: International Reading Association.

Hohmann, M. 2002. *Fee, fie, phonemic awareness: 130 prereading activities for preschoolers.* Ypsilanti, MI: High/Scope Press.

Suggested Time Frame
3-hour workshop

Handout List
4.1
Agenda

4.2
Phonological and Phonemic Awareness

4.3
Tips for Promoting Phonological and Phonemic Awareness

4.4
Using Poetry with Children

4.5
Resources for Rhymes, Chants, and Poetry

4.6
Games for Phonological and Phonemic Awareness

Trainers' Guide to Workshop 4

Essential Messages for This Workshop: Phonological and Phonemic Awareness

- *Phonological awareness* is the ability to hear, identify, and manipulate the sounds of spoken language. This means that children can hear and repeat sounds, separate and blend sounds, identify similar sounds in different words, and hear parts or syllables in words (hel-i-cop-ter).
- *Phonemic awareness* is a more advanced component of phonological awareness. It is the ability to notice, think about, and work with the individual sounds (called phonemes) in spoken words (for example, identifying the three sounds in the word bug as /b/ /u/ /g/).
- *Phonics* is connecting sounds to letters (for example, the letter "b" makes the /b/ sound).
- Before children can learn to read print, they must have awareness of how the sounds in words work (Armbruster and Osborn 2001). They acquire this from hearing the sounds in spoken language and through chants, rhymes, nonsense words, and poetry.

▸▸ *Display Overhead 4.1 or PowerPoint Slide 1: Welcome to Today's Workshop as participants arrive.*

---

1. Opening Activity: Name Play [10 minutes]

Welcome everyone and introduce yourself with an alliterative phrase or sentence; for example, "Workshop Wonder Wendy" or "Delightful, Dynamic Dylan."

▸▸ *Give each participant a blank name tent (see page 316 in Appendix E) and a pen or marker.*

Ask, "Who knows what alliteration means? Turn to your neighbor and share what you think it means." Invite participants to share some responses. Make sure the definition is well understood. (The definition of alliteration is "the repetition of the same sounds or of the same kinds of sounds at the beginning of words.")

▸▸ *Show Overhead 4.2 or PowerPoint Slide 2: Name Play.*

Say, "Find a partner and work together to create alliterative phrases for your names. Use a marker to write the alliterative phrase for your name on your name tent."

Ask, "What are some ways to encourage children's play with language using the sounds in their names?" Invite a few responses. Ideas include: making up nonsense rhyming words with a child's name (Foody Judy) or adding a verb or adjective to a child's name (Jumping Janis or Jolly Holly); playing and singing "Willoughby Wallaby Woo" at circle time; and using silly names to direct children to leave the circle to choose a center or to line up.

Ask, "What are some reasons this will engage children in listening and playing with the sounds of language?" Responses might include: because children love hearing their own names, saying silly sounds, and playing repetitive games. Ask participants what children can learn from playing these games. Examples of responses might include: they will learn each other's names; they will learn to listen for repeating sounds; and they will hear, say, and make up rhyming words.

Say, "Today's workshop will focus on the sounds in language and how to foster children's learning of phonological and phonemic awareness.

Phonological awareness is the ability to hear, identify, and manipulate the sounds of spoken language.

2. Welcome and Logistics [5 minutes]

▸▸ *Distribute* Handout 4.1: Agenda. *Review the agenda and workshop objectives.*

3. Introducing the Topic: Phonological and Phonemic Awareness [20–30 minutes]

Note: If you decide to have participants review books later in the mini-lecture, you will need to estimate the full amount of time required.

▸▸ *Distribute* Handout 4.2: Phonological and Phonemic Awareness.

▸▸ *Show* Overheads 4.3 *and* 4.4 *or* PowerPoint Slides 3 and 4: Phonological Awareness *and review key points.*

Hearing the sounds in spoken language is a listening skill. It is the ability to hear, identify, and manipulate the sounds of spoken language. For example: hearing and repeating sounds; separating and blending sounds; identifying similar sounds in different words; and hearing parts or syllables in words (hel-i-cop-ter).

97

A child with phonological awareness can:
- **identify and make oral rhymes.** When children can string together rhyming words such as *dip, sip, lip, glip* they show us that they are developing phonological awareness.

- **hear, identify, and play with the sounds in words.** Listen to the words sun, sit, and song. What sound do they all begin with? (The /s/ sound). What other words begin with the "sss" sound? Now listen to these words: bite, dot, and sit. What sound do they end with? (The /t/ sound) Which of these words doesn't fit: dust, dog, dig, and stop? (stop) Why not? (It does not start with the /d/ sound.)

- **hear the syllables in words.** Let's clap the sounds in some words. "Hap-py," "lol-li-pop," "el-e-phant." Let's snap for a word. Who would like to suggest a fanciful multi-syllable word?

To support children's development of phonological awareness:
- **use songs, rhyming games, nursery rhymes, and rhyming poetry.**
- **play syllable clapping games.**
- **play games with the sounds in words.** Incorporate playful rhymes with children ("Oh my, we have oodles of noodles for lunch today!" Or after singing the song "Banana Fofanna," say, "Where's my marker marker bo barker? Who has seen my marker?")
- **talk with children about words and sounds in everyday situations.** If you want children to tune into the sounds of language, you must do it, too! Think about times you have drawn children's attention to the way language sounds. Does anyone have an example to share? For example, call attention to alliteration by using it playfully in the opening activity, noting it in read-aloud books or with a poem.
- **choose read-aloud books that focus on sounds.** Invite participants to come up with two or three read-aloud books that are great for the sounds in language. Ideas include *The Summer Noisy Book* and *The Winter Noisy Book* by M. W. Brown, *Animal Lingo* by P. Conrad, and *Joe Joe* by M. Serfozo.

Note: If participants are in groups at tables, you might pause here to give them time to look at and read the books you have put on the tables.

▸▸ *Show* Overhead 4.5 *or* PowerPoint Slide 5: Phonemic Awareness.

- **Phonemic awareness is a more advanced form of phonological awareness.** Phonemic awareness is a component of phonological awareness, but it is a higher-level skill. It is also a listening skill. Phonemic awareness means understanding that words are made up of sounds. Each individual sound in spoken words is called a phoneme. There are 44 phonemes in the English Language. Children must hear the individual sounds in words before they can learn to read print.

■ ■

■ **A child with phonemic awareness can hear, identify, and work with individual sounds (phonemes) in spoken words. For example, "bug" has three sounds (/b/ /u/ and /g/). Add the /l/ sound to "ate" to make "late." And take away the /t/ sound from "train" and get "rain."**

■ **Phonemic awareness is an important step toward learning the alphabetic principle: Words are composed of letters, and each letter in a printed word is connected to a spoken sound.**

■ **Phonemic awareness is different from phonics.** Phonics is a print skill, associating the letter symbol with the sound it makes.

> ➤➤ *Show* Overhead 4.6 *or* PowerPoint Slide 6: Supporting Phonemic Awareness.

Tell the participants that to support children learning phonemic awareness, they can:

■ **use songs, chants, fingerplays, rhyming games, nursery rhymes, and rhyming poetry.** Rhythm, rhyme, and repetition help familiarize children with the sounds and structure of language. Good ones to use are "Open Them, Shut Them" and "The Wheels on the Bus."

■ **play games that ask children to listen for beginning and ending sounds. For example: "If your name begins with the same sound as Ryan's, you may line up to go outside," or "Let's find all the things in our classroom that begin with the same sound as 'soup'."** Play "I Spy" with preschoolers by saying, "I spy something that begins with a 'b' sound." Children then look for something in the room that begins with that sound. For kindergarten children who can do this, you can begin to introduce letters. "I spy something that begins with the letter 'b'." This also adds phonics to the game.

■ **play "What Is Left When We…"** Ask the children what happens when one letter is removed from a word. For example:
   ■ "What is left when we take the /s/ sound away from 'smile'?"
   ■ "What is left when we take the /n/ sound away from 'moon'?"

■ **play games where children segment and blend the sounds in words. For example: "The letters 'st' + 'op' make 'stop.' Without the 'st', it would be 'op'."**

Say, "Let's do an activity now that will give you ideas to help children acquire these skills."

Phonemic awareness is the ability to notice, think about, and work with the individual sounds (called phonemes) in spoken words.

■ ■

4. Activity: Promoting Phonological and Phonemic Awareness [20–25 minutes]

▸▸ *Distribute one Assignment Card per table (see page 104 for assignment cards). If there are more than three groups, give the same assignment to multiple groups.*

Introduce this activity by saying, "Promote phonological and phonemic awareness by incorporating experiences throughout the day that engage children in listening to and playing with the sounds of language. You can do this best when you have a large repertoire of ideas. The next activity will give you a chance to share strategies you use currently and to learn new ideas from your colleagues. Take a moment to read the assignment card on your table. As a group, answer the questions and prepare to share. You will have 15–20 minutes to complete the assignment. Be prepared to share two highlights from your brainstormed list and 'perform' your presentation. Any questions?"

Circulate and check for understanding of the assignment. Clarify the difference between phonological and phonemic awareness. Be sure the ideas they generate specifically address phonological and phonemic awareness. Give participants a 2-minute warning before you call time.

Invite each group to share. If possible, offer to type up all of the lists and distribute.

5. Discussion [10 minutes]

Invite responses after asking, "What new insights do you have as a result of this activity?" "What are the different times during the day when you might use the activities generated today?"

▸▸ *Distribute* Handout 4.3: Tips for Promoting Phonological and Phonemic Awareness.

Say, "As you look over the handout, circle one idea that you already use in your classroom and one or two ideas that you plan to use immediately."

6. Activity: Using Poetry with Children
[30–35 minutes]

▸▸ *Divide participants into groups of four using one of the methods on page 15. Provide each group with one or two poetry books, some chart paper, and markers.*

▸▸ *Show* Overhead 4.7 *or PowerPoint Slide 7: Fuzzy Wuzzy.*

Introduce this activity by saying, "Let's read this traditional poem together."

Fuzzy Wuzzy (Traditional)
Fuzzy Wuzzy was a bear.
Fuzzy Wuzzy lost his hair.
Then Fuzzy Wuzzy wasn't fuzzy,
Was he?

Say, "Listening to and reading material that includes rhythm, rhyme, and repetition helps children become familiar with the sounds and structures of language. Poetry helps children learn phonological and phonemic awareness and, at the same time, teaches them that language can be playful and joyful."

▸▸ *Show* Overhead 4.8 *or PowerPoint Slide 8: Poetry Activity.*

Poetry Activity
■ Choose a poem from one of your collections.
■ Write the poem on a chart so it supports what you want to teach children about the sounds of language and words.
■ Include a few picture clues to help children "read" the poem.

▸▸ *Distribute* Handout 4.4: Using Poetry with Children.

■ Develop a plan for different ways children can repeat recitations, using strategies from the handout Using Poetry with Children or other ideas.
■ Brainstorm different times of the day when you might chant the poem with children.
■ Prepare to present a creative recitation to the whole group.

Say, "In this next activity, you will have a chance to look through some poetry collections, learn a poem, and reflect on ways to engage children in learning the poem. Let's review the steps. First, look through the books. Choose a poem you would like children to learn.

Write the poem on a chart. Think about how you will write it. Do you want to emphasize the rhymes or the sounds in certain words? Do you want to use picture clues to help children read it? You will have 15–20 minutes to work."

Give a 2-minute warning before you call time. Have them post their charts and invite them to take turns presenting their poems. Following each group's presentation, invite others to offer comments.

7. Discussion [10 minutes]

Pose the following questions, inviting responses after each:
- "What are some of the poems you use with children? How do the children respond?"
- "What are some of the ways you use poetry in your classrooms?"
- "As a result of this activity, what is one thing you are excited to try?"

> ▸▸ *Distribute* Handout 4.5: Resources for Rhymes, Chants, and Poetry.

8. Activity: Phonological and Phonemic Awareness Games [35 minutes]

Say, "We have talked today about how books, chants, fingerplays, and poetry help children learn phonological and phonemic awareness. Now let's look at games you can play with children to help them learn specific skills related to phonological and phonemic awareness, including:
- identifying sounds,
- building rhyme awareness,
- building alliteration awareness,
- recognizing letters, and
- developing letter-sound awareness."

> ▸▸ *Distribute* Handout 4.6: Games for Phonological and Phonemic Awareness.

> ▸▸ *Use* Overhead 4.9 or PowerPoint Slide 9: Phonological and Phonemic Awareness Games *to review directions for the activity.*

- **Review and discuss the ideas for games on the handout.**
- **Try each of the games and come up with additional ideas. Practice by alternating between playing the roles of teacher and children.**
- **Think of ways to extend one or two games so children who are ready can begin to learn letter names and their corresponding sounds (phonics).**
- **Prepare to share ideas for one game.**

Provide 20 minutes for participants to work (give a 2-minute warning) and 10 minutes for sharing.

9. Discussion [10 minutes]

Invite responses after saying, "Think about times during the day when you might do some of these activities with children. As you think about doing these activities in your classroom, what challenges do you anticipate? How can you address them up front?"

10. Closure [10 minutes]

Read aloud from one of your favorite books from the booklist (see Appendix A, pages 301-305). Choose a book that is rich in rhyming or alliteration.

Assignment Cards

Promoting Phonological and Phonemic Awareness

Copy this page, cut out each assignment, and distribute one assignment to each group. If you have more than three groups, make copies of this page and give two groups the same assignment.

Assignment One

Brainstorm a list of rhyming games you do with children. You can include games you use, games you have seen others use, or you can invent games! Try to come up with at least six ideas. Identify times of the day when you can use each game.

Make up a rhyming chant. Prepare to present it to the group.

Assignment Two

Brainstorm a list of fingerplays you do with the children in your class. Review and edit your list so it only includes those that support children's development of phonological and phonemic awareness. Make a list of books, tapes, CDs, or other resources that you use to help you with fingerplays.

As a group, memorize one fingerplay that most of you do not know or use. Prepare to present it to the group.

Assignment Three

Brainstorm a list of tongue twisters. Talk about those you knew in your childhood. Identify at least four you can use with children and when during the day you might use them.

As a group, make up a tongue twister. Prepare to present it to the group.

WELCOME TO TODAY'S WORKSHOP

Phonological and Phonemic Awareness

105

Name Play

Create alliterative phrases for your names.

Work together.

Use a marker to write the alliterative phrase for your name on your name tent.

Phonological Awareness

Hearing the sounds in spoken language is a listening skill.

A child with phonological awareness can:

◆ identify and make oral rhymes:
dip, sip, lip, glip
mat, sat, cat, hat

◆ hear, identify, and play with the sounds in words:
sun, sit, and song (all begin with the /s/ sound)
bite, dot, and *sit* (all end with the /t/ sound)
dust, dog, dig, and *stop* (ask which word doesn't fit and why)

◆ hear the syllables in words:
Clap for each sound in your name ("Ra-shan").
Snap for each sound in umbrella (um-brell-a).

The Essential Literacy WORKSHOP BOOK

W
O
R
K
S
H
O
P

4

Phonological Awareness

To support children's development of phonological awareness:

■ **use songs, rhyming games, nursery rhymes, and rhyming poetry;**

■ **play syllable clapping games;**

■ **play games with the sounds in words (for example, group objects by their beginning sounds, ask which word doesn't fit, and so on);**

■ **talk with children about words and sounds in everyday situations; and**

■ **choose read-aloud books that focus on sounds.**

The Essential
Literacy
WORKSHOP
BOOK

Phonemic Awareness

Phonemic awareness is a more advanced phonological awareness skill.

A child with phonemic awareness can hear, identify, and manipulate individual sounds (phonemes) in spoken words, such as:

◆ "bug" has three sounds (/b/ /u/ and /g/);

◆ add the /l/ sound to "ate" to make the word "late"; and

◆ take away the /t/ sound from "train" to get the word "rain."

Phonemic awareness is an important step toward understanding the alphabetic principle: Words are composed of letters, and each letter in a printed word is connected to a spoken sound.

Phonemic awareness is associating the letter symbol with the sound it makes; it is different from phonics.

The Essential
Literacy
WORKSHOP
BOOK

**W
O
R
K
S
H
O
P

4**

Supporting Phonemic Awareness

To support children's development of phonemic awareness:

- ## use songs, chants, fingerplays, rhyming games, nursery rhymes, and rhyming poetry.

- ## play games that ask children to listen for beginning and ending sounds, such as

  - ◆ "If your name begins with the same sound as Ryan's, you may line up to go outside."
  - ◆ "Let's find all of the things in our classroom that begin with the same sound as 'soup'."

- ## play "What Is Left When We..."

  - ◆ "What is left when we take the /s/ sound away from 'smile'?"
  - ◆ "What is left when we take the /n/ sound away from 'moon'?"

- ## play games where children segment and blend the sounds in words. For example:

  - ◆ "The letters 'st' + 'op' make 'stop'. Without the 'st', it would be 'op'."

Fuzzy Wuzzy (Traditional)

Fuzzy Wuzzy was a bear.

Fuzzy Wuzzy lost his hair.

Then Fuzzy Wuzzy wasn't fuzzy,

Was he?

Poetry Activity

Choose a poem from one of your collections.

Write the poem on a chart so it supports what you want to teach children about the sounds of language and words.

Include a few picture clues to help children "read" the poem.

Develop a plan for different ways children can repeat recitations, using strategies from Handout 4.4 or other ideas.

Brainstorm different times of the day when you might chant the poem with children.

Prepare to present a creative recitation to the whole group.

Phonological and Phonemic Awareness Games

Review and discuss the ideas for games on the handout.

Try each of the games and come up with additional ideas. Practice by alternating between playing the roles of teacher and children.

Think of ways to extend one or two games so children who are ready can begin to learn letter names and their corresponding sounds (phonics).

Prepare to share ideas for one game.

Literacy
The Essential
WORKSHOP
BOOK

HANDOUT 4.1

AGENDA

Phonological and Phonemic Awareness

Date:

Trainer:

Contact Information:

OBJECTIVES

In this workshop, participants will:
- gain understanding of phonological and phonemic awareness;
- acquire strategies for teaching phonological and phonemic awareness; and
- collect ideas for using chants, fingerplays, poetry, rhyming books, and songs to promote phonological and phonemic awareness.

1. Opening Activity: Name Play [10 minutes]

2. Welcome and Logistics [5 minutes]

3. Introducing the Topic: Phonological and Phonemic Awareness [20–30 minutes]

4. Activity: Promoting Phonological and Phonemic Awareness [20–25 minutes]

5. Discussion [10 minutes]

6. Activity: Using Poetry with Children [30–35 minutes]

7. Discussion [10 minutes]

8. Activity: Phonological and Phonemic Awareness Games [35 minutes]

9. Discussion [10 minutes]

10. Closure [10 minutes]

Phonological and Phonemic Awareness

Phonological awareness is hearing the sounds in spoken language. It is a *listening skill*.

A child with phonological awareness can:

- identify and make oral rhymes:
  dip, sip, lip, glip
  mat, sat, cat, hat
- hear, identify, and play with the sounds in words:
  sun, sit, and *song* (all begin with the /s/ sound)
  bite, dot, and *sit* (all end with the /t/ sound)
  dust, dog, dig, and *stop* (identify which word doesn't fit and why)
- hear the syllables in words:
  Clap for each sound in his name ("Ra-shan").
  Snap for each sound in the word umbrella (um-brell-a).

To support children's development of phonological awareness:

- use songs, rhyming games, nursery rhymes, and rhyming poetry;
- play syllable clapping games;
- play games with the sounds in words (for example, group objects by their beginning sounds, identify which word doesn't fit, and so on);
- talk with children about words and sounds in everyday situations; and
- choose read-aloud books that focus on sounds.

Phonemic awareness is a more advanced phonological awareness skill. It is a *listening skill*.

A child with phonemic awareness can:

- hear, identify, and manipulate *individual* sounds (phonemes) in spoken words. For example:
  - bug has three sounds (/b/ /u/ and /g/);
  - add the /l/ sound to "ate" to make the word "late"; and
  - take away the /t/ sound from "train" to make the word "rain."

Phonemic awareness is an important step toward understanding the alphabetic principle that words are composed of letters. Each letter in a printed word is connected to a spoken sound.

Phonemic awareness is different from phonics, which is associating a letter symbol with the sound it makes.

Literacy The Essential
WORKSHOP
BOOK

To support children's development of phonemic awareness:

- use songs, chants, fingerplays, rhyming games, nursery rhymes, and rhyming poetry, such as
    - play games that ask children to listen for beginning and ending sounds.
    - "If your name begins with the same sound as Ryan's, you may line up to go outside."
    - "Let's find all the things in our classroom that begin with the same sound as 'soup'."
    - play "What's Left When We..."
    - "What's left when we take the /s/ sound away from 'smile'?"
    - "What's left when we take the /n/ sound away from 'moon'?"
- play games where children segment and blend the sounds in words, such as
    - The letters "st" + "op" make "stop." "Stop" without the "st" would be "op."

Tips for Promoting Phonological and Phonemic Awareness

■ Expose children to alliteration by using it playfully, noting it in read-aloud books and with poetry. (*Alliteration* is the use of repeating initial sounds such as "Peter, Peter, pumpkin eater.")

■ Use children's names to create tongue twisters and alliterations. This will help them develop awareness of initial consonant sounds. ("Benita's brother broke brittle bottles.") Or use alliteration and vocabulary. For example, on a rainy day you might say, "Hello, soggy Sarah" when she arrives in the classroom.

■ If you want children to play with language, you must model it! Find situations when you can use nonsense words. Children will copy you because they delight in the silliness.

■ Incorporate playful rhymes into the day. For example, say, "Oh my, we have oodles of noodles for lunch today!" Or, after singing "Banana Fofanna" with the children, you might say, "Where's my marker marker bo barker? Who has seen my marker?"

■ Make rhymes using children's names and nonsense words (such as Holly's Folly or Shantal Lantal). Be sure children know that the point is to *have* fun, not to *make* fun!

■ Use rhyming fingerplays at transition times.

■ After reading aloud a book that rhymes, take a few minutes to generate a list of words that continue one rhyming pattern from the book. For example, after reading *Green Eggs and Ham,* you might ask, "Sam and ham. What other words can you think of that rhyme with Sam and ham?" You can do the same with alliteration. After reading *Sheep on a Ship,* you might ask, "What other words do you know that start like *sheep* and *ship?"*

■ Reread rhyming books with the children and leave out the rhyming word(s). Encourage the children to guess the word.

■ When doing a rhyme or word play game, keep it short so children stay engaged and want to do it again.

■ Create new rhymes from familiar verses with the children. For example, after reading *Brown Bear, What Do You See?* create a similar rhyme using children's names.

■ Provide opportunities for children to memorize chants, rhymes, and songs.

Using Poetry with Children

Choosing Poems

Many types of poems are valuable to use with children. Some are good for:
- reading aloud to children.
- reciting with children because they are fun.
- memorizing, a valuable to skill to have.
- provoking thought and inviting discussion; for example, metaphors and similes.
- listening to the sounds of language such as alliteration and onomatopoeia*.
- finding wonderful, descriptive words that extend vocabulary.
- relating to a theme.
- relating to a book.
- enlarging on a chart because they are visually interesting in shape or structure.

Memorizing Poems with Children
- Have children do many different recitations.
- Vary the way children recite the poem (whispering, speaking loudly, taking turns with lines, standing, sitting, rapping, using hand gestures, and so on).
- Choose poems for choral reading that have repetitive refrains, suggest simple sound effects, and linger on the tongue.
- Use short and easy-to-learn poems for recitation or memorizing.
- Let children hear some of the poems before they see the written words.

Some Good Poetry Books to Use with Children
A Fine Fat Pig and Other Animal Poems by Mary Ann Hoberman
Father Fox's Pennyrhymes by Clyde Watson
Flicker Flash by Joan Bransfield Graham
Read-Aloud Rhymes for the Very Young collected by Jack Prelutsky
Tomie dePaola's Book of Poems by Tomie dePaola
Winter Eyes by Douglas Florian

* *Onomatopoeia* refers to the use of a word in which the pronunciation sounds like the sound made when the action occurs (*swish, plop,* and so on).

Resources for Rhymes, Chants, and Poetry

Bennett, J. 1987. *Noisy poems*. New York: Oxford University Press.

Bryan, A. (Ed.). 2001. *Ashley Bryan's ABC of African American poetry*. New York: Aladdin.

Church, E. B. 2000. *The great big book of classroom songs, rhymes, and cheers*. New York: Scholastic.

Foster, J. 1998. *Finger rhymes*. New York: Oxford University Press. (John Foster has a series of books called First Verses of which this is one.)

Goldish, M. 1999. *101 science poems and songs for young learners*. New York: Scholastic.

Greenfield, E. 1986. *Honey, I love and other love poems*. New York: HarperCollins.

Greenfield, E. 2003. *In the land of words: New and selected poems*. New York: HarperCollins.

Hale, G. (Ed.). 1997. *Read-aloud poems for young people*. New York: Black Dog & Leventhal.

Hall, D. (Ed.). 2001. *The Oxford illustrated book of American children's poems*. New York: Oxford University Press.

Katz, B. 2001. *Rumpus of rhymes: A noisy book of poems*. New York: Dutton.

Myers, W. D. 1996. *Brown angels: An album of pictures and verse*. New York: HarperCollins.

Prelutsky, J. (Ed.). 2000. *The Random House book of poetry for children*. New York: Random House.

Press, J. 1997. *Alphabet art with a-z animal art and fingerplays*. Charlotte, VT: Williamson Publishing.

Rosen, M. 1994. *Poems for the very young*. Boston, MA: Kingfisher.

Schiller, P., & Moore, T. 2004. *Do you know the muffin man?: Literacy activities using favorite rhymes and songs*. Beltsville: MD: Gryphon House.

Simpson, J. 2005. *Circle time poetry: Math*. New York: Scholastic.

Simpson, J. 2005. *Circle time poetry: Science*. New York: Scholastic.

Warren, J. 1993. *Nursery rhyme theme-a-saurus: The great big book of nursery rhyme teaching themes*. Waldoboro, ME: Totline Publications.

Worth, V. 1996. *All the small poems and fourteen more*. New York: Farrar, Straus and Giroux.

WORKSHOP

Games for Phonological and Phonemic Awareness

4

To support children's learning, play games to help them:

- identify sounds,
- build rhyme awareness,
- build alliteration awareness,
- recognize letters, and
- develop letter-sound awareness.

Phonemic Manipulation

Choose a word and ask the children to think of ways to change it to another word by removing a sound, adding a sound, or changing a sound.

For example, come up with different ways to change the word *cat:*

- What happens if we take away the /c/ sound? *(at)*
- What happens if we change the /at/ sound in cat with a /an/ sound? *(can)*
- What happens if we replace the /t/ sound in cat with a /p/ sound? *(cap)*

Oddity Tasks

Say a short list of words and ask the children to listen for the word that does not belong (based on sound). For example, *man, make,* and *boy (boy)* or *bat, cat, snake,* and *rat (snake).*

Making Rhymes

There are a number of rhyming games you can play at different levels. Some examples are:

- Change the ending words in familiar nursery rhymes. For example, "Jack be nimble, Jack be red, Jack jump over the _____." Have children fill in the blank with word that rhymes with *red.*
- Say simple rhymes. For example, say, "I say 'cat'; you say _____." The child responds with a word that rhymes with *cat.*
- Do rhyme chains. Begin with a word and ask the child for a word that rhymes with it. If you say "cat," the child might say "mat." Continue with "sat," and the child might say "rat," and so on.
- Do rhyme phrases by asking the child to fill in the blank. For example, say, "I will pick a flower, and be back in one _____." The child responds with "hour." Or, "We were resting near a tree, when I was stung by a _____." The child responds with "bee."

The Essential
Literacy
WORKSHOP
BOOK

120

Where's the Sound?

To prepare, label three cups as follows: *beginning, middle,* and *end.* Gather buttons, teddy bear counters, or another item to put into the cups. **Note:** You can also play this game using beanbags and squares made on the floor with masking tape. Label three boxes: *beginning, middle,* and *end.* Ask, "Where do you hear the "l" in 'silly'?" The /l/ sound comes in the middle of the word, so the child drops a button or other marker in the cup labeled *middle.* Or ask, "Where do you hear the /b/ in 'bake'?" The child should drop an item in the cup labeled *beginning.*

Word Chains

You can play this higher-level game one-on-one or with a group. Begin by saying a word. The child then says a word that begins with the final sound in the first word. For example, the last sound in the word *tan* is /n/, so the next word would start with a /n/ sound *(nut).* The next word said would begin with the /t/ sound. This can go on indefinitely. Choose a number of words before beginning ("Let's do a word chain with then words.") **Note:** Keep in mind that the chain is made using the last *sound* of a word, not the last letter. For example, in the word *write* the last letter is "e," but the last sound is /t/.

Sound Trays

You will need a tray or a sturdy paper plate and objects that are on hand or are familiar to the child. Make the tray or plate a sound tray for a particular sound, such as /m/. Write the letter "m" on the plate or on an index card to identify the letter. Begin by putting a marker on the tray to identify the sound /m/. The marker is an object that begins with the "m" sound. Then, put additional objects, one at a time, on the tray. Whatever goes on the tray changes to that sound (in this case, /m/). For example, the child puts a pencil on it and says, "mencil." The next child puts a ruler on the tray and it becomes a "muler."

The Essential Literacy Workshop Book

Creating Environments to Support Literacy

Workshop Objectives

In this workshop, participants will:

- gain a deeper understanding of how to plan and set up preschool and kindergarten learning environments that support emergent literacy and foster active learning;
- acquire strategies for creating developmentally appropriate print-rich environments that facilitate meaningful learning, support diversity, and promote literacy development; and
- collect ideas for literacy materials, props, and ideas to enhance learning centers.

Workshop Materials

- Overhead projector and Overheads 5.1–5.13 or computer and PowerPoint Workshop 5 (on accompanying CD)
- Handouts 5.1–5.5, one copy for each participant
- Chart paper, markers, tape
- Props for activity *Print Has a Purpose* (gift box with a scarf or pair of gloves, birthday card, blank nametag, cell phone, some receipts, phone book or list of phone numbers, and paper with writing that looks like rules)
- Activity Cards for activity *Infusing Literacy in Centers* (see page 135). Precut the page. Depending on the number of groups, you may need to make a copy of the page and assign more than one group the same assignment.

Supplemental Resources

Heroman, C. & Jones, C. 2004. *Literacy: The creative curriculum approach.* Washington, DC: Teaching Strategies.

Owocki, G. 1999 *Literacy through play.* Portsmouth, NH: Heinemann (Chapters 4 and 6).

Schickedanz, J. 1999. *Much more than the ABC's: The early stages of reading and writing.* Washington, DC: NAEYC (Chapter 6).

Trainers' Guide to Workshop 5

Essential Messages for This Workshop: Creating Environments to Support Literacy

- The materials we make accessible to children (or don't make accessible) encourage (or limit) their play. Without varied props to support literacy, we limit children's opportunities to develop literacy skills and knowledge.

- In a print-rich environment, there is liberal inclusion of print that has meaning for children. The print serves a purpose. Signs, labeled centers, wall stories, labeled displays, labeled murals, charts, and poems are just a few ways to display print. This does not mean putting labels on everything in sight such as the door, window, and tables, nor does it mean papering the walls with words.

- By organizing the environment and planning experiences with the intention of incorporating literacy, teachers make reading and writing a meaningful part of children's lives (Schickedanz 1999).

▸▸ *Display* Overhead 5.1 *or* PowerPoint Slide 1: Welcome to Today's Workshop *as participants arrive.*

1. Opening Activity: Focusing on the Literacy Environment [10–15 minutes]

After the participants arrive, divide them into groups of 5–6 people (use one of the strategies outlined on page 15).

Begin by saying, "Today we are going to focus on the environment. Please find all of the literacy materials you have in your possession. Let's see which group can come up with the largest number of items. You can only count a pen once, even if three people in your group have the same item." Possible items include: pen, pencil, marker, crayon, cell phone, pad, address book, a CD, a book, checkbook, file card, takeout menu, credit card, an envelope, a letter, business card, receipt, coupons, family pictures, magazine, date book, calendar, recipe card, map, note, Post-its, journal, notebook, and so on.

Allow time for each group to look through its possessions and find materials to support literacy. After 3–5 minutes, say, "Now, count your group's items and report your totals."

Have the group with the most items show and list each item, one at a time, and describe how it relates to literacy. **Note:** If two groups tie, have a "run-off," with one group showing one item and the other group showing a different item not already shown by the first group. Some of the objects may relate to literacy because people:

- talk about family photos using expressive language;
- read and write recipe cards;

- write in a checkbook;
- listen to music CDs; or
- speak and listen on a cell phone and read the numbers and letters on the keypad.

Make sure that participants include reading, writing, listening, speaking, and viewing, which are the components of literacy. If they do not mention one or some of these, make sure you mention them.

After each group has finished going through its items, ask if any group has something that has not been shown or mentioned yet. Invite them to share that item.

After all the different items have been shown, pose the question, "How many of these items are available in your dramatic play center? Think about what you would do if you did not have a checkbook. You would not be able to write checks. The materials we make accessible to children (or don't make accessible) encourage (or limit) their play. Without varied props to support literacy, we limit children's opportunities to develop literacy skills and knowledge."

Say, "Today's workshop will focus on using the environment and materials to support children's literacy development. "

2. Welcome and Logistics [5 minutes]

▸▸ *Distribute* Handout 5.1: Agenda. *Review the agenda and workshop objectives.*

3. Introducing the Topic: Creating Environments to Support Literacy [40–45 minutes]

Begin by saying, "Knowing that the physical environment affects children's literacy development, many effective teachers carefully and intentionally arrange classroom environments in ways that promote children's literacy learning. The physical environment tells children what they may or may not do (for example, what is expected of them); and the types of materials we provide and the way we arrange them help decide what kind of learning will take place."

▸▸ *Show* Overhead 5.2 *or* PowerPoint Slide 2: Good Environments Promote Literacy (Seefeldt & Galper 2001).

125

Arrange classrooms so children can:

- **construct meaning through firsthand activities that support the use of language.** Arrange the environment into learning centers with materials that are interesting and accessible to children. Materials should be real and reflective of the children's experiences. Children can select among centers and varied materials.

  Ask, "What are some of the ways you promote meaningful firsthand learning in your classroom?" Invite some ideas before continuing to review key points.

- **develop awareness of the purpose and function of print.** The NAEYC and International Reading Association's joint position statement *Learning to Read and Write: Developmentally Appropriate Practices for Young Children* (1998) notes that a central goal of early childhood programs is to expose children to print and develop concepts of print.

- **use language, speaking, listening, reading, and writing in connection with their interactions with the learning environment, materials, peers, and teachers.** Children are active learners. They learn by interacting with their environment, materials, other children, and adults. When children are actively engaged, they find it essential to use both spoken and written language.

- **use language to share information and opinions, persuade others, and solve problems.** As children work in learning centers, they learn social skills such as cooperation and sharing, as well as how to deal with conflict and diverse points of view.

▶▶ *Have participants choose a partner.*

Say, "Share some of examples with your partner of children in your classroom using language in one of these ways." After 2–3 minutes, invite a few people to share a few examples aloud and then continue with the following points:

- **talk to others about their ideas and questions; elaborate on experiences and clarify their thinking.** Children make meaning through experiences. Encourage children to talk through or explain their reasoning. Interact with children in ways that clarify, extend, and expand their language skills and knowledge.

- **feel successful as they learn new skills, vocabulary, and knowledge.** Make sure that materials are varied, open-ended, and available in different levels of difficulty.

Ask, "What are some reasons it is important for children to experience success?" Invite two or three responses.

▶▶ *Show* Overhead 5.3 *or* PowerPoint Slide 3: A Good Learning Environment.

Read the following statement aloud: "A good learning environment encourages children to feel successful and builds self-confidence." Pause for 30 seconds and read it again. Invite participants to comment on ways their classroom environment supports children's feelings of competence and confidence.

▶▶ *Distribute* Handout 5.2: Key Elements in Organizing Space and Materials.

Say, "Take a few minutes to review the handout, and put a + next to those items you do very well, and a √ next to those items you would like to improve." Provide a few minutes for participants to complete this task.

When they are finished, say, "Now, with your partner, find another pair to join you to form a group of four. Share what you wrote for #14: something beautiful that you have in your classroom. Please do not include children. While we know they are beautiful, they are not things!"

Provide 2 minutes for group sharing and then invite a few people to share their responses with the whole group. Say, "Now we are going to focus specifically on literacy in the environment."

▶▶ *Distribute* Handout 5.3: Developing the Literate Play Environment.

Say, "This handout will help you remember many of the key points on the overhead (or PowerPoint), which we will discuss now."

▶▶ *Show* Overhead 5.4 *or* PowerPoint Slide 4: Developing a Literacy-Rich Play Environment (Owocki 1999; Morrow 2002).

Annotate as noted. **Note:** Use a piece of paper to uncover the overhead one line at a time. If using PowerPoint, this will occur naturally.

1. **Infuse the learning environment to support literacy-rich play.** An environment that

supports literacy-rich play is one where teachers and children use written language throughout the day, as needed, to serve real-life tasks in their play and daily routines. If children do not observe and experience that reading and writing serve a purpose in our lives, they have little reason to use them. Your role is to encourage and extend their natural uses of written language and to model and establish its many real-life functions.

Ask, "What are some of the real-life functions of written language? In other words, why is it necessary to read and write?" Solicit a variety of reasons. Then uncover the next section on the overhead and relate participants' responses to the four major functions: Environmental, Occupational, Informational, and Recreational (Owocki 1999).

Examples for each of these categories include:
- *Environmental*—street and traffic signs, store names and department directory signs, schedules, restroom signs, price tags, coupons;
- *Occupational*—menus, message pads, order forms, signs, money, appointment books, licenses, reference materials, plan books, checkbooks;
- *Informational*—calendars, date books, clocks, maps, newspapers, phone books;
- *Recreational*—magazines, storybooks, poems, travel books, birthday cards, invitations, thank-you notes.

2. **Establish a print-rich learning environment.** *A print-rich environment* contains a liberal offering of print that has meaning for children, and the print serves a purpose. Signs, labeled materials and shelves, wall stories (see note below), labeled displays and murals, classroom charts, and poems are a few ways to display print. This does not mean putting labels on everything in sight such as the door, window, tables, and so on; nor does it mean papering the walls with words. It also means that there are books and writing materials in many centers. **Note:** Wall stories, also called chart stories, are simple, short stories made up by children, adapted from text (for example, the very hungry dinosaur), or true to text. Each page or scene of the story is written on a sentence strip, typed in large font, or printed onto chart paper. Children can make illustrations to accompany the text. Wall stories are usually no more than 5–8 pages or chart papers in length. They are hung in sequence at children's eye level to encourage children to read the text. Commercial wall stories are available.

3. **Establish at least one classroom literacy center.** Typically this is an expanded writing center that includes items such as various types, colors, and sizes of paper; markers, crayons, pencils, and colored pencils; stapler; hole punch; tape; blank books; envelopes; cards; stencils; word files (see note below); notebooks; clipboards; Post-its; name cards; stationery; and books. **Note:** A word file is a box similar to a recipe box that holds index cards. The index cards each have a word written on them, usually with an accompanying picture. Some teachers create word files by punching a hole through the index cards and keeping them together with a ring clasp, eliminating the need for a box.

4. **Provide books and varied writing materials in many centers.** Each center should have books or reading materials linked with that center, along with varied materials to write with and on. Consider what children do in that center, and what purposes writing and reading can serve. For example, in the block center, you might add index cards and markers to make signs for children's buildings; a clipboard and ruler to measure their structures; architectural paper and blueprints to support planning a structure; books about the city, castles, traffic signs, farms, buildings; and other props to extend and support their play.

5. **Introduce literacy props based on familiar experiences to centers.** Play props to support literacy should be linked to children's interests and experiences. Observe children's play themes and talk with family members about where children have been and what they have experienced. Most children have been to a grocery store or to a gas station, so it makes sense to provide literacy props to support those kinds of play. On the other hand, not all children have been to an airport. Knowledge for young children is context-bound.

6. **Start a collection of literacy materials.** Collect literacy materials to use for various dramatic play themes. Create a center for dramatic play themes beyond the home living center when possible. For the home living center, think about all of the literacy props used in daily activities in your home and in the children's homes. Start adding these to your collection. Visit real places in the community and ask for literacy materials to support creating that theme center. For example, menus and order pads can be added to create a restaurant; appointment books, eye chart, medical charts, and a message pad can be added to create a doctor's office. Create theme prop boxes to support literacy, for example, for a pet store, a supermarket, a bakery, a florist, a vegetable stand, a car wash, a train station, an office, or a post office. By laminating the signage and gathering or making the necessary props, including those that support literacy, you will have a variety of theme-based centers to add to your classroom over the course of the year.

4. Activity: Print Has a Purpose [15–20 minutes]

▶▶ *You will need two volunteers for this activity.*

Privately, give the volunteers directions for a role-play. One person will play a customer and the other a store clerk. The customer wants to return a present she got for her birthday, but she does not have the receipt. The store clerk will not accept the item back because the store policy is "no returns without a receipt." Instruct them to act this out without talking or using their voices, and using no props.

■ ■

Let the group know that they will observe a role-play for about 1–2 minutes. After a couple of minutes, interrupt the role-play and invite participants to guess what the scene is about. Invite a few guesses but do not give the answer.

Provide the same actors with props for a second role-play. Give the customer a gift box with a scarf or a pair of gloves and a birthday card. Give the clerk a nametag, a cell phone, a few receipts, a phone book or a phone list to look up her supervisor's number, and a paper that looks like policies for returns. Ask them to repeat their scene, still without voices, but now they may use props.

Let the actors do the second role-play for a few minutes or until someone guesses what the scene is about.

Say, "The materials and props we provide for children allow them to take on different roles and learn about the various purposes of print. Providing literacy materials encourages children to explore literacy and learn that print has meaning, and takes different forms."

5. Discussion [10–15 minutes]

Ask, "What literacy props did our actors use?" Responses should include a birthday card, phone book, nametag, cell phone, receipts, and store policy guidelines.

Ask, "What forms, functions, or features of print did they use?" Responses might include: When buying things people get a receipt, and when returning things, people usually need the receipt; receipts are usually lightweight paper; cards go with presents; phone books help us find phone numbers and addresses; nametags are written in large letters; store employees usually wear nametags; stores have policies for returns.

Say, "Let's look around this room. Where do you see print with a purpose in this room?" Possible answers include: exit signs; "Turn Off the Light" signs next to the switch; recycle signs on trash cans; emergency exit sign; notice of an upcoming meeting; and so on.

Ask, "What examples of print with a purpose are in your classroom?" As different participants respond, ask each participant to name the purpose the print serves. Keep in mind the four functions of print—environmental, occupational, informational, recreational.

Give the following example to emphasize the importance of using picture cues with print: "When a child sees a sign next to the toilet that says, 'Please flush' with a picture of a child flushing the toilet, this not only helps the child learn to flush, but also reinforces that print has meaning."

Say, "The print you include in the classroom should contain a simple, clear message or meaning. Print should capture children's attention, so make it large, attractive, and eye-catching." Give some other examples of print that has a purpose in a classroom, such as helper charts, the daily schedule, labels on bins, and labels on shelves to know where to find items and where to put them away.

6. Activity: Infusing Literacy in Centers [20–25 minutes]

▸▸ *Show* Overheads 5.5–5.11 *or* PowerPoint Slides 5–11: Photos for Creating Environments to Support Literacy.

▸▸ *Arrange participants into pairs.*

Say, "Work with your partner to discuss the 'print with a purpose' you see in the seven photos of various centers and areas of the classroom. Jot down your ideas."

After each slide, pause to let pairs talk about the photograph for a minute. Then invite responses. Spend 1–2 minutes for each photo.

▸▸ *Distribute* Handout 5.4: Infusing Literacy in Centers.

Divide the participants into new groups of 4–5 people.

Say: "To infuse language and literacy experiences in learning centers throughout the classroom, consider these three questions:

■ **What materials can you add?**
■ **What specific ideas do children need to guide their work and play so literacy learning is fostered?**
■ **What is your role?**"

▸▸ *Using the precut activity cards (see page 135), assign each group a different center and give them chart paper and markers.*

Note: Precut the Activity Cards: Infusing Literacy in Centers into segments so each group has one of the following centers to use for their assignment: Art, Blocks, Dramatic

Play/House Area, Science/Discovery, Sand/Water, Outside, Table Toys, Music/Movement, Computer, and Library Corner. Depending on how many groups you have, there may be more than one group doing the same assignment or you may not have enough groups to cover all of the centers. Give each group chart paper and markers.

Say, "With your group, work on your assigned center. Think about materials to add and ideas you can use to focus and extend children's literacy learning. It is not necessary to include those materials generally found in that learning center. Combine your ideas on a chart. Your group's chart should include materials you will add, guiding ideas to support children's literacy as they work and play at the center, and the role of the teacher at that center."

7. Discussion [10–15 minutes]

▸▸ *Have each group select a spokesperson to summarize the ideas on their chart paper.*

Summarize this activity by saying, "By adding materials to centers and utilizing appropriate teacher supports (interactions and questions), we can infuse many types of literacy experiences into our classrooms."

8. Activity: Dramatic Play Themes to Support Literacy [30–35 minutes]

Begin this activity by saying, "For this activity, we will explore in more depth the varying functions of written language."

▸▸ *Ask groups to select new facilitators and recorders. Give the recorder chart paper and markers.*

Assign one of the following functions to each group: Environmental, Occupational, Informational, or Recreational. For 5 minutes, have each group brainstorm dramatic play themes that support that area. Stop them after 5 minutes; post the charts on a wall and read the lists aloud. Themes may include office, flower shop, gas station, bakery, repair shop, sporting goods store, hair salon, fast food restaurant, police station, doctor's office, post office, pet store, library, and construction site.

Say, "Each group should choose one of the themes for this last activity."

> ▸▸ *Give each group another sheet of chart paper to record their ideas.*

Note: There will likely be overlap among the lists. That is fine because many themes provide opportunity for children to gain knowledge about the various functions of print. The intention is to develop a list of various dramatic play themes. If you are short on time, assign a dramatic play theme. However, do not assign or include "Supermarket" as most classrooms already use this theme.

> ▸▸ *Show Overhead 5.12 or PowerPoint Slide 12: Dramatic Play Themed Centers for Instructions.*

Say, "After I read the instructions, review these five questions in your groups and discuss how you will motivate children's interest in this theme and ensure that they have the necessary experience to support their play. What materials will you add? How will the theme be organized? What roles are there for the children to play and how can you support children's literacy learning in this play center?"

Read the instructions:
1. **How will this theme be introduced?**
2. **How will you motivate children's interest in this theme and ensure that they have the necessary experience to support their play?**
3. **What materials will be added?**
4. **How will the theme be organized?**
5. **What roles are there to play and how can you support children's literacy learning in this play center?**

Say, "Number your chart paper from 1–5 and answer each of the questions on the overhead (or PowerPoint)."

After 10–15 minutes, have the groups report what they wrote.

9. Discussion [5–10 minutes]

Pose a few of these questions to stimulate dialogue:
- What are some ways teachers can ensure that children have the necessary experience to make this a successful theme center?
- Where can one get materials to support a theme center?
- How do you select themes to expand to a center?
- Which themes have been successful?
- How can a theme help build children's knowledge of the various functions of written language?

10. Closure: Reflections [10 minutes]

▸▸ *Show* Overhead 5.13 *or* PowerPoint Slide 13: Reflection.

Read the words slowly as participants pause to reflect:

Good teachers continually self-evaluate and reflect on their role in facilitating literacy through active learning.
- **Do the children in my class read and write during play?**
- **Are materials meaningful?**
- **Do I take time to capitalize on teachable moments?**
- **What functions does literacy serve in the children's play?**
- **Are the children exploring a variety of genres and forms of written language?**
- **Do the children have the materials they need to explore the features of print?**

▸▸ *Distribute Handout 5.5: Reflection.*

Provide teachers with 5 minutes to reflect on the questions and write an "Aha!" based on today's session. Invite a few to share their "Ahas!"

Activity Cards

Infusing Literacy in Centers

A r t

_____

B l o c k s

_____

D r a m a t i c   P l a y / H o u s e   A r e a

_____

S c i e n c e / D i s c o v e r y

_____

S a n d / W a t e r

_____

O u t s i d e

_____

T a b l e   T o y s

_____

M u s i c / M o v e m e n t

_____

C o m p u t e r

_____

L i b r a r y   C o r n e r

_____

WELCOME TO TODAY'S WORKSHOP

Creating Environments to Support Literacy

Good Environments Promote Literacy

Arrange classrooms so children can:

◆ construct meaning through firsthand activities that support the use of language.

◆ develop awareness of the purpose and function of print.

◆ use language, speaking, listening, reading, and writing in connection with their interactions with the learning environment, materials, peers, and teachers.

◆ use language to share information and opinions, to persuade others, and to solve problems.

◆ talk to others about their ideas and questions, elaborate on experiences, and clarify their thinking.

◆ feel successful as they learn new skills, vocabulary, and knowledge.

(Seefeldt & Galper 2001)

W
O
R
K
S
H
O
P

5

Literacy
The Essential
WORKSHOP
BOOK

**W
O
R
K
S
H
O
P**

5

A Good Learning Environment

A good learning environment

encourages children

to feel successful and

builds self-confidence.

Literacy
The Essential
WORKSHOP
BOOK

Developing a Literacy-Rich Play Environment

1. Infuse the learning environment to support literacy-rich play. The four major functions of written language:
   ◆ environmental
   ◆ occupational
   ◆ informational
   ◆ recreational

2. Establish a print-rich learning environment.

3. Establish at least one classroom literacy center.

4. Provide books and varied writing materials in many centers.

5. Introduce literacy props based on familiar experiences to centers.

6. Start a collection of literacy materials.

(Owocki 1999; Morrow 2002)

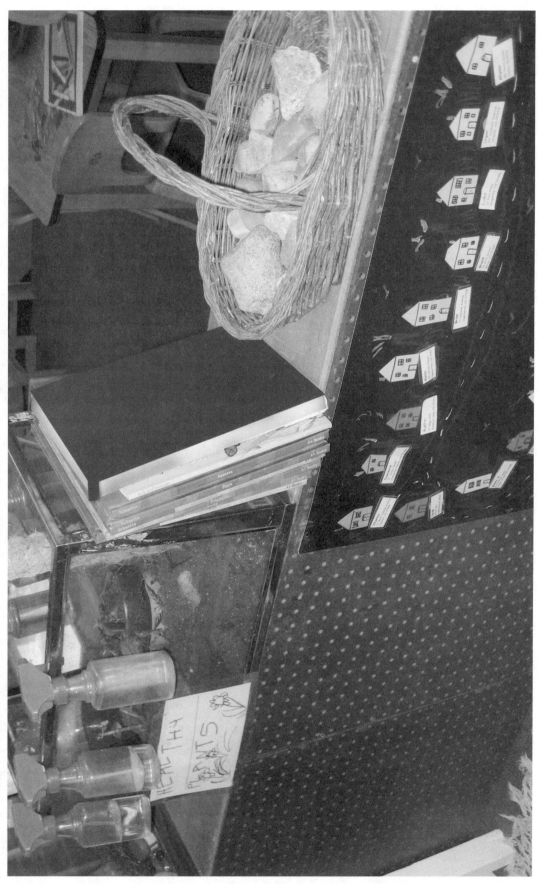

Gryphon House, Inc. grants permission for this page to be photocopied by professionals using *The Essential Literacy Workshop Book*.

Literacy The Essential
WORKSHOP
BOOK

OVERHEAD 5.11

Activity: Dramatic Play Themed Centers

Instructions

1. How will this theme be introduced?

2. How will you motivate children's interest in this theme and ensure that they have the necessary experience to support their play?

3. What materials will be added?

4. How will the theme be organized?

5. What roles are there for the children to play and how can you support children's literacy learning in this play center?

W
O
R
K
S
H
O
P

5

Reflection

Good teachers continually self-evaluate and reflect on their role in facilitating literacy through active learning.

◆ Do the children in my class read and write during play?

◆ Are materials meaningful?

◆ Do I take time to capitalize on teachable moments?

◆ What functions does literacy serve in the children's play?

◆ Are the children exploring a variety of genres and forms of written language?

◆ Do the children have the materials they need to explore the features of print?

W
O
R
K
S
H
O
P

5

AGENDA

Creating Environments to Support Literacy

Date:

Trainer:

Contact Information:

OBJECTIVES

In this workshop, participants will:
■ gain a deeper understanding of how to plan and set up preschool and kindergarten learning environments that support emergent literacy and foster active learning;
■ acquire strategies for creating developmentally appropriate print-rich environments that facilitate meaningful learning, support diversity, and promote literacy development; and
■ collect ideas for literacy materials, props, and ideas to enhance learning centers.

1. Opening Activity: Focusing on the Literacy Environment [10–15 minutes]

2. Welcome and Logistics [5 minutes]

3. Introducing the Topic: Creating Environments to Support Literacy [40–45 minutes]

4. Activity: Print Has a Purpose [15–20 minutes]

5. Discussion [10–15 minutes]

6. Activity: Infusing Literacy in Centers [20–25 minutes]

7. Discussion [10–15 minutes]

8. Activity: Dramatic Play Themes to Support Literacy [30–35 minutes]

9. Discussion [5–10 minutes]

10. Closure [10 minutes]

The Essential **Literacy** WORKSHOP BOOK

149

HANDOUT 5.2

Key Elements in Organizing Space and Materials

1. Establish boundaries between learning centers, creating well-defined centers.

2. Plan traffic patterns purposefully. A clear traffic pattern allows children to move around the room while not interfering with other children's activities.

3. Establish quiet zones and private places. Include soft cozy areas with pillows, cushions, rugs and large stuffed animals in your room.

4. Think about how you will supervise the children in all of the centers. Can you see all parts of the room?

5. Store materials near their use. Locate play spaces near the shelves where the materials are stored.

6. Label bins and shelves with words and pictures; organize materials based on their use and type.

7. Make sure displays are child related. Display appropriate materials for children. Put most of the displays in the room and on the walls at child's eye level. Most of the displays should be children's work with individualized work predominating.

8. Separate quiet areas from noisy centers. Place quiet and active centers in areas of the room so they do not interfere with one another.

9. Display materials attractively and be sure they are easily accessible. Avoid clutter.

10. Put books in many centers in addition to the Library Corner. Place meaningful words, letters, and symbols throughout the room. Put writing materials in many centers in addition to the Writing Center.

11. Make sure the environment promotes an acceptance of diversity, encompassing different races, cultures, ages, abilities, and gender. Materials should show diversity in a positive way and avoid stereotypes. Have many books, pictures, and materials (multiracial or multicultural dolls, music, props, puzzles, clothes, games, manipulatives, and musical instruments) accessible to children.

12. Store teaching materials separately from children's materials.

13. For health and safety reasons, place tissues in convenient areas in the classroom. Provisions for toileting (toilet paper, soap, paper towel, trash) should be convenient and accessible for children. Store all poisons, medicines, and other substances in locked cabinets where they are inaccessible to children. Label these materials "Keep out of reach of children." Cover electrical outlets or childproof them. Make sure there are no loose electrical cords or other major safety or health hazards.

14. Ensure that there is something beautiful to wonder over and ponder about in several places in your room.

The Essential
Literacy
WORKSHOP
BOOK

Developing the Literate Play Environment

1. Literacy is speaking, listening, reading, writing, and viewing.
2. Infuse the learning environment to support literacy-rich play.
3. Establish a print-rich learning environment.
4. Establish at least one classroom literacy center.
5. Provide books and varied writing materials in many centers.
6. Introduce literacy props based on familiar experiences to centers.
7. Start a collection of literacy materials.
8. Store literacy materials for dramatic play themes to allow for easy access for children.
9. Read to children in small groups every day.
10. Continually self-evaluate and reflect on your role in facilitating literacy through active learning.

Knowledge of Written Language

Written language has many purposes, including:
- environmental
- occupational
- informational
- recreational

Written language exhibits a variety of forms. Form is related to purpose, context, and content (menus, lists, thank you notes, signs, and so on).

Written language has significant features.
- Letters and words convey meaning.
- What is said can be written. What is written is always read the same way.
- In the English language, letters form words and are written in a line. We read and write from left to right and top to bottom.
- Letters make sounds. There is a connection between letter patterns and sound patterns.
- Words have a beginning and an end. In written language, there is a space between words and punctuation to note the end of sentences and to reflect pauses and intonation.

The Essential
Literacy
WORKSHOP
BOOK

Activity: Infusing Literacy in Centers

What materials can you add?

What specific ideas do children need to guide their work and play so literacy learning is fostered?

What is your role?

Reflection

Effective teachers continually self-evaluate and reflect on their role in facilitating literacy through active learning.

Do the children in my class read and write during play?

Are materials meaningful?

Do I take time to capitalize on teachable moments?

What functions does literacy serve in the children's play?

Are the children exploring a variety of genres and forms of written language?

Do the children have the materials they need to explore the features of print?

Aha!

The Essential
Literacy
WORKSHOP
BOOK

Supporting Children as Writers

Workshop Objectives

In this workshop, participants will:

- gain understanding of how children develop as writers;
- identify strategies to promote writing throughout the day;
- explore techniques and materials to encourage children's writing in centers;
- learn that becoming a competent writer involves knowing and understanding the forms, function, and features of writing; and
- understand how writing can be integrated throughout the day and within the environment.

Workshop Materials

- Overhead projector and Overheads 6.1–6.12 or computer and PowerPoint Workshop 6 (on accompanying CD)
- Handouts 6.1–6.4, one copy for each participant
- Chart paper, markers and pens, tape
- 5" x 8" index cards
- Children's book, *Click Clack, Moo: Cows That Type* by Doreen Cronin

Supplemental Resources

Schickedanz, J. & Casbergue, R. M. 2004. *Writing in preschool: Learning to orchestrate meaning and marks.* Newark, DE: International Reading Association.

Owocki, G. 1999. *Literacy through play.* Portsmouth, NH: Heinemann (Chapters 3 and 4).

Trainers' Guide to Workshop 6

Essential Messages for This Workshop: Supporting Children as Writers

- Reading and writing develop together. Children who write become better readers.
- Children learn the uses of written language before they learn the many forms writing takes. (**Note:** The forms of writing are not the letter formations, but are instead the style or structure of writing. For example, a shopping list uses a different style of writing than a thank-you note. In a shopping list, words are normally placed one item under the next; whereas a thank-you note begins with "Dear..." followed by complete sentences, and then a closing with a name.)
- Children's writing develops through constant invention and reinvention of the forms of written language. To learn to write, children need many opportunities to practice writing.
- While some teachers may instruct children to practice writing letters or words over and over, children learn to write more effectively when their writing is self-initiated and for real purposes (Morrow, 2005).
- Being a competent writer involves knowing and understanding the forms, function, and features of writing.
- Writing should be integrated into classroom activities and experiences throughout the day and within the environment.

▸▸ *Display* Overhead 6.1 *or* PowerPoint Slide 1: Welcome to Today's Workshop *as participants arrive.*

1. Opening Activity: Acrostic Poem [10–15 minutes]

▸▸ *Distribute one 5" x 8" index card and a marker or pen to each participant.*

Say: "Turn the card vertically and write your first name in capital letters vertically with each letter below the next." For example:

P
A
T

When participants are finished, say, "For each letter of your name, write a word or short phrase that describes you." For example:

JORDAN   or   CASIE

JORDAN	CASIE
Joyful	**C**uddly
Outgoing	**A**ffectionate
Rational	**S**weet tooth
Devilish	**I**ntelligent
Animal Lover	**E**ffervescent
Natural beauty	

To learn to write, children need many opportunities to practice writing.

Allow participants to assist one another. After 5 minutes, give a 2-minute warning to finish.

Invite participants to stand up and walk around the room, holding their index cards in front of them like a sandwich board. Say, "Introduce yourself to people you do not know and read each other's poems."

After allowing a few minutes for participants to share their poems, call them back to their seats. Ask if anyone knows the name of the type of poem they just wrote. If no one responds, tell them that it is an *acrostic* poem. Ask if anyone has written acrostic poems with their class. Tell them that it is one way to support children's writing as well as to point out letter-sound correspondence. Lead into the agenda by saying, "Today's workshop is about supporting children as writers."

2. Welcome and Logistics [5 minutes]

▸▸ *Distribute* Handout 6.1: Agenda. *Review the agenda and workshop objectives.*

3. Introducing the Topic: Supporting Children's Writing [30 minutes]

▸▸ *Open the session using* Overhead 6.2 *or* PowerPoint Slide 2: Children Want to Write.

Invite a volunteer to read the following statement aloud:

Children want to write. Children have been writing since they could first grasp a tool that makes a mark. Before they came to your classroom, they wrote on driveways, sidewalks, walls, mirrors, cabinets, books, and paper with crayons, markers, chalk, pens, pencils, or lipstick. A child's scribbles, symbols, and lines convey his or her sense of being. "I did this. I was here. I am me."

157

Say, "Think for a moment about your own first experiences of writing. What do you remember about writing at home or at school?" Allow a few moments for private reflection before forming groups.

Divide participants into groups of 4–5 using one of the strategies suggested on page 15.

▸▸ *Give each group a piece of paper and a pen.*

Ask participants to share their reflections and discuss the statement with their group. Allow about 5 minutes of discussion. Have them list the ways they see their children as writers. For example, many children attempt to write their names; some children scribble on paper; some children are attracted to colored markers; some children cover the entire paper on the easel with paint, but leave the space with their name written untouched. Invite the participants to discuss the different ways the children in their classrooms write. For example, do they scribble, make cards, write their names, copy words, use journals, add letters to their drawings? Allow 5 minutes for group discussions.

▸▸ *Invite participants to share the ways the children in their classrooms write. Chart their responses on a piece of chart paper.*

Say, "You have described many of the ways children write. Researchers have noted many descriptions of the development of writing. Most agree, though, that if there are stages, they are not well defined or necessarily sequential."

Add, "Young children learn about and use written language long before they receive formal instruction. Children begin to learn written language in the same way they learn to speak. Babies understand the power of speech because of the reinforcement they receive from adults. They are surrounded by adults and other children who use language and expect children to speak as well. Babies learn to make their needs known and to participate in the social world around them. Similarly, children learn about writing by observing others and making their own meaning. They learn about writing by watching adults write for real purposes. The more hands-on experiences children have with written language, the more opportunities they will have to make meaning of writing and reading."

Say, "Let's look at the categories and stages of children's writing."

▸▸ *Show Overhead 6.3 or PowerPoint Slide 3: Categories and Stages of Children's Writing and briefly describe each stage as noted on the following page.*

The Essential Literacy Workshop Book

Relate what participants have shared about children's writing on the chart paper to the different categories. **Note:** Overheads 6.4–6.9 or PowerPoint Slides 4–9 include samples of each stage of writing. Refer to these to show examples of each stage.

Categories and Stages of Children's Writing

■ **Marks and Scribbles:** Children as young as 18–24 months can begin to experiment with making marks and scribbling as they begin to explore what happens as they move a crayon or marker on a piece of paper. Starting with random marks, as children have more experience with writing materials their scribbles become more organized and begin looking like pictures while others look more like writing.

■ **Scribble Writing:** This is scribbling intended as writing. Some children will draw a picture and then make intentional wavy lines to stand for words. Children in dramatic play often use scribble writing as they hand the teacher a message or take a restaurant order on a pad.

■ **Letter-Like Forms and Individual Letters:** These mock letters often look like letters. At this stage, individual letters also start to appear. The initial letter of a child's name is often the first intentional letter a child makes.

■ **Letter Strings and My Name:** These are often sequences of letters from a child's name or other letters the child knows. The child may write them out of order or repeat letters more than once (for example, Mary may write MMAAYAMM). The child's correctly spelled name also appears as it is often practiced most often and is seen most frequently.

■ **Invented Spelling:** Children create their own spellings for words. Sometimes one letter may stand for an entire syllable; sometimes words are not spaced properly. Vowels may be omitted. As the child's writing matures, the words look more like conventional spelling with a letter omitted; for example, *LIK* for *like*).

■ **Conventional Forms:** At this stage, the child's writing resembles standard writing. Spelling errors may appear as errors, not because of invented spelling. Even after a child is able to produce standard writing, he or she will often use mock letters or scribble writing for various purposes, such as making a shopping list.

4. Activity: Constructing Knowledge About Writing [30 minutes]

▸▸ *Begin this activity by dividing participants into groups of five or six. Distribute a piece of chart paper and markers to each group. Ask the groups to brainstorm a list of the types of writing they did this week. Examples might be writing checks to pay bills, making a shopping list, writing an email, writing a child's dictation, and so on. Allow five to seven minutes for this task.*

▸▸ *Show* Overhead 6.10 *or PowerPoint Slide: 10 Why I Write. Ask for a volunteer to read what is on the overhead or PowerPoint slide.*

Everybody has to write. You need to write so you can get along in the world. There's lots of things to write like stories, songs, poems, jokes, riddles, information, cards, letters, emails, text messages, journals, diaries, instructions, grocery lists, checks, signs, labels, or just a note to someone. You have to think about what you are writing, because writing is different for different things. If you are writing a sign or instructions or a grocery list, then you have to write what it is, but when you write a story or a poem, you write what you want to write. You get to use your imagination or to express feelings. Some things like lists or recipes don't have to be in complete sentences but when you write a story, you have to use sentences and paragraphs.

When I start to write a story, I think about what should I say first, how should I start off, and sometimes I think what would be the best way to start and end my story. I have always wanted to get stories out of my mind. I want to be an author because if I was an author then the things I write about to express me would be shown to the world. Writing is a very fun thing. You can write about an adventure that a Hamburger had or you could write about friendship. I love writing very much because it makes me be creative and think about my readers.

—Brooke Ramsier, age 11

Say, "As Brooke has explained so vividly, one must have a reason to write, and the writer has to think about many things when she writes. The purpose or function of writing dictates the form. Let's look at some of the functions of writing."

Ask for one or two examples from the group to model the next part of this activity. For each example, ask the function of the writing and then expand to discuss the form. For example, a person writes a shopping list to remember what to buy at the store; the form for writing a list is to put one item below the next.

Ask, "What opportunities, materials, and strategies do you offer children to learn about the functions and forms of writing?" Ask a few participants to share examples.

▸▸ *Give each group chart paper and markers.*

Instruct each group to revisit their list to discuss the forms and functions of written language, as follows, "What strategies can you use to encourage exploration of the various forms and functions of writing? List some of the ways teachers support writing."

Allow 10–15 minutes for small-group discussions.

Invite the groups to share strategies with the whole group. Strategies may include providing various materials, modeling writing, sharing writing, scaffolding, using environmental print, and so on.

Make links between the functions and forms of writing.

5. Mini-Lecture: Features of Writing [15 minutes]

▸▸ *Display* Overhead 6.11 *or* PowerPoint Slide 11: Significant Features of Written Language *and annotate. Link the information to the forms, functions, and strategies reported previously by the small groups.*

▸▸ *Distribute* Handout 6.2: Understanding Writing.

Significant Features of Written Language

- **Letters and words convey meaning.** This is one of children's earliest discoveries. They learn that print must be present for a teacher to read a story (for example, the difference between a picture book and story book). Children might ask, "What does that say?"
- **Objects can be represented by print.** Children think initially that print simply labels objects. Early on, children expect print to name only what is in the picture; for example, five lines of print say only one word.
- **What is said can be written. What is written is read the same way, always.** Children start to learn that oral language must match written messages. Children will take four lines of their print/scribbles and make them match what they say.
- **There is a right way to write.** Children begin to hypothesize that there is a difference between pretend writing and real writing. They start to realize that scribbling and letter strings are not words.
- **Letters form words and are written in a line.** In the English language, children learn that we read and write from left to right and top to bottom.
- **Letters make sounds.** Children's move to conventional writing begins with understanding that one letter = a syllable, as well as identifying or writing initial consonants.
- **Words have a beginning and an end; words together make sentences.** Children learn that in written language, there is a space between words and punctuation at the end of sentences and to reflect pauses and intonation.

■ ■

6. Activity: Integrating Writing Throughout the Day [30 minutes]

Summarize by saying, "During this workshop, we have looked at the broad categories and stages children use in emergent writing, and the knowledge children need to develop about the forms, functions, and features of writing. We have shared ideas and strategies for supporting writing through the environment and through our actions. Now we are going to focus on the daily routine and how to integrate writing throughout the day."

▸▸ *Distribute* Handout 6.3: Integrating Writing Experiences Throughout the Day.

▸▸ *Have the participants form triads and brainstorm various ways children can experience writing during each segment of the day (arrival, circle time, center time, and so on).*

Allow 10–15 minutes for groups to work, then ask each group to join with another group they do not work with or know well to present their ideas. Allow 5–10 minutes for groups to share with each other, then bring the whole group back together.

Go through each segment of the day and invite participants to share. Solicit three to five ways to integrate writing for each segment. As participants share their ideas, comment on the relation of that idea to children learning about the forms, functions, and features of print.

Note: Comment on using Morning Messages, a strategy many teachers use to support writing. Each day, a message is written on a chart about an event or an interesting question. The content is used as the basis for discussion and the skills and concepts related to print and writing are also discussed. Teachers sometimes write the messages with the children while assembled in a whole group, making their actions explicit. For example, "I need to put a space between the words to show that they are different words." Teachers may have already written the Morning Message and will read it to children while making explicit decoding strategies. For example, if the message is "Today is Monday. We are going to make applesauce today," the teacher might say, "This must say Monday because it starts with the /m/ sound like Mikela." Ask if anyone does this, and invite a few participants to share what they do. Note that with three- and four-year-olds, it is important to keep the message short (one or two sentences) and to include rebus symbols in their writing.

Ask for questions, insights, and new ideas.

7. Discussion [10–15 minutes]

▸▸ *Use* Overhead 6.12 *or* PowerPoint Slides 12: Suggestions to Support Writing *to recap and share additional strategies.*

▸▸ *Distribute* Handout 6.4 Suggestions to Support Writing *to participants.*

Suggestions to Support Writing

■ **Provide a variety of useful writing and drawing materials in all centers.** Match materials with the center (for example, graph paper, Post-it notes, and other materials for signage in the Block Center).

■ **Anticipate emergent forms of writing.**

■ **Encourage children to write their own way.**

■ **Invite children to write or dictate a story.**

■ **Encourage children to write to one another.**

■ **Accept children's additions to your writing.**

■ **Display and send home samples of children's writings.**

■ **Listen to children "read" their writing.**

■ **Make encouraging and specific comments.** State explicitly the strategies you see children use. ("I see you left a space between the words.")

■ **Model the usefulness of writing.** Children need to see you writing for various purposes: writing a note to another teacher, taking a phone message, or using a Post-it note as a reminder.

■ **Make your writing strategies explicit.** Talk as you write, pointing out a specific strategy. For example, when writing Tom's name on his paper, say, "To make a T, I make a straight line down and then one more line across the top.")

■ **Notice environmental print.** Ask children questions such as, "What do you think it says?"

■ **Encourage children to write.**

■ **Provide opportunities and materials for book-making.**

■ **Relate meaningful writing experiences to projects and themes.**

■ **Create a Writing Center and vary the materials in it.** It is important to keep the center interesting by adding new materials to it regularly.

■ **Carefully observe children's writing. Knowing where children are in their thinking enables you to support them based on their current levels of development.** It is important to observe children as they write in their play and to talk to children about their writing.

Say, "It is vital that we provide children with the necessary materials for writing and that we stimulate and support children's writing every day."

8. Closure [10 minutes]

▸▸ *Ask participants to add two or three new ideas they heard today next to the bullets at the bottom of Handout 6:4 Suggestions to Support Writing.*

Ask, "As a result of today's workshop, what is one idea you are excited to try in your classroom?" Hear a few ideas from the group.

▸▸ *Read the children's book,* Click Clack, Moo: Cows That Type. *Comment that just like the cows in the book, children must have a purpose for writing and materials to do it.*

W
O
R
K
S
H
O
P

6

WELCOME TO TODAY'S WORKSHOP

Supporting Children as Writers

165

W
O
R
K
S
H
O
P

6

Children Want to Write

**Children want to write.
They have been writing
since they could first grasp a tool
that makes a mark.
Before they came to your classroom,
they wrote on driveways,
sidewalks, walls, mirrors, cabinets,
books, and paper with crayons,
markers, chalk, pens,
pencils, or lipstick.
A child's scribbles, symbols,
and lines convey
his or her sense of being.
"I did this. I was here. I am me."**

Categories and Stages of Children's Writing

Marks and Scribbles

Scribble Writing

Letter-Like Forms and Individual Letters

Letter Strings and My Name

Invented Spelling

Conventional Forms

Marks and Scribbles

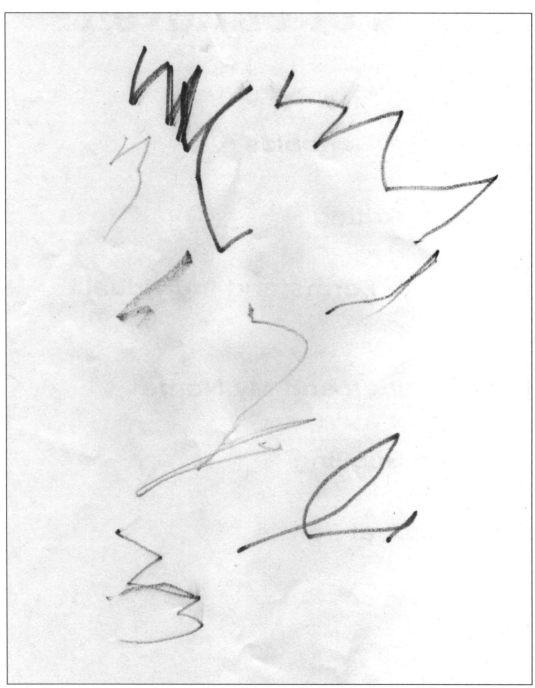

At 17 months, Madison is beginning to make her mark on the world.

Scribble Writing

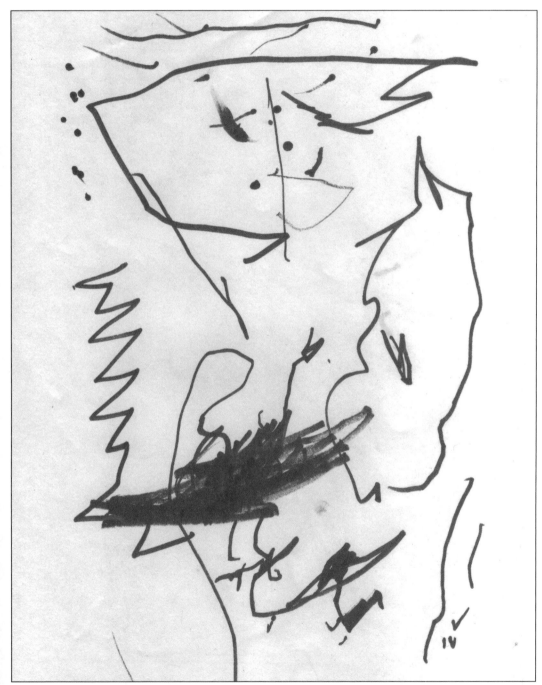

Notice the "M's" Mikela is starting to make as she scribble writes.

W
O
R
K
S
H
O
P

6

Letter-Like Forms and Individual Letters

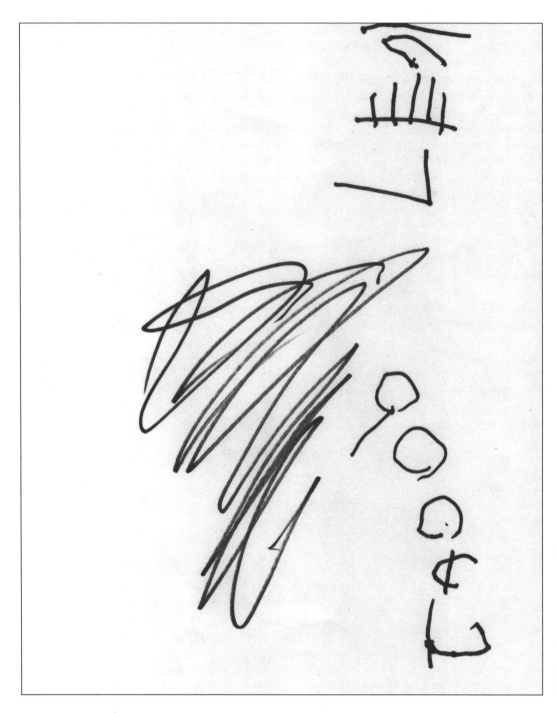

At age 4, Jacob is making forms and letters.

Letter Strings and My Name

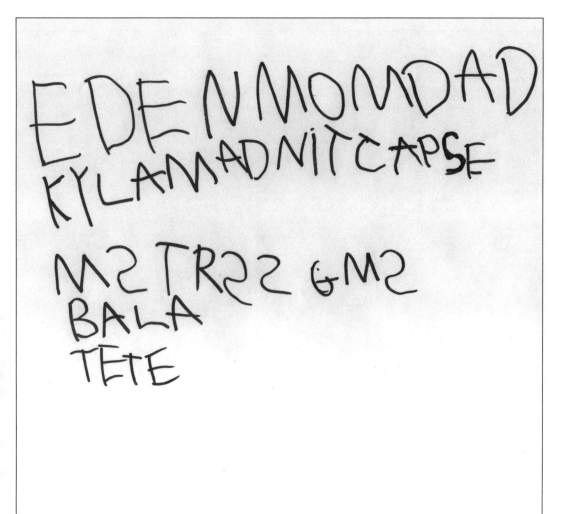

After writing her name and "Mom" and "Dad," Eden writes letter strings to name her friends.

Invented Spelling

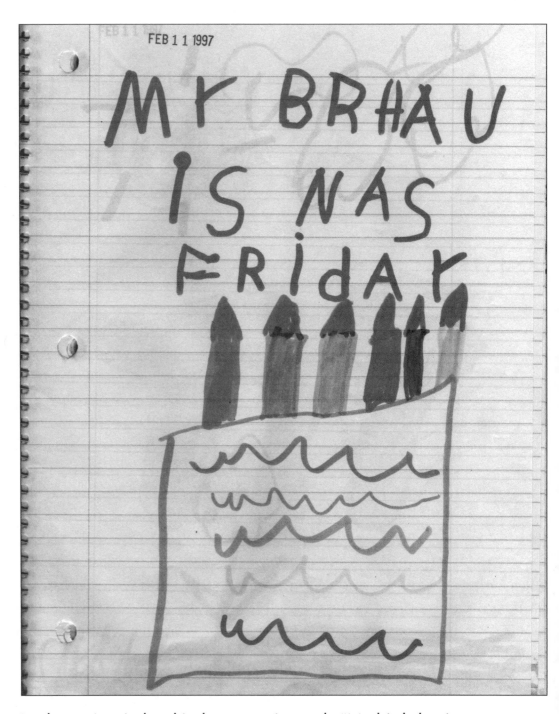

Jordan writes in her kindergarten journal: "My birthday is next Friday." She will turn 6.

Invented Spelling

Spelling progresses as children gain more letter sound recognition and sight words.

Dear Mrs. Forbes,
I am going to Florida and Rhode Island too. Jordan will see you and I might see you in school again. I got new shoes. They are black and they are sparkles.
Love, Alexa

Invented Spelling

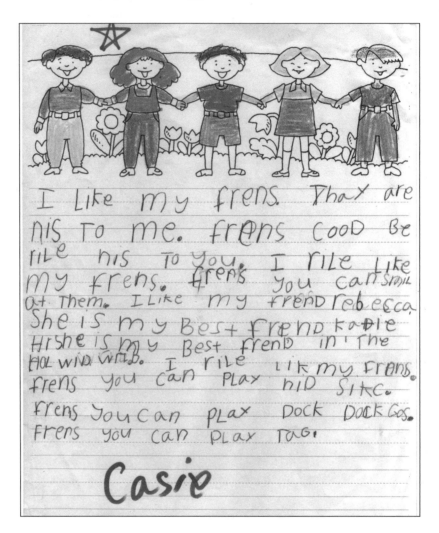

When using invented spelling, children feel comfortable about writing more. Notice the periods.

I like my friends. They are nice to me. Friends could be really nice to you. I really like my friends. Friends you can smile at them. I like my friend Rebecca. She is my best friend. Katie Hersh is my best friend in the whole wide world. I really like my friends. Friends you can play hide and seek. Friends you can play duck duck goose. Friends you can play tag.
Casie

Conventional Forms

> Dear tooth Fariy,
> How are you? I lost another molar! Today I went on a plane all by my self! I am staying at my aunts house. Well see you next time I loose a tooth. Bye Bye.
>
> Love,
> Alexa ♡

It is always helpful to use conventional spelling and form when writing a letter to the Tooth Fairy!

Literacy
The Essential
WORKSHOP
BOOK

Why I Write

Brooke on Writing

Everybody has to write. You need to write so you can get along in the world. There's lots of things to write like stories, songs, poems, jokes, riddles, information, cards, letters, emails, text messages, journals, diaries, instructions, grocery lists, checks, signs, labels, or just a note to someone. You have to think about what you are writing, because writing is different for different things. If you are writing a sign or instructions or a grocery list, then you have to write what it is, but when you write a story or a poem, you write what you want to write. You get to use your imagination or to express feelings. Some things like lists or recipes don't have to be in complete sentences but when you write a story, you have to use sentences and paragraphs.

When I start to write a story, I think about what should I say first, how should I start off, and sometimes I think what would be the best way to start and end my story. I have always wanted to get stories out of my mind. I want to be an author because if I was an author then the things I write about to express me would be shown to the world. Writing is a very fun thing. You can write about an adventure that a Hamburger had or you could write about friendship. I love writing very much because it makes me be creative and think about my readers.

—Brooke Ramsier, age 11

The Essential
Literacy
WORKSHOP
BOOK

Significant Features of Written Language

Letters and words convey meaning.

Objects can be represented by print.

What is said can be written. What is written is read the same way, always.

There is a right way to write.

Letters form words and are written in a line.

Letters make sounds.

Words have a beginning and an end; words together make sentences.

The Essential
Literacy
WORKSHOP
BOOK

Suggestions to Support Writing

- Provide a variety of useful writing and drawing materials in all centers.

- Anticipate various emergent forms of writing.

- Encourage children to write their own way.

- Invite children to write or dictate a story.

- Encourage children to write to one another.

- Accept children's additions to your writing.

- Display and send home samples of children's writings.

- Listen to children "read" their writing.

- Make encouraging and specific comments.

- Model the usefulness of writing.

- Make your writing strategies explicit.

- Notice environmental print.

- Encourage children to write.

- Provide opportunities and materials for book-making.

- Relate meaningful writing experiences to projects and themes.

- Create a Writing Center and vary the materials in it.

- Carefully observe children's writing. Knowing where children are in their thinking enables you to support them based on their current levels of development.

AGENDA

Supporting Children as Writers

Date:

Trainer:

Contact Information:

OBJECTIVES

In this workshop, participants will:

- gain understanding of how children develop as writers;
- identify strategies to promote writing throughout the day;
- explore techniques and materials to encourage children's writing in centers;
- learn that becoming a competent writer involves knowing and understanding the forms, function, and features of writing; and
- understand how writing can be integrated throughout the day and within the environment.

1. Opening Activity: Acrostic Poem [10–15 minutes]

2. Welcome and Logistics [5 minutes]

3. Introducing the Topic: Supporting Children's Writing [30 minutes]

4. Activity: Constructing Knowledge About Writing [30 minutes]

5. Mini-Lecture: Features of Writing [15 minutes]

6. Activity: Integrating Writing Throughout the Day [30 minutes]

7. Discussion [10–15 minutes]

8. Closure [10 minutes]

Literacy The Essential
WORKSHOP
BOOK

Understanding Writing

"Knowledge of the forms and functions of print serves as a foundation from which children become increasingly sensitive to letter shapes, names, sounds, and words." (IRA/NAEYC, 1998, 35)

Categories and Stages of Writing

Marks and Scribbles
Drawing
Scribble Writing
Letter-Like Forms and Individual Letters
Letter Strings
Invented Spelling
Conventional Forms

The Process of Writing

Writing and reading develop together.
A writer needs a purpose or reason for writing.
A writer selects a form for writing.

Significant Features of Written Language

Letters and words convey meaning.
Objects can be represented by print.
What is said can be written. What is written is read the same way, always.
There is a right way to write.
Letters form words and are written in a line.
Letters make sounds.
Words have a beginning and an end; words together make sentences.

The Essential
Literacy
WORKSHOP
BOOK

Activity: Integrating Writing Experiences Throughout the Day

Arrival/Circle Time	
Center Time	
Meals	
Small Group	
Outside	
Music Time	

HANDOUT 6.4

Suggestions to Support Writing

- Provide a variety of useful writing and drawing materials in all centers. Add new materials to support children's interests.
- Anticipate emergent forms of writing.
- Encourage children to write in their own way.
- Invite children to write or dictate a story.
- Encourage children to write to one another.
- Accept children's additions to your writing.
- Display and send home samples of children's writings.
- Listen to children "read" their writing.
- Make encouraging and specific comments.
- Model the usefulness of writing.
- Make your writing strategies explicit.
- Notice environmental print.
- Encourage children to write.
- Provide opportunities and materials for book-making.
- Relate meaningful writing experiences to projects and themes.
- Create a Writing Center and vary the materials in it.
- Carefully observe children's writing. Knowing where children are in their thinking enables you to support them based on their current levels of development.

Using Literacy Centers in Kindergarten

Workshop Objectives

In this workshop, participants will:

■ understand the importance of centers for young children;

■ identify ways to promote literacy in centers during choice time and during your scheduled literacy/language arts period; and

■ acquire practical tips for making centers successful in kindergarten classrooms.

Workshop Materials

■ Overhead projector and Overheads 7.1–7.7 or computer and PowerPoint Workshop 7 (on accompanying CD)

■ Handouts 7.1–7.4, one for each participant

■ Chart paper, markers, pens, tape

■ 2 charts for opening activity *Pick a Prop,* one labeled "The Teacher's Role" and the other "Characteristics of Activity"

■ Props for opening activity, such as a rubber band, light bulb, kitchen utensils (spatula, strainer, whisk, egg beater, or wooden spoon), coin, Slinky, magnifying glass, kaleidoscope, paper clip, magnet, card file box, and change purse, displayed on a table or in a large bin. Be sure to have as many props as participants (using two or three of the same item is fine).

■ Materials for each of the five center activities (see Kindergarten Literacy Centers Activity Cards on pages 192-194 for specific materials). Prepare five center activities by placing materials on tables around the room or in bins ready to be placed on tables.

■ 5 index cards, labeled with the names of the five literacy centers (one per card)

■ Copies of the Kindergarten Literacy Centers Activity Cards for each center activity

■ Timer

■ Center Assignment Cards: Label index cards with names of centers for activity #8 *Enriching Learning Centers with Literacy.* Depending on your audience, determine which centers or interest areas you want participants to explore in this activity and create assignment cards accordingly. Refer to Overhead 7.7 or PowerPoint Slide 7: *Enriching Learning Centers with Literacy* for a list of centers.

Suggested Time Frame
3-hour workshop

Handout List
7.1
Agenda

7.2
Literacy Learning in Centers in the Kindergarten Classroom

7.3a, b, c
Kindergarten Literacy Centers (Rotation Activity) (3 pages)

7.4
Learning Centers vs. Literacy Centers

Supplemental Resources

Hong Xu, S., & Rutledge, A.L. 2003. "Chicken starts with ch! Kindergartners learn through environmental print." *Young Children.* 58 (2). 44–51.

Owocki, G. 2001. *Make way for literacy: Teaching the way young children learn.* Portsmouth, NH: Heinemann & Washington, DC: National Association for the Education of Young Children. (Chapter 10 discusses sociodramatic play and literacy; pages 164–180 of the chapter address literacy-enriched centers.)

Trainers' Guide to Workshop 7

Essential Messages for This Workshop: Using Literacy Centers in Kindergarten

- Children are motivated to learn when they are actively engaged, working independently and with others, and able to make decisions and choices.
- Literacy activities in centers should promote purposeful learning and provide children with interesting problems to solve.
- The tasks expected of learners in centers are open-ended in ways that are responsive to different levels of learners.
- Center experiences should be designed so children can figure out what to do and feel successful in their endeavors.

1. Opening Activity: Pick a Prop [10–15 minutes]

Begin this activity as participants arrive and continue for 10–15 minutes.

▸▸ *Before the workshop begins, set up a table by the door with a variety of props (such as a rubber band, light bulb, kitchen utensils, and so on). Make a sign that says, "Choose a prop and take it to your table."*

▸▸ *Display* Overhead 7.1 *or* PowerPoint Slide 1: Welcome to Today's Workshop *with activity directions.*

Directions: Use the prop as a metaphor to finish this sentence: "My role as teacher is like a (fill in the prop) because (fill in your explanation)."

▶▶ *Post two charts, one labeled "The Teacher's Role" and the other "Characteristics of Activity."*

To start the workshop, divide the participants into groups of 4–6 and invite them to share their metaphors and explanations with others in their group. After 5 minutes, say, "Let's hear some of the metaphors. Please share those you heard rather than those you invented." Listen to five or six responses. As you hear ideas that relate to the teacher's role in making centers work, list them on the "Teacher's Role" chart. Ideas might include: flexibility, facilitation, keeping many things going at the same time, keeping things organized, creative, and inventive.

Ask, "How would you describe this activity? What are its characteristics? Let's hear some ideas." Elicit a few responses and write them on the "Characteristics of Activity" chart. Ideas to listen for and record include: literacy-focused (use of metaphors), open-ended (no "right" answers), makes you think, allows you to make choices and decisions, encourages problem solving, and involves talking and sharing.

Say, "Today's workshop is about using meaningful literacy centers in your classroom. The activity you just did offers many reasons why centers are important. As we go through the day, we will examine your role [point to the Teacher's Role chart] and the qualities of centers that make them valuable for children [point to the Characteristics of Activity chart]."

Center experiences should be designed so children can figure out what to do and feel successful in their endeavors.

2. Welcome and Logistics [5 minutes]

▶▶ *Distribute* Handout 7.1: Agenda. *Review agenda and workshop objectives.*

3. Introducing the Topic: Using Literacy Centers in Kindergarten [15–20 minutes]

Ask, "How many of you have centers in your classrooms?" (Show of hands.) "How many of you have center time daily? A few times each week? Today we will talk about using centers to foster literacy learning in kindergarten and we will address two ways to do this: during free choice time in learning centers and during your scheduled literacy/language arts period." **Note:** If you know that all teachers in this workshop are using a reading program, acknowledge that their programs include ideas for literacy centers like the ones you will discuss today. Be sure to validate what they are doing with their reading programs.

185

■ ■

Say, "Let's begin by reflecting on why centers are important for kindergarten children. Take a minute to talk with the person next to you. What are some reasons centers are valuable for young children?"

After 2–3 minutes, invite a few participants to share their responses.

▸▸ *Show* Overhead 7.2 *or* PowerPoint Slide 2: Literacy Learning in Kindergarten Centers. *Distribute* Handout 7.2: Literacy Learning in Centers in the Kindergarten Classroom.

Review the top section of the handout and overhead or slide, making links to the ideas offered by participants:

Literacy Learning in Kindergarten Centers
■ **Why are centers important for young children?**
  ■ **Center-based learning responds to how young children think and learn. Effective Centers:**
    ■ **offer purposeful, hands-on, active learning;**
    ■ **engage children in thinking and problem-solving;**
    ■ **allow for decision-making and choice;**
    ■ **are open-ended and responsive to different levels of learners; and**
    ■ **allow children to work independently, collaboratively, and successfully.**
■ **Use learning centers and literacy-focused centers to promote literacy learning.**
  ■ **Include a portion of each day for children to choose learning centers.**
  ■ **Use focused literacy centers during a literacy block so children can work independently while the teacher works with small groups.**

▸▸ *Show* Overheads 7.3 *and* 7.4 *or* PowerPoint Slides 3 and 4: Tips for Successful Centers.

Say, "Review the tips for successful centers on the bottom half of your handout (Handout 7.2). Put an asterisk or a checkmark next to two strategies you are currently using in your classroom. Put a question mark next to an idea you would like to know more about. When your group is ready, share your reflections." **Note:** Participants should still be sitting in their groups from the opening activity.

Circulate to hear comments and issues raised in groups so you can refer to them when you review the discussion.

After 5–7 minutes, call time. Review the list and invite participants to offer examples of how they apply these strategies in their classrooms. Address questions.

■ At the beginning of the year, have fewer centers and keep them simple until children learn the routines.

■ ■

- ■ Establish predictable times on the schedule for centers so children can anticipate when and for how long they can work.
- ■ Teach children predictable routines for working in centers.
- ■ Use morning circle time or meeting to teach routines.
- ■ Think carefully about the materials you include in centers.
- ■ Teach children the proper care and use of materials.
- ■ Teach children procedures for getting, cleaning up, and storing materials.
- ■ Label materials in storage bins with pictures and words so they are easy for children to take from and return to shelves.
- ■ Establish a clear system for making choices and moving through centers and teach it to children.
- ■ Use a planning board or choice chart for children to choose centers.
- ■ Establish procedures for children and teachers to keep track of children's choices.
- ■ Vary the materials in centers to keep children interested.
- ■ Observe children at work; if a center is not working well, talk with children and encourage them to help determine necessary changes.
- ■ Ensure that there is room in each center for three to five children, depending on the center.
- ■ Use a checklist or other record-keeping method for centers so you can keep track of where children go.

4. Activity: Literacy Centers Rotation [50 minutes]

▸▸ *Make a copy of the Kindergarten Literacy Centers Activity Cards (pages 192-194) and cut out each activity.*

Set up five literacy centers on tables or in other areas of the room. Place the activity card, suggested materials, and an index card with the name of the activity on it at each center.

Note: Ideas are provided for five centers. The activity is designed so participants spend 10 minutes at each center. Depending on the number of participants and the amount of time you have, participants can rotate through three or four centers.

Introduce this activity by saying, "In this activity, you will rotate through five centers, each designed to foster engaged, independent, and collaborative learning of important literacy skills."

▸▸ *Show participants where the centers are located. Ask them to count off to form five groups (one group at each center).*

After they are settled in their new groups, say, "Each center time will last 10 minutes. This is a simulation. Ten minutes is not an appropriate duration for centers and we would not expect children to rotate through five centers in one work period. I will give you a 1-minute warning for cleanup, which is also not appropriate for young children. When the timer goes off, your group should proceed to the next center."

At the end of the rotation, ask participants to return to their seats.

▸▸ *Distribute* Handout 7.3: Kindergarten Literacy Centers (Rotation Activity).

5. Discussion [10–15 minutes]

▸▸ *Show* Overhead 7.5 *or* PowerPoint Slide 5: Discussion: Literacy Centers Rotation.

Say, "Talk with others in your group about the center activities you did. Respond to the questions on the screen and record your responses on your handout: Kindergarten Literacy Centers."

- **What were some qualities of the center activities that you found valuable?**
- **What were some of the specific decisions and choices you made to accomplish tasks at the centers?**
- **How did the activities in each center address the diverse skill levels of learners?**

Provide time for discussion. Invite two to three responses to each question.

Ask, "What are some ways you can demonstrate the activities to children in advance so they can be independent and successful?" Invite a few responses. Check for questions.

6. Activity: Extending Literacy Centers
[15–20 minutes]

Ask, "Brainstorm five ways you can provide a rich literate environment for children in ways that cultivate and nurture their development and appreciation of literacy." Provide 2–3 minutes for them to talk with their group. Elicit a few ideas.

Say, "Drill and practice does not cultivate and nurture successful literacy development. It takes engagement and enthusiasm. Centers, both open-ended or literacy-focused, can make literacy come alive in your classrooms through careful planning and consideration of the key principles we discussed earlier today. Let's briefly revisit them. You can find them on your Handout 7.2: Literacy Learning in Centers in the Kindergarten Classroom." Invite individual participants to read each bullet aloud.

Effective learning centers:

- **promote purposeful, active, hands-on learning;**
- **engage children in thinking and problem-solving;**
- **allow for decision-making and choice;**
- **are open-ended and responsive to different levels of learners; and**
- **allow children to work independently, collaboratively, and successfully.**

Say, "Think about the centers you just rotated through. Let's consider ways to extend them by applying these principles."

▸▸ *Show Overhead 7.6 or PowerPoint Slide 6: Extending Literacy Centers to explain and clarify the directions. Refer back to Handout 7.3: Kindergarten Literacy Centers (Rotation Activity) where there is space for participants to add ideas. Provide 10 minutes for participants to work. Give a 2-minute warning and let them know they are expected to present their ideas to the whole group.*

7. Discussion [10 minutes]

Invite each group to share one idea. Ask participants to offer comments or questions after each group shares.

Provide 2–3 minutes for participants to reflect on one idea they will try when they return to their classrooms.

8. Activity: Enriching Learning Centers with Literacy [25 minutes]

Note: Chapter 10 (pages 157–182) in *Make Way for Literacy* (Owocki 2001) on sociodramatic play and literacy will provide excellent background knowledge for this segment of the workshop.

▸▸ *Distribute* Handout 7.4: Learning Centers vs. Literacy Centers. *Invite participants to read the handout silently, underlining ideas that stand out for them. After a few minutes, invite them to share ideas and explanations.*

Say, "Literacy centers, when well designed, provide children with open-ended opportunities to learn and practice specific literacy skills. Well-designed learning centers provide similar opportunities when teachers plan with intention. Let's think about the block area and different ways it can be enriched to support literacy."

Ask them to talk at their tables for a few minutes to generate some ideas.

▸▸ *Write "Block Area" across the top of a piece of chart paper so you can list participants' ideas as they share them.*

Note: If the idea of themes hasn't been raised by participants, consider asking another question such as, "Suppose your class is doing a theme about houses in the neighborhood. What are some ways you could support and extend literacy learning in the block area?" Elicit a few ideas.

▸▸ *Show* Overhead 7.7 *or* PowerPoint Slide 7: Enriching Learning Centers with Literacy.

Introduce the overhead or slide by saying, "To enrich learning centers throughout the classroom with language and literacy learning, you must be purposeful. Here are some things to think about."

Materials to add: Adding materials to a center should always be purposeful. When you add things without introducing them to children, they become clutter. (For each item on the list, invite participants to think of one or two examples of what can be added to make literacy connections and enrich children's learning.)
- **books or other text**
- **photographs or signs**
- **props**
- **writing tools**
- **open-ended questions to ponder** For example, in the science area, post a question on a chart next to fruit placed on a tray that says, "What is happening to our apples? Record your observations."

Ideas to prompt learning: Adding materials often requires facilitation from the teacher.
- **Have a discussion.**

- **Read a book.**
- **Brainstorm as a group.**
- **Ask questions.**

Skills and standards: As a result of the change to the center, what new learning is possible?
- **Clarify your purpose.**
- **Help children make connections.**

Determine in advance how you will assign groups to centers. Distribute the Center Assignment Cards (described in the materials list). Have the group form triads and give each triad a different center assignment, for example, Writing Center, Listening Center, Block Center, and so on.

▸▸ *Distribute chart paper and markers to each group.*

Say, "Work on your assigned center in your triads. Think about materials to add and ideas to focus and extend children's literacy learning. As you develop your ideas, think about the literacy skills and standards children can attain, as well as those from other curriculum areas. Record your ideas on a chart."

Provide about 10 minutes to work.

9. Discussion [5–10 minutes]

▸▸ *Post charts for a gallery walk (see Appendix E, page 316). Tell participants that as they review the charts, they should write down one idea they plan to try. When everyone returns to their seats, invite questions and insights.*

10. Closure [10 minutes]

Pose these questions and ask participants to do a written reflection: "As a result of today's workshop, what is one idea you are really excited to try in your classroom? What is one thing you anticipate will be a challenge for you? How can you make the challenge a learning opportunity?"

Hear a few "excited abouts" and then invite a few challenges and learning opportunities.

Kindergarten Literacy Centers Activity Cards

#1 SEQUENCE THE STORY

M a t e r i a l s

Familiar storybooks such as: *Blueberries* for Sal by Robert McCloskey; *Goodnight Moon* by Margaret Wise Brown; *The Very Hungry Caterpillar* by Eric Carle; and *A Chair for My Mother* by Vera B. Williams

3 different colored index cards: one labeled "beginning," another color labeled "middle," and the other labeled "end"

A s s i g n m e n t

■ Read a story.
■ What happened in the story?
■ Use the cards to draw and write about what happened at the beginning, middle, and end of the story.

#2 MAKE WORDS AND SENTENCES

M a t e r i a l s

Magnetic letters
Magnetic boards or cookie sheets
Picture cards
Chicka Chicka Boom Boom by Bill Martin, Jr. and John Archambault
3 or 4 task cards (Suggestions include "Make your name," "Make the word on the picture card," "Copy words from the book," and "Write a sentence")

A s s i g n m e n t

Choose task cards and perform the task!

#3 TAPE YOUR READING

Materials

1 or 2 wordless books such as: *The Apple Bird* by Brian Wildsmith; *The Snowman* by
   Raymond Briggs; *Pancakes for Breakfast* by Tomie dePaola; *Frog, Where Are You?*
   by Mercer Mayer; and *Good Dog, Carl* by Alexandra Day

A tape recorder

A blank tape

Assignment

■ Take turns reading the story.

■ Record your words as you read.

■ When you are finished, play the tape and listen to the story.

#4 MAKE YOUR NAME

Materials

Alphabet strip (with all letters)

Paper and markers

5 or 6 alphabet books such as: *On Market Street* by Arnold Lobel; *Miss Spider's ABC*
   by David Kirk; *A Garden Alphabet* by Isabel Wilner; *ABC Kids* by Laura Williams;
   Alphabet City by Stephen Johnson; *Amazon Alphabet* by Martin Jordan; *ABC Drive:
   A Car Trip Alphabet* by Naomi Howland; and *Eating the Alphabet* by Lois Ehlert

Assignment

■ Take a piece of drawing paper for each letter of your name.

■ Choose an alphabet book.

■ Find the letters in your first name in the book.

■ For each letter of your name, copy the letter, draw the picture in the book, or
   draw your own picture of something that begins with each letter in your name.

#5 FIND THE SAME SOUNDS

Materials

Clipboards

Markers, crayons, or pencils

Bin with 7–10 objects with different initial consonant sounds (for example, banana, hat, scissors, pencil, marker, and so on)

Paper with one initial consonant written at the top (have more papers and consonants than objects)

Assignment

- Select an object from the bin.
- Find the paper that has the letter sound that matches the first sound in your object.
- Take a clipboard and marker.
- Find at least five objects in the room that begin with the same initial sound.
- Write the word or draw a picture on your paper.

The Essential Literacy Workshop Book

WELCOME TO TODAY'S WORKSHOP

Using Literacy Centers in Kindergarten

Arrival Activity: Pick a Prop

- Select a prop from the prop table and take it with you to your table.

- Use the prop as a metaphor to finish this sentence:

"My role as teacher in the classroom is like a ____ (your prop) because ____ (your explanation) ."

WORKSHOP 7

Literacy Learning in Kindergarten Centers

Why are centers important for young children?

- **Center-based learning responds to how young children think and learn. Effective centers:**
    - offer purposeful, hands-on, active learning;
    - engage children in thinking and problem-solving;
    - allow for decision-making and choice;
    - are open-ended and responsive to different levels of learners; and
    - allow children to work independently, collaboratively, and successfully.

Use learning centers and literacy-focused centers to promote literacy learning.

- Include a portion of each day for children to choose learning centers.
- Use focused literacy centers during a literacy block so children can work independently while the teacher works with small groups.

Tips for Successful Centers

■ At the beginning of the year, have fewer centers and keep them simple until children learn the routines.

■ Establish predictable times on the schedule for centers so children can anticipate when and for how long they can work.

■ Teach children predictable routines for working in centers.

■ Use morning circle time or meeting to teach routines.

■ Think carefully about the materials you include in centers.

■ Teach children the proper care and use of materials.

■ Teach children procedures for getting, cleaning up, and storing materials.

■ Label materials in storage bins with words and pictures so they are easy for children to take from and return to shelves.

The Essential Literacy WORKSHOP BOOK

WORKSHOP 7

Tips for Successful Centers (continued)

- Establish a clear system for making choices and moving through centers and teach it to children.

- Use a planning board or choice chart for children to choose centers.

- Establish procedures for children and teachers to keep track of children's choices.

- Vary the materials in centers to keep children interested.

- Observe children at work; if a center is not working well, talk with children and encourage them to help determine necessary changes.

- Ensure that there is room in each center for three to five children, depending on the center.

- Use a checklist or other record-keeping method for centers so you can keep track of where children go.

The Essential **Literacy** WORKSHOP BOOK

Discussion: Literacy Centers Rotation

As you describe your center activity to others in your group, discuss the following questions:

■ What were some qualities of the center activities that you found valuable?

■ What were some of the specific decisions and choices you made to accomplish tasks at the centers?

■ How did the activities in each center address the diverse skill levels of learners?

Literacy
The Essential
WORKSHOP
BOOK

W O R K S H O P 7

Extending Literacy Centers

Collaborate with others at your table.

Choose one center from the previous activity to focus on first.

Identify two or three ways you can extend or adapt the activity.

Keep in mind:

■ the standards addressed by the activity;

■ decisions and choices children can make;

■ different levels of learners; and

■ demonstrating the activity to children so that they can work independently.

If you have time, reflect on a second center.

**The Essential
Literacy
WORKSHOP
BOOK**

Enriching Learning Centers with Literacy

WRITING CENTER

LISTENING CENTER

LIBRARY

ART CENTER

DRAMATIC PLAY

BLOCK CENTER

SCIENCE CENTER

MATH CENTER

MUSIC

COMPUTER CENTER

OUTDOOR PLAY

MANIPULATIVES CENTER

SAND AND WATER (SENSORY) CENTER

THINK ABOUT

Materials to add:
- books or other text
- photographs or signs
- props
- writing tools
- open-ended questions to ponder

Ideas to prompt learning:
- Have a discussion.
- Read a book.
- Brainstorm as a group.
- Ask questions.

Skills and standards:
- Clarify your purpose.
- Help children make connections.

The Essential Literacy WORKSHOP BOOK

HANDOUT 7.1

AGENDA

Using Literacy Centers in Kindergarten

Date:

Trainer:

Contact Information:

OBJECTIVES

In this workshop, participants will:
- understand the importance of centers for young children;
- identify ways to promote literacy in centers during choice time and during your scheduled literacy/language arts period; and
- acquire practical tips for making centers successful in kindergarten classrooms.

1. Opening Activity: Pick a Prop [10–15 minutes]

2. Welcome and Logistics [5 minutes]

3. Introducing the Topic: Using Literacy Centers in Kindergarten [15–20 minutes]

4. Activity: Literacy Centers Rotation [50 minutes]

5. Discussion [10–15 minutes]

6. Activity: Extending Literacy Centers [15–20 minutes]

7. Discussion [10 minutes]

8. Activity: Enriching Learning Centers with Literacy [25 minutes]

9. Discussion [5–10 minutes]

10. Closure [10 minutes]

The Essential
Literacy
WORKSHOP
BOOK

Literacy Learning in Centers in the Kindergarten Classroom

- Center-based learning responds to how young children think and learn. Effective centers:
    - offer purposeful, hands-on, active learning;
    - engage children in thinking and problem-solving;
    - allow for decision-making and choice;
    - are open-ended and responsive to different levels of learners; and
    - allow children to work independently, collaboratively, and successfully.
- Use learning centers and literacy-focused centers to promote literacy learning.
    - Include a portion of each day for children to choose learning centers.
    - Use focused literacy centers during literacy block so children can work independently while the teacher works with small groups.

Tips for Successful Centers

- At the beginning of the year, have fewer centers and keep them simple until children learn the routines.
- Establish predictable times on the schedule for centers so children can anticipate when and for how long they can work.
- Teach children predictable routines for working in centers.
- Use morning circle time or meeting to teach routines.
- Think carefully about the materials you include in centers.
- Teach children proper care and use of materials.
- Teach children procedures for getting, cleaning up, and storing materials.
- Label materials in storage bins with words and pictures so that they are easy for children to take from and return to shelves.
- Establish a clear system for making choices and moving through centers and teach it to children.
- Use a planning board or choice chart for children to choose centers.
- Establish procedures for children and teachers to keep track of children's choices.
- Vary the materials in centers to keep children interested.
- Observe children at work; if a center is not working well, talk with children and encourage them to help determine changes.
- Ensure that there is room in each center for three to five children (depending on the center).
- Use a centers checklist or other record-keeping method so you can keep track of where children go.

The Essential Literacy WORKSHOP BOOK

Kindergarten Literacy Centers
(Rotation Activity)

#1 SEQUENCE THE STORY

Materials
Familiar storybooks such as: *Blueberries for Sal* by Robert McCloskey; *Goodnight Moon* by Margaret Wise Brown; *The Very Hungry Caterpillar* by Eric Carle; and *A Chair for My Mother* by Vera B. Williams
3 different colored index cards: one labeled "beginning," another color labeled "middle," and the other labeled "end"

Assignment
- Read a story.
- What happened in the story?
- Use the cards to draw and write about what happened at the beginning, middle, and end of the story.

Ideas for extensions and adaptations:

#2 MAKE WORDS AND SENTENCES

Materials
Magnetic letters
Magnetic boards or cookie sheets
Picture cards
Chicka Chicka Boom Boom by Bill Martin, Jr. and John Archambault
3 or 4 task cards (Suggestions include "Make your name," "Make the word on the picture card," "Copy words from the book," and "Write a sentence")

Assignment
Choose task cards and perform the task!

Ideas for extensions and adaptations:

The Essential
Literacy
WORKSHOP
BOOK

#3 TAPE YOUR READING

Materials
1 or 2 wordless books such as: *The Apple Bird* by Brian Wildsmith; *The Snowman* by
   Raymond Briggs; *Pancakes for Breakfast* by Tomie dePaola; *Frog, Where Are You?*
   by Mercer Mayer; and *Good Dog, Carl* by Alexandra Day
Tape recorder
Blank tape

Assignment
- Take turns reading the story.
- Record your words as you read.
- When you are finished, play the tape and listen to the story.

Ideas for extensions and adaptations:

#4 MAKE YOUR NAME

Materials
Alphabet strip (with all letters)
Paper and markers
5 or 6 alphabet books such as: *On Market Street* by Arnold Lobel; *Miss Spider's ABC*
   by David Kirk; *A Garden Alphabet* by Isabel Wilner; *ABC Kids* by Laura Williams,
   Alphabet City by Stephen Johnson; *Amazon Alphabet* by Martin Jordan; *ABC
   Drive: A Car Trip Alphabet* by Naomi Howland; and *Eating the Alphabet* by Lois
   Ehlert

Ideas for extensions and adaptations:

The Essential
Literacy
WORKSHOP
BOOK

#5 FIND THE SAME SOUNDS

Materials

Clipboards

Markers, crayons, or pencils

Bin with 7–10 objects with different initial consonant sounds (for example, banana, hat, scissors, pencil, marker, and so on)

Paper with one initial consonant written at the top (have more papers with consonants than objects)

Assignment

- Select an object from the bin.
- Find the paper that has the letter sound that matches the first sound in your object.
- Take a clipboard and marker.
- Find at least five objects in the room that begin with the same initial sound.
- Write the word or draw a picture on your paper.

Ideas for extensions and adaptations:

The Essential
Literacy
WORKSHOP
BOOK

Learning Centers vs. Literacy Centers*

*Written by Laura Brown, a kindergarten teacher in Columbia, Maryland.

There are distinct differences between choice-time learning centers and content-specific literacy centers.

Learning Centers comprise a distinct portion of the day. Children are allowed to choose from a variety of activities or areas in the classroom. The options in each area are not dictated or prescribed to the child and are primarily open-ended rather than product-oriented tasks. The environment is carefully planned to foster social interaction, independence, vocabulary development, and to promote learning across the curriculum in a meaningful and developmentally appropriate manner. The learning objectives for each center are numerous and ever-changing. An individual center could potentially address objectives from many curricular areas at the same time. Specific materials can be added to promote literacy and math learning. The centers are often represented in distinct areas of the classroom, such as a dramatic play corner, a block area, an easel, or a science table. The teacher may or may not be directly involved with children in the centers. Learning centers during choice time present a rich opportunity for gaining valuable information about children through observational assessment. Moreover, the interaction among children that takes place during this time provides extensive opportunities for scaffolded learning.

Literacy Centers directly support the goals and objectives of language arts during designated instructional times. Often, these centers are used to engage children purposefully in literacy-related activities while the teacher is meeting with other children in small groups for instructional purposes during language arts block. The activities in each center can be open-ended or product-oriented and commonly relate to current units of study or provide skill reinforcement. The use of literacy centers provides a valuable opportunity for differentiation of instruction during the language arts block to meet the varying academic levels of children in a kindergarten classroom.

During the language arts block, it is recommended that the center options correlate specifically with literacy objectives. While some child-selected center choices may overlap with those offered during literacy centers, (listening, library corner, games, and so on), it is more likely that the choices in each type of center time are distinct from one another. One option might be to designate literacy centers in a different manner, such as in tubs, tote trays, or baskets, to be used during the language arts block only. It is also more likely that the teacher may direct the rotation of children through literacy centers, as well as the child groupings in each.

Literacy
The Essential
WORKSHOP
BOOK

Using Music to Support Literacy

Workshop Objectives

In this workshop, participants will:
- gain understanding of how music supports literacy learning;
- acquire strategies for supporting literacy with musical activities throughout the day; and
- learn how to support children's expressive and receptive language development by creating new words and themes for familiar songs.

Workshop Materials

- Overhead projector and Overheads 8.1–8.6 or computer and PowerPoint Workshop 8 (on accompanying CD)
- Handouts 8.1–8.5, one copy for each participant
- Music CD or cassette from the list on Handout 8.3
- Chart paper, markers, tape
- Chart for activity *Exploring Literacy Connections with a Song* with the words and blank spaces for the song "If You're Happy And You Know It."
- Index cards and pens (one per participant)
- Materials for activity *Creating Music Picture Books:*
    - 12" x 18" construction paper (at least 1 sheet per participant)
    - Stapler
    - Crayons and/or markers
    - Old magazines (at least 2–3 per group)
    - Scissors (1–2 pairs per group)
    - Glue sticks or squeeze bottles of glue (1–2 per group)
    - Activity Cards precut into four pieces. Each group needs one assignment: A, B, C, or D. Depending on the number of groups, more than one group can do the same assignment.
- Enough books from Handout 8.5: Good Picture Books That Are Songs for each group to have two or three
- Activity Cards for activity: *Connecting Music and Literacy* precut into four pieces. Each group needs one assignment; depending on the number of groups, more than one group can do the same assignment
- One book from Handout 8.5: Good Picture Books That Are Songs to read aloud for Closure Activity.

Trainers' Guide to Workshop 8

Essential Messages for This Workshop: Using Music to Support Literacy

■ Children should have many opportunities to sing, listen to music, and respond to music in a variety of ways throughout the day because:

- ■ music supports the development of phonological awareness as children tune in to the rhythms, rhymes, and patterns when they sing and respond to music with rhythm instruments and props;

- ■ singing and listening to the words in songs helps children develop expressive and receptive language skills; and

- ■ creating their own songs using familiar tunes supports high-level thinking and the use of new vocabulary words.

■ Music of varied genres and from many cultures should be available in every classroom.

■ Musical expression is a form of communication; for many children, singing is a first step toward oral language in the classroom. This is often true for English language learners.

▸▸ *Hang three pieces of chart paper in different parts of the room.*

Write one of the following titles across the top of each chart:

This music makes me feel _____ or think about _____.
A song or piece of music I heard on my way to this workshop is _____.
A song or musical activity the children in my class enjoy is _____.

▸▸ *Display* Overhead 8.1 *or* PowerPoint Slide 1: Welcome to Today's Workshop *so participants can see the directions for completing the charts.*

1. Opening Activity: Music Is a Part of Our Lives [5 minutes]

▸▸ *Play one of the CDs or cassettes from* Handout 8.3: Great CDs/Cassettes to Use with Rhythm Instruments *as participants arrive. Invite them to add their ideas about music to the charts on the wall.*

After everyone has had a chance to write on the charts, turn off the background music. Say, "Let's look at the charts." Briefly review what the participants wrote. Continue by saying, "You can see from the different responses that even though we have individual tastes and interests as adults and early childhood teachers, music is a part of all of our lives. Today's workshop will focus on how we can create musical experiences to foster literacy development. This includes phonological and phonemic awareness, expressive and receptive language development, supporting listening skills, and reinforcing written language."

2. Welcome and Logistics [5 minutes]

▸▸ *Distribute* Handout 8.1: Agenda. *Review the agenda and workshop objectives.*

3. Activity: Exploring Literacy Connections with a Song [30 minutes]

Say, "I imagine everyone is familiar with this song. If you know the words, please sing along with me."

If you're happy and you know it, clap your hands.
If you're happy and you know it, clap your hands.
If you're happy and you know it, and you really want to show it,
If you're happy and you know it, clap your hands.

Say, "Let's try something new. Substitute the word *happy* with your name and substitute *clap your hands* with something you like to do and make up a hand gesture to emphasize what you are singing about."

If you're Janis and you know it, play the guitar. (pretend to strum a guitar)
If you're Janis and you know it, play the guitar. (pretend to strum a guitar)
If you're Janis and you know it, and you really want to show it,
If you're Janis and you know it, play the guitar. (pretend to strum a guitar)

Break into groups of 4–6. Invite the participants to go around their table, taking turns singing the song using each person's name. (All groups do this at the same time.)

Ask, "What are some reasons children would enjoy this version of the song?" Listen for ideas such as:
■ Children love hearing their own names.
■ They can tell everyone about the things they like to do.
■ It is a safe and comfortable way for some children to express themselves in a group.

211

Ask, "What are some things children learn from singing this song?" Listen for ideas such as:
- They learn each other's names.
- They learn to use the rhythmic pattern of the song in a new way.
- They use their own words to express something personal.
- They learn new words in the different versions of the song.

Emphasize the ideas that support literacy.

Note: The following section is designed to show how to connect a song with written language.

▸▸ *Post a chart on which you have written the following information:*

If you're _____ and you know it, _____
If you're _____ and you know it, _____
If you're _____ and you know it, and you really want to show it,
If you're _____ and you know it, _____

▸▸ *Give each person an index card and a pen.*

Say, "Let's connect this musical experience to written language. As you can see on this chart, I have left out part of the words to "If You're Happy and You Know It." You will have two minutes to make a symbolic representation of *happy* and *clap your hands*. On one side of your index card, make a symbol for *happy*. On the other side, make a symbol for *clap your hands*.

After two minutes, invite everyone to sing the song. As you point to the blanks on the chart, ask each person to hold up his or her card.

Ask, "How does this activity support writing and word recognition in young children?" Responses may include: children see how the words in the song look in written form; they notice the similarities and differences of words; they see that the words of the song have letters and spaces; they see letters that look like letters in their names; and they realize that words can be represented by picture symbols or letters.

Ask the participants to discuss with their group songs that work well for charting the words. Have them share a few ideas and discuss why certain types of songs make good charts or rebuses (mention that a rebus is a term used when pictures are substituted for some written words). Their ideas may include songs that have repeating words, have few words, are easy to memorize, and have words that are easy to make into picture form.

212

▶▶ *Distribute* Handout 8.2: If You're Happy and You Know It *for participants to take back to their classrooms as a reminder of this experience.*

Summarize by saying, "We have taken a familiar song, created new words that are unique for each person, listened to each other's words, and explored these words in written and picture form. We have begun to link music and literacy. Children benefit from repeated opportunities to associate print with what they know. Explore these types of music and graphic associations with your class."

Of the eight multiple intelligences described in his book, Frames of Mind, Howard Gardner says the earliest to emerge in children is musical intelligence (Gardner 1983).

4. Introducing the Topic: Using Music to Support Literacy [30 minutes]

▶▶ *Show* Overhead 8.2 *or* PowerPoint Slide 2: Musical Intelligence.

Of the eight multiple intelligences described in his book, *Frames of Mind*, Howard Gardner says the earliest to emerge in children is musical intelligence (Gardner 1983).

Note: The seven other multiple intelligences defined in the book are linguistic, logical/mathematical, spatial, naturalistic, interpersonal, intrapersonal, and bodily/kinesthetic.

Provide a minute for participants to read the overhead or PowerPoint slide. Then invite them to reflect on what it means and to share their ideas with their group. After a minute or two, ask for volunteers to share a few ideas aloud. Their responses may include that babies can hear music while they are still in the womb, babies respond to musical mobiles above their cribs, family members rock their babies to sleep, children often mimic melodies and words of songs before they can speak, and so on.

Say, "We know that children come to our classrooms with musical intelligence. It is our responsibility to cultivate it and use it to support literacy development."

▶▶ *Show* Overhead 8.3 *or* PowerPoint Slide 3: Inventing Music. *Make the key points below.*

All children should have opportunities to invent music and lyrics in order to develop their vocabulary by:
- **singing songs from a variety of genres and cultures;**
- **singing familiar and new songs; and**
- **making up their own songs.**

213

Early experiences "playing" with musical lyrics support children's comfort with creating:

- poetry;
- prose;
- rhymes; and
- rhythms.

Describe ways in which children have unique experiences, concepts, and words that they can share. Talk about incorporating words and phrases from other languages. Provide examples by singing "Good Morning" songs or songs listing the days of the week in other languages.

⇒ *Distribute* Handout 8.3: Great CDs/Cassette Tapes to Use with Rhythm Instruments.

Invite participants to add to the list, choosing from a broad range of different types of music that utilize rhythms from many genres (adaptations of folk music, rock music, music from many cultures and countries, and traditional children's songs).

After each person has added to his or her own list, divide participants into new groups of 4–6 and ask each group to vote on the two best selections to share with the whole group. Invite each group to share their ideas.

⇒ *Show* Overhead 8.4 *or* PowerPoint Slide 4: Responding to Music.

All children should have opportunities to respond to music in order to develop their listening skills, vocabulary, and phonological awareness as they focus on the rhythms they hear:

- using their bodies (clapping, dancing, and so on);
- using rhythm instruments (including commercially made instruments and those made by teachers and children);
- using props (scarves, puppets, and so on); and
- using words ("This song makes me feel ____.").

Stress the following key points:

- As children respond to music with parts of their bodies (clapping, head shaking, toe tapping, dancing, or marching), rhythm instruments, or props, they develop phonological awareness skills. These skills include listening to beginning and ending sounds in words, rhyming and rhythmic patterns, and the sounds and segmentation of the melodies.
- Expressing their emotions and reactions with words supports expressive language development and cognition.

214

■ ■

▶▶ *Show* Overhead 8.5 *or* PowerPoint Slide 5: Listen to and Enjoy Music, *and make these key points below:*

All children should have opportunities to listen to and enjoy music that helps them relax, laugh, and, at the same time, attend.

As you present each bullet point below, invite participants to give examples:

■ **Example of relaxing music** ("Rock-a-bye, Baby" and other lullabies);

■ **Example of music that supports laughter** ("Peanut Butter and Jelly," "Apples and Bananas" and "Down by the Bay");

■ **Example of music that helps children pay attention** ("She'll Be Comin' 'Round the Mountain," "I Know an Old Lady Who Swallowed a Fly," and various cleanup songs).

Expressing their emotions and reactions with words supports children's expressive language development and cognition.

5. Activity: Supporting Phonological Awareness with Rhythm Instruments [20 minutes]

▶▶ *Distribute* Handout 8.4: Supporting Phonological Awareness with Rhythm Instruments.

Go over the statement at the top of the handout:
As children use commercial or homemade instruments, they are attentive to the segmented sounds of music. This helps them to develop phonological awareness, which includes hearing the specific sounds, called phonemes, that make up words.

Briefly discuss what this means.

Say, "Fill in the list of rhythm instruments typically used in preschool classrooms." Quickly review this list. These should include cymbals, drums, triangles, rhythm sticks, tambourines, bells, sand blocks, and so on.

Say, "Look around the room and find any item that can be used as a rhythm instrument. You can use any item except a part of your body." Give participants several minutes to find an "instrument." If they need clarification, offer following examples: a shoe, a book (bang it on the table), or keys.

▶▶ *Play a song from the CD used earlier (or another CD or cassette from* Handout 8.3: Great CDs/Cassette Tapes to Use with Rhythm Instruments) *and invite participants to use their rhythm instrument to play along with the song.*

■ ■

Note: Make sure to play a song that invites rhythmic response. If time allows and the level of participation warrants, play a second song and have participants trade instruments. The second song should be from a different CD or cassette with a different type of rhythm.

6. Discussion [10 minutes]

To complete the rest of the Handout, ask each person to think of objects in the classroom that can be used as rhythm instruments. Responses may include such things as empty yogurt containers filled with crayon pieces from the art area, a wooden spoon and pot from the dramatic play area, and so on.

Each group—the same groups as for the prior activity—shares their list among themselves.

End this segment by saying, "Remember that as we create different experiences for young children to hear and respond to music with rhythm instruments, we are supporting their phonological development in a developmentally appropriate way."

7. Activity: Creating Music Picture Books
[25–35 minutes]

Say, "Our next activity involves collaboration among children and is something you can do with a small group of children. For this activity, we will break up into triads. Move around as needed so you are in a group of three. To help you practice what you can do with children in your classroom, each triad will receive an activity card with an assignment on it. We will go over the assignment together."

▶▶ *Distribute one Creating Music Picture Books Activity Card (see page 219) to each group.*

Give each group one assignment (A, B, C, or D). Depending on the number of groups, you may give the same assignment to different groups. Give each participant a piece of 11" x 18" construction paper. Distribute markers, crayons, magazine pictures, scissors, glue, and a stapler to each group or put these items on a materials table. If you think participants will benefit from seeing you model the activity first, you might use the theme "family" and the tune "The Farmer in the Dell" to discuss and create one verse.

216

▸▸ *Show* Overhead 8.6 *or* PowerPoint 6: Directions for Activity: Creating Music Picture Books.

Review the directions:
- ■ **Read your group's assignment.**
- ■ **Sing the first verse of your tune to make sure everyone is familiar with it.**
- ■ **Create new lyrics to the song; the lyrics must connect to your assigned theme.**
- ■ **Each person must write a verse and create a page for your group's book.**
- ■ **Use pictures, words, and symbols for your page.**
- ■ **After your pages are completed, assemble your book.**
- ■ **Decide on a title.**
- ■ **Make a cover.**

8. Discussion [5–10 minutes]

Say, "Let's reflect on the literacy skills children use, focusing on similarities and differences for three- and four-year-olds."

Invite responses, which might include for three-year-olds talking, story-telling through dictation (child talks, teacher writes), marks or scribble writing to represent images and words, and turning pages in a book. For four-year-olds, skills also include beginning to make representational pictures, attempts at making letters and words, thinking about the sounds they hear in words, and attempts at printing their names on their page.

▸▸ *Distribute* Handout 8.5: Good Picture Books That Are Songs. *Give participants a few minutes to go over the list. Invite comments and additions to the list.*

▸▸ *Give two or three picture books from this handout to each group.*

Explain to participants that after reading a book to their class, they should place the book in the library area for children to reread individually or in small groups. Ask participants to share other strategies learned in this workshop to extend these books. Responses may include:
- ■ using rhythm instruments in a music center or during class meetings to accompany the book;
- ■ changing words in the book to relate to new themes;
- ■ putting the words onto charts or rebuses;
- ■ making new song books; and
- ■ using puppets or other props to act out the song.

9. Activity: Making Connections in the Classroom [15–20 minutes]

▸▸ *Distribute Activity Card for Connecting Music and Literacy (see page 221). Break into new groups of 4–6 (see page 15 for suggestions for breaking into groups).*

Precut this handout into three pieces. Give each group one assignment (A, B, or C). Depending on the number of groups, more than one group may do the same assignment.

▸▸ *Give each group a piece of chart paper and a marker.*

Say, "Let's brainstorm and share specific examples of songs and musical activities that support literacy skills at different centers and different times of day. Spend 10 minutes completing your assignment and record your ideas on chart paper."

After 10 minutes, say, "Pass your chart paper to another group. Each group should add comments and additional ideas to the chart paper. Put a question mark next to any ideas you do not understand."

Note: Each group should work on two assignments in 15 minutes.

10. Discussion [10 minutes]

▸▸ *Post charts. Have participants take a gallery walk (see Appendix E, page 316) to review charts they have not seen. Discuss question marks on charts.*

11. Closure [10 minutes]

Say, "Write a response to the following question on the back of your workshop agenda: As a result of this workshop, what is one thing you are excited to try?"

Read one of the books from Handout 8.5: Good Picture Books That Are Songs. Choose a book that invites participants to sing along.

218

Activity Card: Creating Music Picture Books

GROUP A

Your Theme: Families
Your Tune: "The Farmer in the Dell"
Your Task: Sing the first verse of the song.

The farmer in the dell,
The farmer in the dell,
Hi-ho the derry-o,
The farmer in the dell.

Create new lyrics to the song, making sure the lyrics connect to your assigned theme. Each person must write a verse. Using construction paper, markers, crayons, and/or magazine pictures, draw or cut out pictures, words, or symbols that represent the verse in the song. After the pages are completed, assemble your book, decide on a title, make a cover, and prepare to present your book to another group. As a group, design a cover for your book.

GROUP B

Your Theme: Friends
Your Tune: "Ring Around the Rosie"
Your Task: Sing the first verse of the song.

Ring around the rosie,
A pocket full of posies.
Ashes, ashes, we all fall down!

Create new lyrics to the song, making sure the lyrics connect to your assigned theme. Each person must write a verse. Using construction paper, markers, crayons, and magazine pictures, draw or cut out pictures, words, or symbols that represent the verse in the song. After the pages are completed, assemble your book, decide on a title, make a cover, and prepare to present your book to another group. As a group, design a cover for your book.

GROUP C

Your Theme: My School
Your Tune: "London Bridge Is Falling Down"
Your Task: Sing the first verse of the song.

London Bridge is falling down,
Falling down, falling down.
London Bridge is falling down,
My fair lady.

Create new lyrics to the song, making sure the lyrics connect to your assigned theme. Each person must write a verse. Using construction paper, markers, crayons, and magazine pictures, draw or cut out pictures, words, or symbols that represent the verse in the song. After the pages are completed, assemble your book, decide on a title, make a cover, and prepare to present your book to another group. As a group, design a cover for your book.

GROUP D

Your Theme: My Body
Your Tune: "The Wheels on the Bus"
Your Task: Sing the first verse of the song.

The wheels on the bus go round and round,
Round and round, round and round.
The wheels on the bus go round and round,
All around the town.

Create new lyrics to the song, making sure the lyrics connect to your assigned theme. Each person must write a verse. Using construction paper, markers, crayons, and magazine pictures, draw or cut out pictures, words, or symbols that represent the verse in the song. After the pages are completed, assemble your book, decide on a title, make a cover, and prepare to present your book to another group. As a group, design a cover for your book.

Activity Card for Connecting Music and Literacy

ASSIGNMENT A

Setting: Morning Meeting
Identify two songs or musical activities that support listening skills.

1.

2.

Identify two songs or musical activities that support writing.

1.

2.

ASSIGNMENT B

Setting: Transition Time
Identify two songs or musical experiences that help children focus and use rhyme at cleanup time.

1.

2.

Identify two songs or musical experiences that help children focus and use rhyme before naptime.

1.

2.

ASSIGNMENT C

Setting: Music Center

Identify four items or activities that support literacy in the Music Center. Do not include recorded music or instruments, CD or cassette players, or furniture.

1.

2.

3.

4.

WELCOME TO TODAY'S WORKSHOP

Using Music to Support Literacy

> **Please add your ideas
> to the three charts
> posted around the room.**

W
O
R
K
S
H
O
P

8

Musical Intelligence

Of the eight multiple intelligences described in his book, *Frames of Mind,* Howard Gardner said that the EARLIEST to emerge in children is Musical Intelligence.

(Gardner 1983)

Inventing Music

All children should have opportunities to invent music and lyrics in order to develop their vocabularies by:

- singing songs from a variety of genres and cultures;
- singing familiar and new songs; and
- making up their own songs.

Early experiences "playing" with musical lyrics supports children's comfort with creating:

- poetry;
- prose;
- rhymes; and
- rhythms.

Literacy The Essential
WORKSHOP
BOOK

WORKSHOP 8

Responding to Music

All children should have opportunities to respond to music in order to develop their listening skills, vocabulary, and phonological awareness as they focus on the rhythms, words, and melodies

they hear:

- using their bodies (clapping, dancing);
- using rhythm instruments (including commercially made instruments and those made by teachers and children);
- using props (scarves, puppets, and so on); and
- using words ("This song makes me feel _____.").

Listen to and Enjoy Music

All children should have opportunities to listen to and enjoy music that helps them relax, laugh, and, at the same time, attend.

- **Example of relaxing music**

- **Example of music that supports laughter**

- **Example of music that helps children pay attention**

Literacy
The Essential
WORKSHOP
BOOK

Directions for Activity: Creating Music Picture Books

- Read your group's assignment.
- Sing the first verse of your tune to make sure everyone is familiar with it.
- Create new lyrics to the song; the lyrics must connect to your assigned theme.
- Each person must write a verse and create a page for your group's book.
- Use pictures, words, and symbols for your page.
- After your pages are completed, assemble your book.
- Decide on a title.
- Make a cover.

The Essential
Literacy
WORKSHOP
BOOK

AGENDA

Using Music to Support Literacy

Date:

Trainer:

Contact Information:

OBJECTIVES

In this workshop, participants will:
- gain understanding of how music supports literacy learning;
- acquire strategies for supporting literacy with musical activities throughout the day; and
- learn how to support children's expressive and receptive language development by creating new words and themes for familiar songs.

1. Opening Activity: Music Is a Part of Our Lives [5 minutes]

2. Welcome and Logistics [5 minutes]

3. Activity: Exploring Literacy Connections with a Song [30 minutes]

4. Introducing the Topic: Using Music to Support Literacy [30 minutes]

5. Activity: Supporting Phonological Awareness with Rhythm Instruments [20 minutes]

6. Discussion [10 minutes]

7. Activity: Creating Music Picture Books [25–30 minutes]

8. Discussion [5–10 minutes]

9. Activity: Making Connections in the Classroom [15–20 minutes]

10. Discussion [10 minutes]

11. Closure [10 minutes]

The Essential
Literacy
WORKSHOP
BOOK

If You're Happy and You Know It

8

If you're _____ and you know it,

_____ .

If you're _____ and you know it,

_____ .

If you're _____ and you know it,

And you really want to show it.

If you're _____ and you know it,

_____ .

Great CDs/Cassette Tapes to Use with Rhythm Instruments

Delacre, L. 1992. *Arroz con leche: Popular songs and rhymes from Latin America.* CD/cassette. New York: Scholastic.

Gill, N. 1992. *Friends.* CD/cassette. Chicago: Etcetera Records.

Greg and Steve. 1986. *We all live together volume 1.* CD/cassette. Los Angeles: Youngheart Records.

Hunter, T. 1990. *Bits and pieces.* CD/cassette. Bellingham, WA: The Song Growing Company.

Jenkins, E. 1996. *Jambo and other call-and-response songs and chants.* CD/cassette. New York: Smithsonian/Folkways.

Jenkins, E. 1996. *Songs children love to sing.* CD/cassette. Washington, DC: Smithsonian/Folkways.

Orozco, J-L. 2004. *De colores and other Latin American folk songs for children.* CD/cassette. Berkeley, CA: Arcoiris Recording.

Sweet Honey in the Rock. 1994. *I got shoes.* CD. Redway, CA: Music for Little People.

Raffi. 1991. *Raffi in concert with the rise and shine band.* CD/cassette. Hollywood, CA: MCA Records.

Raffi. 1993. *Raffi on broadway: a family concert.* CD/cassette. Universal City, CA: MCAe.

Various Artists. 1992. *Reggae for kids: a collection of music for kids of all ages.* CD/cassette. Washington, DC: RAS Records.

Zydeco, B. 1994. *Choo choo boogaloo: zydeco music for families.* CD. Redway, CA: Music for Little People.

Additions to this list:

■ _____

■ _____

■ _____

■ _____

The Essential **Literacy** WORKSHOP BOOK

W
O
R
K
S
H
O
P

8

Supporting Phonological Awareness with Rhythm Instruments

As children use commercial or homemade instruments to experiment with rhythm, they are attentive to the segmented sounds of music. This helps them to develop phonological awareness, which includes hearing the specific sounds, called phonemes, that make up words.

Rhythm instruments typically used in preschool:

- _____
- _____
- _____
- _____
- _____
- _____
- _____
- _____
- _____

New ideas for rhythm instruments:

- _____
- _____
- _____
- _____
- _____
- _____
- _____
- _____
- _____

Good Picture Books That Are Songs

Chicken Soup with Rice: A Book of Months by Maurice Sendak

Do Your Ears Hang Low? by Caroline Jayne Church

The Lady with the Alligator Purse by Nadine Bernard Westcott

Like Me and You by Raffi and Debi Pike

Miss Mary Mack by Mary Ann Hoberman

Miss Polly Has a Dolly by Pamela Duncan Edwards

One Light, One Sun by Raffi

One Wide River to Cross by Barbara Emberley

Over in the Meadow by Jane Cabrera

Over in the Meadow: An Old Nursery Counting Rhyme by Paul Galdone

The Seals on the Bus by Lenny Hort

Shake It to the One That You Love the Best by Cheryl Warren Mattox

She'll Be Comin' 'Round the Mountain by Philemon Sturges

There Was an Old Lady Who Swallowed a Fly by Simms Taback

This Little Light of Mine by E. B. Lewis

Tingalayo by Raffi

Today Is Monday by Eric Carle

Twinkle, Twinkle, Little Star by Iza Trapani

What a Wonderful World! by George David Weiss and Bob Thiele

Wheels on the Bus by Raffi

Zin! Zin! Zin! A Violin by Lloyd Moss

Additional Teacher Resources

Blevins, W. 2004. *Phonemic awareness songs & rhymes.* New York: Scholastic.

Delacre, L. 1992. *Arroz con leche: Popular songs and rhymes from Latin America.* New York: Scholastic, Inc.

Edwards, L.C., Bayless, K.M., & Ramsey, M.E. 2005. *Music: A way of life for the young child, fifth edition.* Upper Saddle River, NJ: Prentice Hall.

Jalongo, M.R. 1996. "Using recorded music with young children: A guide for nonmusicians." *Young Children* (51)5, July, 1996.

Jenkins, E. 1993. *Ella Jenkins' this is rhythm.* Bethlehem, PA: Sing Out Publication.

McDonald, D.T. 2002. *Music in our lives: the early years, tenth edition.* Washington, DC: National Association for the Education of Young Children.

Ringgenberg, S. 2003. "Music as a teaching tool: Story songs." *Young Children* (58)5, September, 2003.

Yopp, H.K. & Yopp, R.H. 2003. *Oo-pples and Boo-noo-noos: Songs and activities for phonemic awareness.* New York: Harcourt.

This website links to songs that support phonological awareness for preschool children: www.songsforteaching.com.

Literacy The Essential Literacy WORKSHOP BOOK

Literacy to Support Diversity and Inclusion

Workshop Objectives

In this workshop, participants will:

■ explore and share their own ethnic and cultural backgrounds and family histories using children's books and other literacy materials;

■ gain an understanding of how to incorporate families into the literacy curriculum;

■ discuss how to support diversity with literacy experiences;

■ learn about the range of special needs in children and the meaning of inclusion;

■ acquire strategies to help children express, share, and celebrate their uniqueness and commonalities; and

■ analyze children's books for biases and stereotypes.

Note: If you have not done Workshop 3: Supporting English Language Learners, do the 35–40 minute activity *Supporting Cultural Diversity* (including Handout 3.7: Taking a Look Within) from Workshop 3. It will help participants explore their own biases prior to engaging in the activities in this workshop.

Workshop Materials

■ Overhead projector and Overheads 9.1–9.8 or computer and PowerPoint Workshop 9 (on accompanying CD)

■ Handouts 9.1–9.5, one copy for each participant (two copies of handout 9.3 for each participant)

■ Chart paper, markers, tape

■ One of the books from Handout 9.4: Children's Books That Support Diversity/Inclusion that focuses on a family experience for the Opening Activity (see activity for suggestions)

■ One book from the handout for each group for Activity 4: *Analyzing Books for Bias*

■ Children's picture books that feature people as characters (1–2 books for each group); they may be fairy tales, folk tales, or other types of stories, and should have a plot

■ Post-it notes or index cards (enough for each participant to have two or three) and pens

■ Art materials to make stick puppets (construction paper, scissors, glue, crayons, markers, craft sticks, yarn for hair, and fabric or scrap materials for clothing)

Suggested Time Frame
3-hour workshop

Handout List

9.1
Agenda

9.2
Analyzing Children's Books for Bias (4 pages)

9.3
Sample Family History Questionnaire

9.4
Children's Books That Support Diversity/Inclusion

9.5
Reflections on Using Literacy to Support Diversity and Inclusion

- Multicultural skin color crayons, colored pencils, and/or markers. (Multicultural skin color paints for the puppet-making portion of Activity 4 are optional.) Multicultural crayons are available from various school supply stores and catalog companies. Some crayon sets have as many as 24 skin colors. You will need one set for each group of five to six participants.

Supplemental Resources

Beaty, J.J. 1996. *Building bridges with multicultural picture books: For children 3-5.* Upper Saddle River, NJ: Prentice Hall.

Hull, K., Goldhaber, J., & Capone, A. 2002. *Opening doors: An introduction to inclusive early childhood education.* Boston, MA: Houghton Mifflin.

NAEYC Position Statement: Responding to Linguistic and Cultural Diversity. 1996. Washington, DC: National Association for the Education of Young Children.

Neugebauer, B. (Ed.) 1992. *Alike and different: Exploring our humanity with young children.* Washington, DC: National Association for the Education of Young Children.

Teaching Tolerance Project. 1997. *Starting small: Teaching tolerance in preschool and the early grades.* Montgomery, AL: Southern Poverty Law Center.

http://www.fpg.unc.edu/~pfi/pdfs/diversity_booklist.pdf (This 22-page bibliography lists children's books about people who are culturally, linguistically, and/or ability-diverse.)

Trainers' Guide to Workshop 9

Essential Messages for This Workshop: Literacy to Support Diversity and Inclusion

- Children come from diverse backgrounds and abilities.
- All children have the right to inclusion—to participate actively in regular classroom settings with typically developing peers.
- Early childhood educators must provide opportunities for children to integrate their home and family experiences into their literacy curriculum.
- Using diversity picture books and related activities can support children's developing self-esteem.

▸▸ *Display* Overhead 9.1 *or* PowerPoint Slide 1: Welcome to Today's Workshop *as participants arrive.*

■■■ ■ ■

1. Opening Activity: Family Memories [20 minutes]

▸▸ *Read one of the books from* Handout 9.4: Children's Books That Support Diversity/Inclusion.

Choose a book that tells a story about a family experience, such as *"More More More," Said the Baby* by Vera B. Williams; *Honey, I Love* by Eloise Greenfield; *Tortillas and Lullabies/Tortillas y cancioncitas* by Lynne Reiser and Corazones Valientes; or *When I Was Young in the Mountains* by Cynthia Rylant.

Say, "This book shares a special family experience with its audience. Does it remind you of a memory of something special in your own family? Close your eyes and try to visualize that memory."

After 1–2 minutes, say, "Gather into groups of five or six. Each person should share that memory briefly and then think about the similarities and differences in each person's memory."

After 8 minutes, invite a spokesperson from one group to share the similarities and differences within their group with the whole group.

Say, "Today we are going to explore diversity in the children and families with whom we work and how we can make connections to literacy as we help children learn about themselves and one another and celebrate who they are."

2. Welcome and Logistics [5 minutes]

▸▸ *Distribute* Handout 9.1: Agenda. *Review the agenda and workshop objectives.*

3. Introducing the Topic: Diversity, Inclusion, and Their Links to Literacy [30–40 minutes]

▸▸ *Show* Overhead 9.2 *or* PowerPoint Slide 2: Who Do We Include in a Definition of Diversity? *and explain:*

237

Who do we include in a definition of diversity?

■ **Children from various cultural backgrounds**—Depending on our classroom setting, the mainstream group will always be different. In one class, a girl from Mexico may have a very different background than the rest of the class who are predominantly from Colombia. Within the same cultural groups, be aware that there are differences in family values. Class, religion, gender, who is raising the child, and other factors are all tied into a child's cultural identity. We need to learn about and incorporate our children's cultures into our classrooms.

■ **Children who are English language learners (non-English speaking or of limited English proficiency)**—Approximately 329 languages are spoken in the United States, and almost 10,000,000 students are English language learners (Morrow 2005). It can be very scary for a child to come to a school where he or she does not understand the language. We need to support the child's home language by encouraging families to use their native language at home as we incorporate much of the child's home language into our classrooms through music, books, and other means.

■ **Children with learning differences (gifted, learning disabled, ADHD, and so on)**—Giftedness is often identified by a high intelligence quotient (at least 130) or by a high proficiency in a particular skill or ability (such as playing a musical instrument or drawing or painting at a level much higher than their peers). Learning-disabled children perform at a level outside the typical range of development for their age due to language processing problems. Children with ADHD typically have short attention spans and have trouble staying focused and sitting still.

■ **Children who are at risk**—Some children come to us from homes that are experiencing extreme stress related to illness or death of a family member, a family's financial or work-related problems, drug or alcohol dependency of one or more family members, homelessness, divorce or separation, or various other factors.

■ **Children who have physical impairments (visual, hearing, mobility, communication and language disorders)**—Children who have visual impairments may be able to use books with large print if they have some vision. Children who are hearing-impaired may need to be close to teachers when they are reading or speaking to the whole group. If children use sign language, the teacher should learn key words and phrases and teach these to the other children. Children with various diseases such as cerebral palsy, muscular dystrophy, and rheumatoid arthritis have typically developing cognitive skills but often have mobility difficulties. Teachers may have to use assistive technology to help them write, use a computer, or even participate at various centers. Children who have communication and language disorders experience speech and language problems such as severe stuttering, abnormal loudness, or other voice issues, or are language delayed (outside the typical range of development for language) (Morrow, 2005).

Say, "Take a minute and think about the most challenging child you have had in one of your classes. Identify a child you felt you were not prepared to handle. Close your eyes and remember what that child looked like, how the child sounded, and how he or she behaved."

Pause and allow a minute or two for participants to reflect before continuing, "Now, imagine that child smiling! Write down one thing you learned from that child and one thing the other children learned from that child. Take a few minutes to share your two ideas with a partner in your group."

Have a couple of volunteers share their ideas with the whole group. Summarize the reflections and draw conclusions about what teachers and children learn from one another.

Ask, "What does this help us understand about diversity?" Answers should include ideas about all children contributing something to the class, about other children learning patience and tolerance, and about teachers learning to individualize their classrooms.

▶▶ *Show* Overhead 9.3 *or* PowerPoint Slide 3: What Is Inclusion? *Read and annotate:*

Inclusion **is the right of all children, no matter their diverse abilities, to participate actively in regular classroom settings with typically developing children. It involves:**

■ **bringing support services to children wherever possible rather than taking them out of the classroom.** Services may include a special education teacher or aide, a physical therapist, occupational therapist, speech and language therapist, vision specialist, or technology specialist. The child may need a special computer or other adaptive equipment or furniture. Early childhood teachers collaborate with the other specialists.

■ **the belief that this experience is beneficial for typically developing children and their families, as well as for children with special needs and their families.** Children learn to be comfortable around people with disabilities by interacting, playing, and learning together. Mutual understanding, friendships, and respect among all types of families are supported.

■ **legal mandates that include ADA, IDEA, and IFSPs or IEPs.** The *Americans with Disabilities Act (ADA)* is a civil rights law that was passed in 1990. The law prohibits discrimination and guarantees equal opportunities for all people with disabilities in child care, school, work, transportation, and government. ADA requires that early childhood programs make reasonable accommodations to include children with special needs; for example, rearranging a room to accommodate a wheelchair.

The *Individuals with Disabilities Education Act (IDEA)* was passed in 1986 as PL99-457 and amended in 1991. The law entitles children five years of age and younger who have developmental disabilities and health problems that can affect their education abilities to outreach services, parent involvement services, and assessment services.

■ ■

The *Individualized Family Service Plan (IFSP)* for children up to 36 months of age, or the *Individualized Education Program* (IEP) for children 3–21 years of age are contracts, usually with the child's school or "local education agency" (LEA) that identify an educational plan for the child.

➡ *Show* Overhead 9.4 *or* PowerPoint Slide 4: Linking Diversity, Inclusion, and Literacy.

Read and annotate:

Linking Diversity, Inclusion, and Literacy

■ **Every child is a unique individual.** A child comes to school with unique experiences tied to family culture, language, and physical, emotional, and cognitive strengths and challenges.

■ **Identifying each child's special needs is the teacher's first step in supporting diversity.** As we become aware of children's needs, we can help them fit into the classroom community and design experiences that support their literacy development.

■ **When we respect children's diverse backgrounds and abilities, we support their self-image.** We must give children the opportunities, tools, and language to see themselves in a positive light.

Pause before making the final point on this slide and say, "Raise your hand if you include in your classroom crayons, paints, and markers that are reflective of a variety of skin colors."

Divide participants into new groups of 4–6 (see page 15 for suggestions on dividing into groups).

➡ *Distribute one set of skin color crayons, markers, or colored pencils (and paints, if you have them) to each group.*

Say, "If we want to acknowledge and celebrate all children for who they are, we must give them the tools to draw themselves, their families, and their friends accurately. Simply having a peach crayon and a brown crayon is not enough. We also must give them the language to express their skin colors in positive ways."

Say, "Authors who write children's books that support diversity often find new words to describe skin colors other than peach, tan, or brown. In her book, *All the Colors of the Earth,* Sheila Hamanaka talks about children who come in all the colors of the earth. She uses phrases such as "roaring browns of bears and soaring eagles" to describe skin color and mentions "hair like bouncy baby lambs."

■ ■

▸▸ *Give each participant an index card and a pen.*

Identifying each child's special needs is the teacher's first step in supporting diversity.

Say, "Write one phrase on your index card to describe your skin color and one phrase to describe your hair. Try to use descriptive, beautiful words that remind you of something wonderful from nature, a food, or a fragrance. Take five minutes to think of your two phrases. For example: My hair is _____ like _____. My skin is _____ like _____."

Allow 5 minutes for this activity, then invite groups to share descriptions among themselves. Ask for a few volunteers to share their descriptions with the whole group.

Summarize by saying, "We can help children learn to use new words to talk about themselves as unique individuals by introducing words like these in our class meetings and by reading diversity books that use eloquent adjectives and expressive language."

▸▸ *Return to the overhead or slide and read and annotate as noted:*

■ **Meaningful conversations and activities involving children's identity, home, and family are critical components in supporting literacy skills.** These conversations take place in response to stories read by the teacher, to listening to stories about diverse characters, to viewing pictures of people who look the same or look different. They are infused in themes, props, toys, dolls, and other literacy materials in centers.

▸▸ *Display* Overhead 9.5 *or* PowerPoint Slide 5: Guidelines for Selecting Diversity/Inclusion Books for Classroom Libraries.

Say, "In selecting books for our classroom libraries, make sure to include books that support diversity."

Guidelines for Selecting Diversity/ Inclusion Books for Classroom Libraries

■ **Children can get to know and love characters who are different than they are. They have an opportunity to get to know children and families they would not ordinarily meet.** Books should include fiction and non-fiction and stories from a variety of genres (fairy tales, folk tales, humor, poetry, story contexts in past and present-day settings, and so on). They should offer a variety of illustrations (including photos, paintings, line drawings, collage, realistic art, and impressionistic art.) A classroom library should include books about typically and non-typically developing children and families from many cultures; books that take place in many types of

241

settings (urban, suburban, rural) with many types of family configurations (not just two-parent homes). Books should include characters of different ages, different body types, different skin color, and so on.

- **Some books should include characters who reflect the individuals in the classroom population.** Every child wants to see himself or herself reflected in a character in a book. We must make sure to have books with characters who look like our children and their families and who live in settings similar to where they live.

- **Books should be free of bias and stereotyping.** Many books pass on subtle stereotypes prevalent in our society such as "blond-haired, blue-eyed girls are the prettiest" and "boys are heroes who must save the weaker girls."

- **Make sure to include books about children with special needs.**

Ask, "Does anyone know a good picture book that relates to any special needs or inclusion that you could share with us?"

After participants share with the whole group, explain that there is a need for more developmentally appropriate books in this domain.

> ▸▸ *Distribute* Handout 9.4: Children's Books That Support Diversity/Inclusion.

Say, "This annotated booklist will help you find new books that focus on a range of diversities, including ethnic and cultural diversities, and physical and cognitive challenges."

4. Activity: Analyzing Books for Bias [30–40 minutes]

Say, "We are going to take a critical look at children's books to see if any of the books we use contain bias and stereotyping. But, before we do that, let's spend a minute listing all of the groups of adults and children that may experience bias or discrimination." Invite responses from the participants.

> ▸▸ *Record their responses on a chart.*

Their responses should include African Americans, Latinos, Asians, and other ethnic groups; girls/women and boys/men (gender bias); gays/lesbians; people who are overweight; older people (ageism); people who wear glasses; people who are short;

people who are tall; people with cognitive challenges; people with physical challenges (blindness, deafness, people in wheelchairs). Make a comprehensive list.

Say, "It is important when we read to children that we do not unconsciously promote biases or stereotypes, so each group will take a critical look at one or two books." (Note: Participants will stay in the same group as for the prior activity.)

▸▸ *Display* Overhead 9.6 *or* PowerPoint Slide 6: Analyzing Children's Books for Bias *and distribute* Handout 9.2: Analyzing Children's Books for Bias.

Make the following points. All of the informatin is on Handout 9.2, so you do not have to cover each point completely, if time is short.

1. **Analyze the illustrations.**
   ■ *Look for Stereotypes.* A stereotype is an oversimplified generalization about a particular group, race, or gender that usually carries derogatory implications. Some infamous, overt stereotypes of African Americans are the poor, gun-carrying criminal who lives in a slum; stereotypes of women include the overly domesticated mother; the demure, doll-loving little girl; or the wicked stepmother. Stereotypes of Native Americans include the naked savage or the primitive craftsperson and his squaw. While you may not always find stereotypes in the blatant forms described, look for variations that in any way demean or ridicule characters based on their ethnicity, race, gender, sexual orientation, or physical disabilities.

   ■ *Look for Tokenism.* If there are people of color in the illustrations, do they look just like whites except for being tinted or colored in? Do all of their faces look stereotypically alike, or are they depicted as genuine individuals with distinctive features? Do the illustrations portray an accurate picture of any physical disabilities?

   ■ *Who's Doing What?* Do the illustrations depict people of color or other groups or individuals in subservient and passive roles or in leadership and action roles? Are males the active doers and females the passive observers?

2. **Analyze the story line.** The following checklist suggests subtle forms of bias to watch for:
   ■ *Standard for Success.* Does it take "white" behavior standards for a person of color to "get ahead"? Is "making it" in the dominant white society projected as the only ideal? To gain acceptance and approval, do non-whites have to exhibit extraordinary qualities (excel in sports, get A's)? In friendships between white and non-white children or boys and girls, is it the non-white or the girl who does most of the understanding and forgiving? Do persons with physical challenges take on a passive role? If the story is about animals, do males dominate?

- *Resolution of Problems.* How are problems presented, conceived, and resolved in the story? Are people of color considered to be "the problem"? Are the oppressions faced by people of color and women represented as casually related to an unjust society? Are the reasons for poverty and oppression explained, or are they accepted as inevitable? Does the story line encourage passive acceptance or active resistance? Is a particular problem faced by a person of color resolved through the benevolent intervention of a white person? If the story is about animals, do they take on stereotypical male/female roles? If there are people with physical challenges, do they resolve their own problems or are they dependent on others?

- *Role of Women.* Are the achievements of girls and women based on their own initiative and intelligence, or are they due to their good looks or to their relationship with boys? Could the same story be told if the genders were reversed?

- *Watch for Loaded Words.* A word is loaded when it has offensive overtones. Examples of loaded adjectives (usually racist) are "savage," "primitive," "conniving," "lazy," "superstitious," "treacherous," "wily," "crafty," "inscrutable," "docile," and "backward."

Look for bias language and adjectives that exclude or in any way demean girls or women or people with physical challenges. Look for use of the male pronoun to refer to both males and females. While the generic use of the word "man" was accepted in the past, its use today is outmoded. The following examples show how sexist language can be avoided: ancestors instead of forefathers; chairperson instead of chairman; community instead of brotherhood; firefighters instead of firemen; manufactured instead of man-made; human family instead of family of man.

3. **Look at the lifestyles.** Are persons from non-Western cultures and their settings depicted in such a way that they contrast unfavorably with the unstated norm of white, middle-class suburbia? If the people of color in question are depicted as "different," are negative value judgments implied? Are people of color depicted exclusively in ghettos, barrios, or migrant camps? If the illustrations and text attempt to depict another culture, do they go beyond over-simplifications and offer genuine insights into another lifestyle? Look for inaccuracy and inappropriateness in the depiction of culture. Watch for instances of the quaint-natives-in-costume syndrome (most noticeable in areas like clothing and customs, but extending to behavior and personality traits, as well).

4. **Weigh the relationships among people.** Do the whites or males in the story possess the power, take the leadership, and make the important decisions? Do people of color, people with physical challenges, and women function in supporting, subservient roles?

How are family relationships depicted? In African American families, is the mother always dominant? In Latino families, are there always lots of children? If the family is separated, are societal conditions (unemployment, poverty) cited among the reasons for the separation?

The above principles also apply to gender and familial roles in stories about animals.

5. **Note the heroes.** For many years, books depicted only "safe" heroes who were people of color—those who avoided serious conflict with the white establishment of their time. Underrepresented groups today (including those with physical challenges) are insisting on the right to define their own heroes (of both sexes) based on their own concepts and struggles for justice.

When heroes who are people of color (or people with physical challenges) appear, are they admired for the same qualities that have made white heroes famous or because what they have done has benefited the group in power? Ask this question, "Whose interests is a particular hero really serving? The interests of the hero's own people or the interests of the group in power?"

6. **Consider the effects on a child's self-image.** Are norms established that limit any child's aspirations and self-concepts? What effect can it have on children of color to be continuously bombarded with images of the color white as the ultimate in beauty, cleanliness, and virtue, and the color black as evil, dirty, or menacing? Does the book reinforce or counteract positive associations with the color white and negative associations with the color black?

What happens to a girl's self-image when she reads that only boys perform the brave and important deeds? What about a girl's self-esteem if she is not fair of skin and slim of body? In a particular story, are there one or more persons with whom a child of color can readily identify to a positive and constructive end? Are children with physical challenges seen as less capable than typically developing children?

7. **Consider the author's and illustrator's background and perspective.** Analyze the biographical material on the jacket flap or the back of the book. If a story deals with a theme relating to a particular ethnic group, what qualifies the author or illustrator to deal with the subject? If the author and illustrator are not members of the group being written about, is there anything in their background that would specifically recommend them to create such a book?

No author or illustrator can be entirely objective. All authors write and illustrate from a cultural as well as a personal context. In the past, children's books have traditionally come from authors and illustrators who were white and who were members of the middle class, with the result that a single ethnocentric perspective has dominated children's literature in the United States. With any book in question, read carefully to determine whether the author's or illustrator's perspective substantially weakens or strengthens the value of his or her written work. Is the perspective patriarchal or feminist? Is it solely Eurocentric or do other perspectives also surface?

8. **Look at the copyright date.** Books with themes focusing on people of color, usually hastily conceived, suddenly began appearing in the mid- and late-1960s. There followed a growing number of books to meet market demand, but these books were still written by white authors, edited by white editors, and published by white publishers, therefore reflecting a white point of view. Not until the early 1970s did the children's book world begin to reflect the realities of a pluralistic society. This new direction resulted from the emergence of diverse authors writing about their own experiences in an oppressive society. Non-sexist books, with rare exceptions, were not published before 1972 to 1974.

Copyright dates can provide a clue as to how likely the book is to be overtly biased, although a recent copyright date is no guarantee of a book's relevance or sensitivity. The copyright date represents the year the book was published. It usually takes two years (often much longer) from the time a manuscript is submitted to the publisher until it is printed and goes on the market. This time lag meant very little in the past, but in a period of rapid change and new consciousness, when children's book publishing is attempting to be relevant, it is becoming increasingly significant. Beginning in the mid-1990s, a genre of diversity picture books began to enter the children's book world. There are now many excellent books of this type.

Say, "Each group is going to review one or two children's books critically to see if they contain any elements of bias. Go over each of the eight points on the handout with your group. You will have 25 minutes for this activity. First, pick one person in the group to read the story and show the illustrations as he or she reads the book."

▶▶ *The group can either have one person come to a central table to choose two books or you can distribute two books to each group.*

Ideally, each group should have one book from Handout 9.4: Books That Support Diversity/Inclusion and one commonly used children's picture book (fairy tale, folk tale, or another type of story that has a plot) that has characters who are people.

5. Discussion [10 minutes]

After 20 minutes, give a 5-minute warning. When the time is up, invite groups to share some of the positive and negative things they found in the books they analyzed. Invite responses for at least four to five books.

Summarize and lead into the next activity by saying, "Now that we see how we can choose good books that support diversity in all of our children and families, let's look even more closely at individual families. We have a responsibility to learn about the families of our students so we can create language-rich experiences within the classroom that support families."

6. Activity: Family Questionnaire [35–45 minutes]

▸▸ *Display* Overhead 9.7 *or* PowerPoint Slide 7: "We Must..." *and say:*

We Must:

- **recognize that all children are linguistically and emotionally tied to the language and culture of their homes**—We must support these experiences with literacy opportunities, such as inviting family members to read or tell stories in their language, sing songs or share CDs of cultural music, donate household items for dramatic play, and so on.

- **understand that children demonstrate their knowledge and capabilities in many different ways**—We must find ways to communicate with all children, including those with speech and language delays, those whose first language is not English, and those who are not yet comfortable talking to adults.

- **involve families in their children's literacy development**—Families are their children's first teachers. Providing literacy workshops for families, sending books home for families on themes of particular interest to specific families, and sharing articles with families are a few ways to encourage this involvement.

- **learn about children's home and family life**—Some early childhood teachers conduct home visits. In other programs, family members pick up and drop off their children, which is often a time for teachers and family members to talk. Additionally, we can send home family questionnaires to gain information about each family.

- **incorporate diverse languages and perspectives into our classroom literacy environment as we create and support opportunities for reading**—(revisiting books in the library area that have been introduced by the teacher and books shared from children's homes), **writing** (helping children create their own books about themselves and their families), **listening** (incorporating music, words, and stories about children and families who are similar and different, and listening to a variety of languages), **speaking** (encouraging children and families to share their interests, strengths, culture, language with toys and props from diverse cultures integrated into every center), and **viewing** (having illustrations, photos, posters of diverse children and adults, and utilizing software that supports diversity).

▸▸ *Distribute* Handout 9.3: Sample Family History Questionnaire. *You may want to give each participant two copies, one for the activity and one for their classroom.*

Say, "Please complete the questionnaire as if you were a parent or guardian of a young child. Use your own family experiences to answer the questions. When you are finished, exchange your questionnaire with someone in your group by counting off "1, 2, 1, 2 within your group. Each 1 will work with a 2. If you have an odd number in your group, raise your hand and I will find you a partner from another group. Reflect on the similarities and differences between your answers and your partner's answers."

Allow 15 minutes for participants to complete their questionnaires and trade with their partners.

Then, say, "Look back at your own questionnaire and think about the person you chose when you answered the question, 'Tell a story about a special relative or friend who is important to your family.' Make a stick puppet of that person. You will have 15 minutes to make your puppet."

▸▸ *Have the materials for this activity ready for each of the groups. (**Note:** These are the same groups prior to breaking into pairs.)*

Note: Materials must include construction paper, scissors, glue, crayons, markers, and craft sticks. Also suggested are yarn for hair, and bits of fabric and scrap materials for clothing. Make sure to include multicultural crayons, markers, or paints.

After 15 minutes, say, "Now we are going to link our family puppets to literacy activities in the classroom. Tell the other people in your group about your puppet and link that puppet to a children's book, poem, or song and then decide on one center where you might play with your puppet in the classroom." Members of the group should help each other with this task.

Here is an example: "My puppet is my Uncle Bob who is a construction worker. He used to help me build things when I was a child. When I went to his house, we would find pieces of scrap wood and he would give me a little hammer and nails to make little trains. The book I would link him to is *Freight Train* by Donald Crews or *Changes, Changes* by Pat Hutchins. I would play with my Uncle Bob puppet in the block area or the woodworking table."

▸▸ *Give each group a piece of chart paper and a marker.*

▸▸ *Display Overhead 9.8 or PowerPoint Slide 8: Instructions for Activity: Linking Family Puppet and Literacy and read the instructions:*

1. Identify one person in the group to be the scribe.
2. The scribe makes three columns on the chart paper.
3. In column one, list the name of each person's family puppet.
4. In column two, next to each family puppet's name, identify a book, song, or poem that relates to the puppet. (You do not have to identify the author if you use a book.)
5. In column three, identify a center where children might play with the puppet and appropriate props you might add to that center.
6. Each group completes one chart.
7. When finished, hang your charts on the wall.

Go over the example:

Name of puppet	Book/Poem/Song	Center
Uncle Bob Construction Worker	*Freight Train* by Donald Crews or *Changes, Changes* by Pat Hutchins	Block Center or woodworking table—add hard hat and blueprints of buildings

7. Discussion [5–10 minutes]

▶▶ *Look at the different charts and summarize them. Ask a few questions about one or two of the puppets that look like they are linked to interesting books, songs, poems, or centers.*

Say, "By finding out about families and including this information in our day-to-day activities, we help support literacy through play with language interactions, music, and art activities. We read books in the whole group, small group, individual contexts, and throughout our centers."

8. Closure [10 minutes]

Say, "Today we have looked at many different ways to incorporate the diversity of children and families into our curriculum and to link literacy to diversity. Let's reflect on what we have learned by completing this last handout."

Please take a few minutes to list two new ways you will support diversity and inclusion with literacy and two things you learned today that you had never thought about before.

▸▸ *Distribute* Handout 9.5: Reflections on Using Literacy to Support Diversity and Inclusion.

Invite a few participants to share their responses.

WELCOME TO TODAY'S WORKSHOP

Literacy to Support Diversity and Inclusion

W
O
R
K
S
H
O
P

9

Who Do We Include in a Definition of Diversity?

- **Children from various cultural backgrounds**

- **Children who are English language learners (non-English speaking or of limited English proficiency)**

- **Children with learning differences (gifted, learning disabled, ADHD, and so on)**

- **Children who are at risk**

- **Children who have physical impairments (visual, hearing, mobility, communication and language disorders)**

The Essential
Literacy
WORKSHOP
BOOK

What Is Inclusion?

Inclusion is the right of all children, no matter their diverse abilities, to participate actively in regular classroom settings with typically developing children.

It involves:

■ bringing support services to children wherever possible rather than taking them out of the classroom;

■ the belief that this experience is beneficial for typically developing children and their families, as well as for children with special needs and their families; and

■ legal mandates that include ADA, IDEA, and IFSPs or IEPs.

The Essential
Literacy
WORKSHOP
BOOK

W
O
R
K
S
H
O
P

9

Linking Diversity, Inclusion, and Literacy

■ **Every child is a unique individual.**

■ **Identifying each child's special needs is the teacher's first step in supporting diversity.**

■ **When we respect children's diverse backgrounds and abilities, we support their self-image.**

■ **Meaningful conversations and activities involving children's identity, home, and family are critical components in supporting literacy skills.**

The Essential Literacy WORKSHOP BOOK

Guidelines for Selecting Diversity/ Inclusion Books for Classroom Libraries

■ Children can get to know and love characters who are different than they are. They have an opportunity to get to know children and families they would not ordinarily meet.

■ Some books should include characters who reflect the individuals in the classroom population.

■ Books should be free of bias and stereotyping.

■ Make sure to include books about children with special needs.

Literacy
The Essential
WORKSHOP
BOOK

W
O
R
K
S
H
O
P

9

Analyzing Children's Books for Bias

1. Analyze the illustrations.

2. Analyze the story line.

3. Look at the lifestyles.

4. Weigh the relationships among people.

5. Note the heroes.

6. Consider the effects on a child's self-image.

7. Consider the author's and illustrator's background and perspective.

8. Look at the copyright date.

We Must...

- recognize that all children are linguistically and emotionally tied to the language and culture of their homes;

- understand that children demonstrate their knowledge and capabilities in many different ways;

- involve families in their children's literacy development;

- learn about children's home and family life; and

- incorporate diverse languages and perspectives into our classroom literacy environment as we create and support opportunities for reading, writing, listening, speaking, and viewing.

W
O
R
K
S
H
O
P

9

Instructions for Activity: Linking Family Puppet and Literacy

1. Identify one person in the group to be the scribe.

2. The scribe makes three columns on the chart paper.

3. In column one, list the name of each person's family puppet.

4. In column two, next to each family puppet's name, identify a book, song, or poem that relates to the puppet. (You do not have to identify the author if you use a book.)

5. In column three, identify a center where children might play with the puppet.

6. Each group completes one chart.

7. When finished, hang your charts on the wall.

Example:

Name of puppet	Book/Poem/Song	Center
Uncle Bob, Construction worker	*Freight Train* by Donald Crews or *Changes, Changes* by Pat Hutchins	Block Center or woodworking table

AGENDA

Literacy to Support Diversity and Inclusion

Date:

Trainer:

Contact Information:

OBJECTIVES

In this workshop, participants will:

- explore and share their own ethnic and cultural backgrounds and family histories using children's books and other literacy materials;
- gain an understanding of how to incorporate families into the literacy curriculum;
- discuss how to support diversity with literacy experiences;
- learn about the range of special needs in children and the meaning of inclusion;
- acquire strategies to help children express, share, and celebrate their uniqueness and commonalities; and
- analyze children's books for biases and stereotypes.

1. Opening Activity: Family Memories [20 minutes]

2. Welcome and Logistics [5 minutes]

3. Introducing the Topic: Diversity, Inclusion, and Their Links to Literacy [30– 40 minutes]

4. Activity: Analyzing Books for Bias [30– 40 minutes]

5. Discussion [10 minutes]

6. Activity: Family Questionnaire [35–45 minutes]

7. Discussion [5–10 minutes]

8. Closure [10 minutes]

Literacy
The Essential
WORKSHOP
BOOK

HANDOUT 9.2a

Analyzing Children's Books for Bias

(Adapted from *10 Quick Ways to Analyze Books for Racism and Sexism*. Council on Interracial Books for Children, Volume 5, No. 3, 1974)

Both in school and out, young children are exposed to bias attitudes. These attitudes, expressed over and over in books and in other media, gradually distort their perceptions until stereotypes and myths about ethnic groups, women, gender roles, and various other groups are accepted as reality. If teachers and children can detect bias in a book, perhaps they can transfer the perception to wider areas. The following guidelines are offered as a starting point in evaluating children's books from this perspective.

1. Analyze the Illustrations

■ **Look for stereotypes.** A stereotype is an oversimplified generalization about a particular group, race, or gender that usually carries derogatory implications. Some infamous, overt stereotypes of African Americans are the poor, gun-carrying criminal who lives in a slum; stereotypes of women include the overly domesticated mother; the demure, doll-loving little girl; or the wicked stepmother. Stereotypes of Native Americans include the naked savage or the primitive craftsperson and his squaw. While you may not always find stereotypes in the blatant forms described, look for variations that in any way demean or ridicule characters based on their ethnicity, race, gender, sexual orientation, or physical disabilities.

■ **Look for Tokenism.** If there are people of color in the illustrations, do they look just like whites except for being tinted or colored in? Do all of their faces look stereotypically alike, or are they depicted as genuine individuals with distinctive features? Do the illustrations portray an accurate picture of any physical disabilities?

■ **Who's Doing What?** Do the illustrations depict people of color or other groups or individuals in subservient and passive roles or in leadership and action roles? Are males the active "doers" and females the passive observers?

2. Analyze the Story Line

The following checklist suggests some of the subtle forms of bias to watch for:

■ **Standard for Success.** Does it take "white" behavior standards for a person of color to "get ahead"? Is "making it" in the dominant white society projected as the only ideal? To gain acceptance and approval, do non-whites have to exhibit extraordinary qualities (excel in sports, get A's)? In friendships between white and non-white children or boys and girls, is it the non-white or the girl who does most of the understanding and forgiving? Do persons with physical challenges take on a passive role? If the story is about animals, do males dominate?

■ **Resolution of Problems.** How are problems presented, conceived, and resolved in the story? Are people of color considered to be "the problem"? Are the oppressions faced by people of color and women represented as casually related to an unjust society? Are the reasons for poverty and oppression explained, or are they accepted as inevitable? Does the story line encourage passive acceptance or active resistance? Is a particular problem faced by a person of color resolved through the benevolent intervention of a white person? If the story is about animals, do they take on stereotypical male/female roles? If there are people with physical challenges, do they resolve their own problems or are they dependent on others?

■ **Role of Women.** Are the achievements of girls and women based on their own initiative and intelligence, or are they due to their good looks or to their relationship with boys? Could the same story be told if the genders were reversed?

■ **Watch for Loaded Words.** A word is loaded when it has offensive overtones. Examples of loaded adjectives (usually racist) are "savage," "primitive," "conniving," "lazy," "superstitious," "treacherous," "wily," "crafty," "inscrutable," "docile," and "backward."

Look for bias language and adjectives that exclude or in any way demean girls or women or people with physical challenges. Look for use of the male pronoun to refer to both males and females. While the generic use of the word "man" was accepted in the past, its use today is outmoded. The following examples show how sexist language can be avoided: ancestors instead of forefathers; chairperson instead of chairman; community instead of brotherhood; firefighters instead of firemen; manufactured instead of man-made; human family instead of family of man.

Examples of Gender Stereotypes

Male Stereotypes		Female Stereotypes	
Active	Expressing anger	Passive	Controlling anger
Brave	Unemotional	Frightened	Emotional
Strong		Weak	
Rough		Gentle	
Competitive		Giving up easily	
Inventive		Unoriginal	
Intelligent, logical		Silly, illogical	
Quiet, easygoing		Shrewish, nagging	
Decisive, problem-solving		Confused	
Messy		Neat	
Mechanical		Inept	
Independent		Dependent	
Leader, innovator		Follower, conformer	
Unconcerned about appearance		Concerned about appearance	
As parent, playing with children		As parent, nurturing children	
Having innate need for adventure		Having innate need for marriage and motherhood	

The Essential
Literacy
WORKSHOP
BOOK

3. Look at the Lifestyles

Are persons from non-Western cultures and their settings depicted in such a way that they contrast unfavorably with the unstated norm of white, middle-class suburbia? If the people of color in question are depicted as "different," are negative value judgments implied? Are people of color depicted exclusively in ghettos, barrios, or migrant camps? If the illustrations and text attempt to depict another culture, do they go beyond over-simplifications and offer genuine insights into another lifestyle? Look for inaccuracy and inappropriateness in the depiction of culture. Watch for instances of the quaint-natives-in-costume syndrome (most noticeable in areas like clothing and customs, but extending to behavior and personality traits, as well).

4. Weigh the Relationships Among People

Do the whites or males in the story possess the power, take the leadership, and make the important decisions? Do people of color, people with physical challenges, and women function in essentially supporting, subservient roles?

How are family relationships depicted? In African-American families, is the mother always dominant? In Latino families, are there always lots of children? If the family is separated, are societal conditions (unemployment, poverty) cited among the reasons for the separation?

The above principles also apply to gender and familial roles in stories about animals.

5. Note the Heroes

For many years, books depicted only "safe" heroes who were people of color—those who avoided serious conflict with the white establishment of their time. Underrepresented groups today (including those with physical challenges) are insisting on the right to define their own heroes (of both sexes) based on their own concepts and struggles for justice.

When heroes who are people of color (or people with physical challenges) appear, are they admired for the same qualities that have made white heroes famous or because what they have done has benefited the group in power? Ask this question, "Whose interests is a particular hero really serving? The interests of the hero's own people or the interests of the group in power?"

6. Consider the Effects on a Child's Self-Image

Are norms established that limit any child's aspirations and self-concepts? What effect can it have on children of color to be continuously bombarded with images of the color white as the ultimate in beauty, cleanliness, and virtue, and the color black as evil, dirty, and menacing? Does the book reinforce or counteract positive associations with the color white and negative associations with the color black?

Gryphon House, Inc. grants permission for this page to be photocopied by professionals using *The Essential Literacy Workshop Book.*

What happens to a girl's self-image when she reads that boys perform all of the brave and important deeds? What about a girl's self-esteem if she is not "fair" of skin and slim of body? In a particular story, are there one or more persons with whom a child of color can readily identify to a positive and constructive end? Are children with physical challenges seen as less capable than typically developing children?

7. **Consider the Author's and/or Illustrator's Background and Perspective**
Analyze the biographical material on the jacket flap or the back of the book. If a story deals with a theme relating to a particular ethnic group, what qualifies the author or illustrator to deal with the subject? If the author and illustrator are not members of the group being written about, is there anything in their background that would specifically recommend them to create such a book?

No author or illustrator can be entirely objective. All authors write and illustrate from a cultural as well as a personal context. In the past, children's books have traditionally come from authors and illustrators who were white and who were members of the middle class, with the result that a single ethnocentric perspective has dominated children's literature in the United States. With any book in question, read carefully to determine whether the author's or illustrator's perspective substantially weakens or strengthens the value of his or her written work. Is the perspective patriarchal or feminist? Is it solely Eurocentric or do other perspectives also surface?

8. **Look at the Copyright Date**
Books with themes focusing on people of color, usually hastily conceived, suddenly began appearing in the mid- and late-1960s. There followed a growing number of books to meet market demand, but these books were still written by white authors, edited by white editors, and published by white publishers, therefore reflecting a white point of view. Not until the early 1970s did the children's book world begin to reflect the realities of a pluralistic society. This new direction resulted from the emergence of diverse authors writing about their own experiences in an oppressive society. Non-sexist books, with rare exceptions, were not published before 1972 to 1974.

Copyright dates can provide a clue as to how likely the book is to be overtly biased, although a recent copyright date is no guarantee of a book's relevance or sensitivity. The copyright date represents the year the book was published. It usually takes two years (often much longer) from the time a manuscript is submitted to the publisher until it is printed and goes on the market. This time lag meant very little in the past, but in a period of rapid change and new consciousness, when children's book publishing is attempting to be relevant, it is becoming increasingly significant. Beginning in the mid-1990s, a genre of diversity picture books began to enter the children's book world. There are now many excellent books of this type.

Sample Family History Questionnaire

Dear Families,

This questionnaire will give us information that will help us get to know your family and your child and incorporate the richness of your heritage and culture into our program. We want to share ideas and learn from each family's traditions.

Sincerely,

_____

Child's Name: _____   Place of Birth: _____

Mother's Name: _____   Place of Birth: _____

Father's Name: _____   Place of Birth: _____

Mother's Parents live/lived in: _____

Father's Parents live/lived in: _____

Child lives with: _____

Languages spoken at home: _____

Does the family have special customs or traditions you would like to share? Tell us about some of these. _____

_____

_____

_____

Tell a story about a special relative or friend who is important to your family. _____

_____

_____

_____

_____

_____

_____

Can you remember special toys or games you (parents/guardians) liked to play with as a child?_____

_____

_____

_____

_____

_____

Some favorite foods the family enjoys are: _____

_____

_____

If you would like to come to school and sing a favorite song; tell a favorite story; do a favorite dance; or send in a favorite photo, CD, DVD, video, cassette tape, or children's book, please describe what you would like to do. _____

_____

_____

_____

Are there items of clothing representative of traditional clothing worn by your family that you would like to show us or donate to our classroom for our dramatic play area? If so, please describe: _____

_____

_____

_____

Please use the rest of this page to write more about any of the questions above, or to add anything else you think would be interesting for us to know about your family heritage or that you would like your child to share with other children in the class.

Children's Books That Support Diversity/Inclusion

Annotated Bibliography

Abuela by Arthur Dorros (grandmother/grandchild relationship in urban NY setting)

All Kinds of Friends, Even Green! by Ellen B. Sensisi (spina bifida)

All the Colors of the Earth by Sheila Hamanaka (racial/diversity)

All the Colors We Are/Todos los colores de nuestra piel by Katie Kissinger (racial diversity)

Arnie and the New Kid by Nancy Carlson (wheelchair/crutches)

Bein' with You This Way by W. Nikola-Lisa (racial/ethnic diversity)

Brothers and Sisters by Laura Dwight (hearing disability, Down syndrome)

The Colors of Us by Karen Katz (racial diversity)

Families by Ann Morris (diverse families)

Family pictures/Cuadros de familia by Carmen Lomas Garza (family memoir in rural setting)

Friends at School by Rochelle Bunnett (inclusion)

Hairs/Pelitos: A story in English and Spanish from The House on Mango Street by Sandra Cisneros (family memoir)

Hats Off to Hair! by Virginia L. Kroll (self-esteem, ethnic/cultural diversity)

Here Are My Hands by Bill Martin, Jr. and John Archambault (racial diversity)

Honey, I Love by Eloise Greenfield (family memoir)

I Can, Can You? by Marjorie W. Pitzer (Down syndrome)

I Look Like a Girl by Sheila Hamanaka (gender)

I Love My Hair! by Natasha Anastasia Tarpley (self-esteem for an African American girl)

Isla by Arthur Dorros (grandmother/grandchild relationship set in Puerto Rico)

Loving by Ann Morris (diverse families)

"More more more," said the baby by Vera B. Williams (diverse family traditions)

My Friend Isabelle by Eliza Woloson (Down syndrome)

My Friend Leslie: The Story of a Handicapped Child by Maxine B. Rosenberg (inclusion in a kindergarten class)

The Other Side by Jacqueline Woodson (racial bias)

Play by Ann Morris (ethnic/cultural diversity)

Rolling Along: The Story of Taylor and His Wheelchair by Jamee Riggio Heelan (mobility challenges)

Shoes, Shoes, Shoes by Ann Morris (ethnic/cultural diversity)

The Skin You Live In by Michael Tyler (self-esteem, diversity)

Someone Special, Just Like You by Tricia Brown (hearing, sight, mobility challenges)

Something Beautiful by Sharon Dennis Wyeth (finding beauty in a poor urban neighborhood)

Somos un arco iris/We Are a Rainbow by Nancy Maria Grande Tabor (racial/ethnic diversity)

This Is the Way We Eat Our Lunch by Edith Baer (cultural diversity)

Tortillas and lullabies/Tortillas y cancioncitas by Lynn Reiser (intergenerational family memoir)

We Are All Alike We Are All Different by the Cheltenham Elementary School Kindergarteners (cultural/ethnic diversity)

We Can Co It! by Laura Dwight (spina bifida, Down syndrome, cerebral palsy, blindness)

We Go in a Circle by Peggy Perry Anderson (physical therapy)

Weddings by Ann Morris (ethnic/cultural diversity)

When I Was Little: A Four-Year-Old's Memoir of Her Youth by Jamie Lee Curtis (self-esteem)

When I Was Young in the Mountains by Cynthia Rylant (memoir in rural setting)

Whoever You Are by Mem Fox (ethnic diversity)

Reflections on Using Literacy to Support Diversity and Inclusion

Two new ways I will support diversity and inclusion with literacy are:

■

■

Two things I learned today that I had never thought about before or now think about in a new way are:

■

■

Literacy Across the Curriculum

Workshop Objectives

In this workshop, participants will:

- learn ideas for teaching literacy while simultaneously addressing content across many subject areas;
- use a planning web to support teaching literacy across the curriculum; and
- develop practical lesson plans to use in their classrooms.

Workshop Materials

- Overhead projector and Overheads 10.1–10.8 or computer and PowerPoint Workshop 10 (on accompanying CD)
- Handouts 10.1–10.7, one copy for each participant
- Chart paper, markers, tape
- Timer
- Collections of found materials for participants to sort and classify such as buttons, shells, keys, bread tabs, and plastic bottle caps. Prepare sets of about 20–30 items in separate boxes or baskets, one collection per group. **Note:** Found items, as contrasted with commercial manipulative materials such as bears or cubes, allow for a wide range of inventive sorting methods, descriptive language, and conversation.
- Picture book about collections. Ideas include *Hannah's Collections* by Marthe Jocelyn; *I Like Things* by Margaret Hillert; *Josephina: The Great Collector* by Diana Engel; *The Button Box* by Margarette Reid; and *The Puddle Pail* by Elisa Kleven.
- Picture book for the activity *Using Books*. We recommend *Just a Little Bit* by Ann Tompert. Alternate suggestions of books with a rich narrative, a variety of interesting language, and subject-specific content include *The Little Red Hen (Makes a Pizza)* by Philemon Sturges and *Shoes from Grandpa* by Mem Fox.
- Books from the list of content and concept books (see handout 10.7) for the activity: *Content or Concepts*. Each group will need 3–4 books representing one concept category. (Assign different concepts to each group.)
- Index cards to make assignment cards for the activity: *Content or Concepts*

■ Charts for the activity: *Using a Theme Approach,* labeled as follows (see activity for additional directions):

   ■ Literacy Ideas
   ■ Ideas for Math, Science, Social Studies, Art, Music
   ■ Ways to Enrich Centers
   ■ Good Questions to Ask
   ■ How to Involve Families
   ■ How to Keep Track of Children's Learning

Trainers' Guide to Workshop 10

Essential Messages for This Workshop: Literacy Across the Curriculum

■ Young children thrive on "becoming experts" because it makes them feel powerful and confident, which in turns leads to more talking, thinking, and questioning.

■ Expertise for young children comes from opportunities to make connections over time as they engage with books, concepts, and topics.

■ When children hear books again and again, they can go beyond recall to higher order thinking and questioning as they make inferences, connections to their own experiences, and connections to concepts and content about the world around them.

■ Helping children make connections and become experts requires careful thinking and planning.

▸▸ *Display* Overhead 10.1 *or* PowerPoint Slide 1: Welcome to Today's Workshop *as participants arrive.*

1. Opening Activity: Collections [15–20 minutes]

▸▸ *Before participants arrive, place a box or basket with a collection of found materials (see the workshop materials list on the previous page for suggestions) on each table.*

This opening activity is designed for groups of five or six people sitting at tables. Set up tables with five or six chairs at each table.

▸▸ *Use* Overhead 10.2 *or* PowerPoint Slide 2: Collections Directions *for activity directions.*

■ ■

▸▸ *Give each group index cards and pens.*

When children hear books again and again, they can go beyond recall to higher order thinking and questioning.

Welcome the group and say, "Today we will be talking about literacy across the curriculum. To get you started, you will find collections in the middle of each of your tables. Dump out the contents of the box or basket and take a few minutes to play with them. You will have about 5 minutes. Write down all of the different words your group uses to describe the collection."

Give participants a two-minute warning.

▸▸ *After a quick cleanup, put up* Overhead 10.3 *or* PowerPoint Slide 3: Two Minutes–Two People *for follow-up directions.*

Say, "When I start the timer, you will have 2 minutes to find two people to talk to. With each person, share three things: what collection you had; two ways your group used the collection; and skills and concepts you explored and used while playing with the collection." Start the timer and call time after 2 minutes.

▸▸ *Read aloud a picture book about collections (see suggestions on the workshop materials list on page 269).*

After reading the book, ask, "Have you heard this book before? What are some other children's books that relate to collecting things? What are some words you heard in the story that you wrote down when you were working in your groups? What skills and concepts did you explore as you played with your collections and listened to the story?"

Invite responses then lead into the agenda by saying, "Take 2 minutes to talk to a neighbor about three or four ways you connect literacy to other areas of the curriculum such as math, science, and social studies." Hear a few ideas before reviewing the agenda and outcomes.

2. Welcome and Logistics [3–5 minutes]

▸▸ *Distribute* Handout 10.1: Agenda. *Review the agenda and workshop objectives.*

271

■ ■

3. Introducing the Topic: Literacy Across the Curriculum [15–20 minutes]

▸▸ *Distribute* Handout 10.2: Literacy Across the Curriculum.

Say, "As we go through the workshop, we will think about how to help children make meaningful connections as they learn. Our focus today is on literacy and how to incorporate and extend it across the curriculum in ways that help children make connections."

▸▸ *Show* Overhead 10.4 *or* PowerPoint Slide 4: Literacy Across the Curriculum *and make the key points below.*

Help children become experts. Young children thrive on "becoming experts." Think about the children you teach. They feel proud when they can tell you something they learned recently or about a favorite book. Being an expert makes children feel powerful and confident, which leads them to talk, think, and question things more.

Think about essential learning. All learning experiences should be planned with a purpose. Always ask yourself, "Why am I doing this with the children? What do I want them to learn?" When you are clear about what you want them to learn, you can help them become experts.

Use literacy connections to help children make meaningful connections. Learning is about making connections. Expertise for young children develops from repeated opportunities to engage in meaningful content over time and in a variety of ways. This helps them see that what they are learning connects to other things they have learned, to their own lives, and to their experiences. When you choose a book to read to them, think about how you can help them connect the book to other experiences in their lives. Does the book remind them of other stories they have heard? Does the book remind them of experiences they have had at home? Think about content connections. How does the book relate to math or science or social studies? This will foster literacy learning across the curriculum in meaningful ways.

There are many ways to foster literacy learning and at the same time help children make connections across the curriculum.

- The first is to begin with a book and extend it. This is sometimes described as using "stretching stories."
- A second way is to identify content or a specific concept related to a particular subject that you want to teach; for example, opposites or positional words. As you plan learning experiences to help children learn the concept, consider ways to help them make connections.

272

■ A third approach is to use themes to make literacy connections and subject area (content or concepts) connections.

The activities we do during today's workshop will let you practice each approach. Regardless of your entry point—a book, a concept, or a theme—you have to plan.

>> *Determine whether you want to present all three approaches to the participants. If not, use the first approach (starting with a book) and then choose between the second approach (content/concept) and the third approach (theme).*

>> *Show* Overhead 10.5 *or* PowerPoint Slide 5: Planning Web *to explain the web.*

>> *Distribute several copies of* Handout 10.3: Planning Web *and one copy of* Handout 10.4: Steps for Using the Planning Web *to each participant.*

Say, "Use a web to organize your thinking. Webs are good planning tools because they help you consider different components. At the center of this web is your focus—the approach you have chosen as your starting point: the book, concept, or theme."

Let the participants know that as you describe the web, the descriptions are on their handout. The text below is on the handout with some elaborated text for you to add.

1. **Select your starting point. It might be:**
   ■ a good book,
   ■ a specific skill or concept within a subject area, or
   ■ a theme.

2. **Consider essential learning.** Ask yourself, "Why am I doing this? What is my purpose? What do I want children to learn so they come away from this experience having made meaningful connections, feeling competent, and having engaged in valuable learning?" Another way to think about essential learning is the big ideas or important concepts or skills that children will use again in other situations.

3. **Identify literacy opportunities.** Think about the ways you can address literacy learning. Things to consider include:
   ■ What different types of text are available? Fiction, non-fiction, poetry, song lyrics?
   ■ What questions will you ask to extend children's language and thinking?
   ■ How will you help children learn concepts of print, language and vocabulary, comprehension (listening and reading), phonological and phonemic awareness, letters and words, and writing?

4. **Explore subject area connections (math, science, social studies, art, music).** If you started with a subject area concept, look for connections to other subjects.

5. **Enrich your classroom centers or interest areas.** What props or experiences can you add to centers that extend children's learning? (For example, blocks, manipulatives, dramatic play, listening, cooking, and so on.)

6. **Think about family connections.** Always keep in mind ways to include families. For example, invite a family member to read the story to a small group. If you started with a book, you might get a copy of the book in a second language spoken by children in your classroom and invite a parent to read it to the class.

7. **Plan for assessment.** Think about what you want to observe and document about children's learning and how you will do it.

Summarize by saying, "Many teachers prefer one approach to another, always starting with a book, always using a theme. Flexibility has virtue. Use different approaches depending on what it is you are trying to accomplish. In our next activity we will practice using the planning web with a book as our starting point."

---

4. Activity: Using Books [45 minutes]

▶▶ *Divide participants into new groups of five or six (see page 15 for suggestions on dividing into groups).*

Introduce the activity by saying, "Using books is a powerful way to extend literacy across the curriculum because we know that children not only benefit from having good books read to them more than once, they love hearing them again and again. Why?"

Invite responses. Ideas might include:
- When children hear books again and again, they connect the stories to their own lives.
- They go beyond recall to higher-order thinking and questioning.
- They make inferences, connections to other books, poems, or songs they know, and connections to concepts and content about the world around them.
- They befriend the books and take ownership of them.

Say, "When you select a book to read to children, think of ways to extend the story. Each time you read the book, modify and adapt the reading so the essential learning is enriched. For example, when you read *Shoes from Grandpa* by Mem Fox for the first time, children learn to appreciate a good story. After reading the book, ask the children what they liked about the story or about gifts they have received. After the next reading, you might focus on recall, encouraging children to recall all of the items Jessie received. After the third reading, you might emphasize the rhyming aspect of the story."

Invite participants to think of ways they have adapted the focus of books after repeated readings. Then add, "Whatever book you select, as you plan for repeated readings, consider the literacy concepts best taught through the book. Notice the literacy ring on the planning web. In addition, reflect on how the book's content relates to other subject areas. For example, when you listened to [title of the collection book you read aloud in the warm-up activity], the story provided many links to math and social studies. This connects to the third ring on the web."

Check for questions or comments.

Say, "We will try different approaches today. With each one, we will explore different aspects of the planning web as a tool. Let's begin with a book. I will read aloud *Just a Little Bit* by Ann Tompert."

Note: If you select a different book for this activity, modify the comments below to fit the book selected.

▸▸ *Use* Overhead 10.6 *or* PowerPoint Slide 6: Responding to the Book *to set up group discussion.*

Say, "You have 3–5 minutes to reflect on two questions. 1) What are some ways children might respond to this story? 2) What is the essential learning children can take away from this story and the extended activities?"

Invite a few responses for essential learning. Listen for ideas including: different things weigh different amounts; vocabulary related to weights and measures and describing things; when others help out, tasks can be accomplished successfully.

Remind teachers that different books address different aspects of literacy learning. Do a group brainstorm of ways in which this book supports literacy learning and connections to children's lives and learning. As you chart their ideas, suggest that they record the information in the literacy ring on their webs. Ideas to listen for include:

■ Repetitive phrasing is engaging, helps children with comprehension, and helps them understand the concepts of *heavy, light,* and *balance.* Invite them to think about open-ended questions to ask in group discussions. Brainstorm a few ideas for retellings (using a felt board, making a book). What are some ways to help children experiment with weight and balance?

■ Invite them to think about the vocabulary they have heard. How might they engage children with these words?

■ Be sure to point out the alliteration (phonological awareness).

■ ■

Provide 5–7 minutes for groups to discuss one or two subject area experiences that logically extend the book. For example, helping children make meaningful connections to size, weight, and balance, and designing small-group or center activities for children (you could put a balance scale in the manipulatives or math area, make seesaws or build parks in the block area, and so on).

5. Discussion [5 minutes]

Say, "Subject area content and concepts are essential learning goals. *Just a Little Bit* supports children's learning about measurement, specifically about size and weight. In the boxes related to subject on your webs, be sure you note what it is that children can learn. In the boxes for centers, think about how you can design experiences that help them learn."

Invite a few people to share their ideas by telling the group what they wrote in the subject boxes and the center boxes.

Point out that every aspect of the web will not be filled in each time they plan. The intent is to highlight meaningful connections.

▶▶ *Distribute* Handout 10.5: Extending Read-Alouds to Centers. *Let participants know this is a resource for them.*

Ask, "What are other books or poems that deal with size and weight? Record them on your web."

Note: Depending on your time and the needs of the group, you may select one of the next two activities.

6. Activity: Content or Concepts [30–35 minutes]

Divide participants into new groups of 4–6.

▶▶ *Write "Math," "Science," or "Social Studies" on an index card and place one index card (assignment card) on each table.*

■ ■

▸▸ *Depending on the books you choose from the book list (see Handout 10.7), create an assignment card for each group: Math, Science, and Social Studies. Depending on the books you choose, you might be more specific with concepts. For example, one group might have **math: measurement** and another group might have **math: shapes**. It is likely that multiple groups will have the same subject.*

Using books is a powerful way to extend literacy across the curriculum.

Give each group a collection of four or five concept books related to the subject area. Distribute Handout 10.6: Thinking About Content and Concepts and explain that it is designed to help them think about what children are learning. It is not comprehensive and may not include specific learning standards from your setting. **Note:** You may modify this handout if your setting has specific standards you want teachers to learn.

Say, "A second way to approach planning is to focus on subject area content. Look at your handout Thinking About Content and Concepts. Each subject area has key concepts and skills for children to learn. Let's revisit our collections task once more. Who sorted and classified the collections?" (Show of hands.) "Imagine that my lesson plan focused on math and science. The essential learning goals were: asking questions; observing and describing the properties of objects; sorting and classifying; and using language to describe things. To make a literacy connection, I selected a book that extended your thinking about different kinds of collections and how to describe them. With your group, think about other kinds of literacy connections you could encourage."

Provide 2–3 minutes and invite ideas. Make sure their ideas include creating a number line from 1–10 of different collections (children can write the numbers to go with the collections) and making collections books (children can draw and write about collections at their homes).

Discuss ways this experience can connect to center experiences. Elicit suggestions. Ideas might include: highlight sorting games in manipulatives; add collections of books about similar kinds of objects into bins in the library area; organize dramatic play shelves with the children; play clean-up games in the block area and emphasize describing, sorting, and categorizing blocks.

▸▸ *Display* Overhead 10.7 *or* PowerPoint Slide 7: Content/Concept Planning.

Say, "Your group has been assigned subject-specific content. Talk with your colleagues about ways to help children make connections to this content. You also have four to five books related to the concept. Design a series of learning experiences using the planning web. Remember: You do not need to fill in every section of the web. You want to help children make connections. How will you help them connect this concept to their own lives? To stories? Think of activities that will help them think about the concept through active problem-solving."

Provide 15 minutes for them to work.

Ask the participants to form triads with two people from two other groups to share. Allow 7–10 minutes for sharing.

7. Discussion [5 minutes]

Invite comments, questions, and insights.

Ask, "What were some of the differences you experienced planning with a book as your focus versus planning with a content focus?"

▸▸ *Distribute* Handout 10.7: Content and Concepts Books.

8. Activity: Using a Theme Approach [25–30 minutes]

Say, "Let's review what we have talked about today. We started with a book and looked at ways to extend it to address other areas of the curriculum and, at the same time, help children acquire literacy skills. Next, we looked at specific content or content from other subjects that you want to teach and identified ways to promote literacy learning by using books, fostering vocabulary development, encouraging writing, and so on."

Ask, "How many of you use themes in your classroom? Based on your experiences, what do you find valuable about thematic teaching for young children?" Responses might include that using themes:

- helps children make meaningful connections to their own lives;
- engages children with content to help them feel knowledgeable, competent, and powerful;
- builds children's knowledge and experience; encourages talking, thinking, problem-solving; questioning; and extends their vocabulary; and
- organizes the curriculum in ways that ensure that literacy as well as content from many subject areas are being addressed.

Ask, "What are some themes you have used with children?" Invite four to five responses. Listen for ideas such as stories, transportation, insects, and so on.

■ ■

▸▸ *Show* Overhead 10.8 *or* PowerPoint Slide 8: Theme Brainstorming.

▸▸ *Select a theme topic that is developmentally appropriate and can be explored firsthand by children ages three to five. You can choose from the ideas generated by the group or select one from the ideas above.*

Say, "For this activity, instead of working individually on webs, we will generate ideas for the web collectively using carousel brainstorming. I have posted charts labeled according to different parts of the web: incorporating ideas for literacy and ideas for other subjects; ways to enrich centers; good questions to ask; how to involve families; and how to keep track of what children are learning. As you think about literacy, focus on ways to promote language, writing, and experiences with a wide range of text." **Note:** If necessary, explain how to do carousel brainstorming (see Appendix E, page 316).

Review the directions on Overhead 10.8 or PowerPoint Slide 8.

▸▸ *Form groups by counting off by the number of charts and ask participants to go to their chart.*

Note: This is a carousel brainstorming activity. Participants rotate to different charts to add ideas, spending about 3 minutes at each chart. Prepare charts ahead of time with a number and a title. Hang them around the room so there is space between each chart. Determine the number of charts based on the number of participants and the amount of time you allocate for this activity. You might have one chart for each of the following: literacy, including different types of text; each subject area; centers; families; lower/higher order questions; and observing and documenting children's learning.

▸▸ *Send groups to the charts. Provide 3–4 minutes at the first chart, depending on how long it takes them to get started. When you see that each group has at least two or three ideas, call time. Then allow three minutes for each subsequent chart so groups can read the charts and add at least one or two new ideas. Groups should return to their original chart and review it.*

Ask participants to return to their seats.

9. Discussion [5–7 minutes]

Address any question marks on the charts. Invite comments and insights. You can make the following points, "We talked today about literacy experiences and ways to connect them to other subject areas. Let's look at the charts and the webs we developed earlier in this workshop and recall literacy ideas besides books."

Invite a few ideas and ask, "What are some ways we highlighted vocabulary? Phonological and phonemic awareness?"

10. Closure [5 minutes]

Say, "Jot down one idea you are excited about trying. I will set the timer for 2 minutes. Find two people you have not talked to today and share your ideas."

When the timer rings, send people back to their seats. Hear one or two ideas. Remind them to take their webs and to experiment with different approaches in their classrooms.

WELCOME TO TODAY'S WORKSHOP

Literacy Across the Curriculum

The Essential **Literacy** WORKSHOP BOOK

Collections Directions

1. **Dump your collection in the middle of the table.**

2. **Play with your collection!**

3. **Write down the different words your group uses to describe the objects in your collection.**

Two Minutes—Two People

Our collection was:

Two ways we used our collection were:

Skills and concepts we explored while playing included:

W
O
R
K
S
H
O
P

1 0

Literacy Across the Curriculum

- **Help children become experts.**

- **Think about essential learning.**

- **Use literacy experiences to help children make meaningful connections.**

  - Start with a book and extend it to other subjects.

  - Start with a subject-related content or concept and connect it to literacy.

  - Start with a theme and make literacy connections and subject area connections.

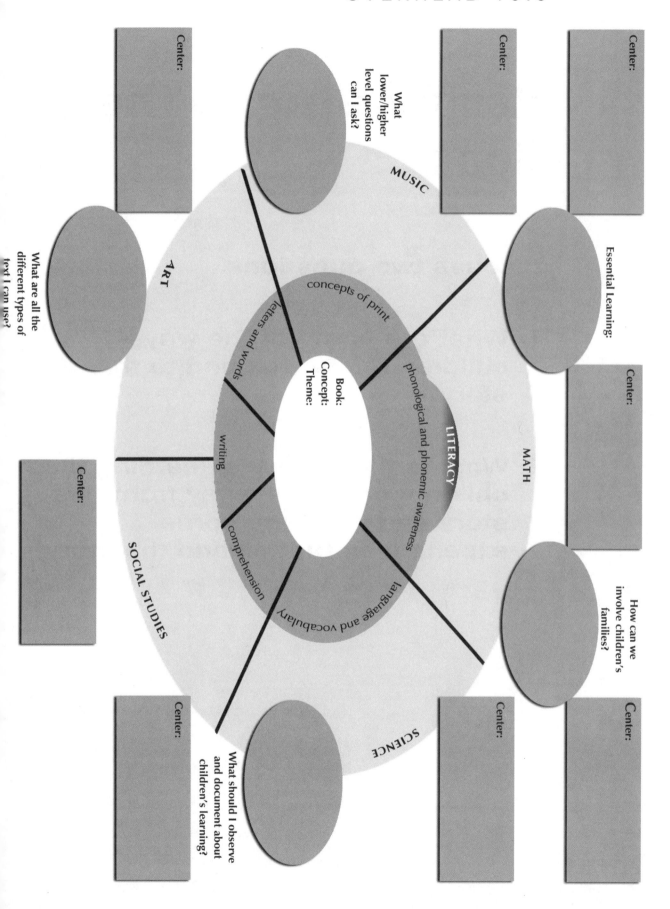

Center:

Center:

Center:

What lower/higher level questions can I ask?

MUSIC

ART

What are all the different types of text I can use?

concepts of print

letters and words

Book:
Concept:
Theme:

LITERACY

phonological and phonemic awareness

writing

comprehension

language and vocabulary

SOCIAL STUDIES

MATH

SCIENCE

Essential Learning:

Center:

How can we involve children's families?

Center:

Center:

Center:

Center:

What should I observe and document about children's learning?

Center:

W
O
R
K
S
H
O
P

10

Responding to the Book

Discuss two questions.

1. What are some of the ways children might respond to this story?

2. What is the essential learning that children can take away from this story and what are some experiences that extend the story?

Activity: Content/Concept Planning

- Look at your subject-specific content assignment.
- Brainstorm ways you might help children make connections to this content.
- Review the books related to the concept.
- What is the essential learning you want children to acquire related to the content?
- Which books can be most helpful?
- What other literacy connections can you make?
    - What vocabulary opportunities are there?
    - What open-ended questions can you ask?
    - What writing experiences could connect?
    - Do you have ideas for centers?
    - How will you observe and document children's learning?

Everyone in the group should keep track of ideas generated.
- Prepare to share the following:
    - your concept
    - ideas for essential learning
    - 1–2 books you selected
    - a center connection

The Essential
Literacy
WORKSHOP
BOOK

W
O
R
K
S
H
O
P

10

Theme Brainstorming

- **Brainstorm ideas for your section of the web.**

- **You will have a few minutes at each chart.**

- **When the timer rings, rotate clockwise to the next chart.**

- **When you come to a new chart, review it and:**
  - Put a checkmark (√) if you agree with the idea
  - Put a question mark (?) if you disagree or have a question
  - Add new ideas

- **When you return to your original chart:**
  - Note how it has changed
  - Prepare to address question marks

AGENDA

Literacy Across the Curriculum

Date: _____

Trainer: _____

Contact Information:

OBJECTIVES

In this workshop, participants will:
- learn ideas for teaching literacy while simultaneously addressing content across many subject areas;
- use a planning web to support teaching literacy across the curriculum; and
- develop practical lesson plans to use in their classrooms.

1. Opening Activity: Collections [15– 20 minutes]

2. Welcome and Logistics [3–5 minutes]

3. Introducing the Topic: Literacy Across the Curriculum [15–20 minutes]

4. Activity: Using Books [45 minutes]

5. Discussion [5 minutes]

6. Activity: Content or Concepts [30–35 minutes]

7. Discussion [5 minutes]

8. Activity: Using a Theme Approach [25–30 minutes]

9. Discussion [5–7 minutes]

10. Closure [5 minutes]

The Essential Literacy WORKSHOP BOOK

Literacy Across the Curriculum

■ Help children become experts. Young children thrive on becoming experts.

■ Think about essential learning. Be clear about your purpose.

■ Use literacy experiences to help children make meaningful connections. Learning is about making connections. There are many ways to foster literacy learning and at the same time help children make connections across the curriculum. You might:

> ■ start with a **book** and extend it to other subjects,

> ■ start with **subject-related content or concept** and connect it to literacy, or

> ■ select a **theme** and look for meaningful literacy connections as well as other connections across different subject areas.

The Essential
Literacy
WORKSHOP
BOOK

Planning Web

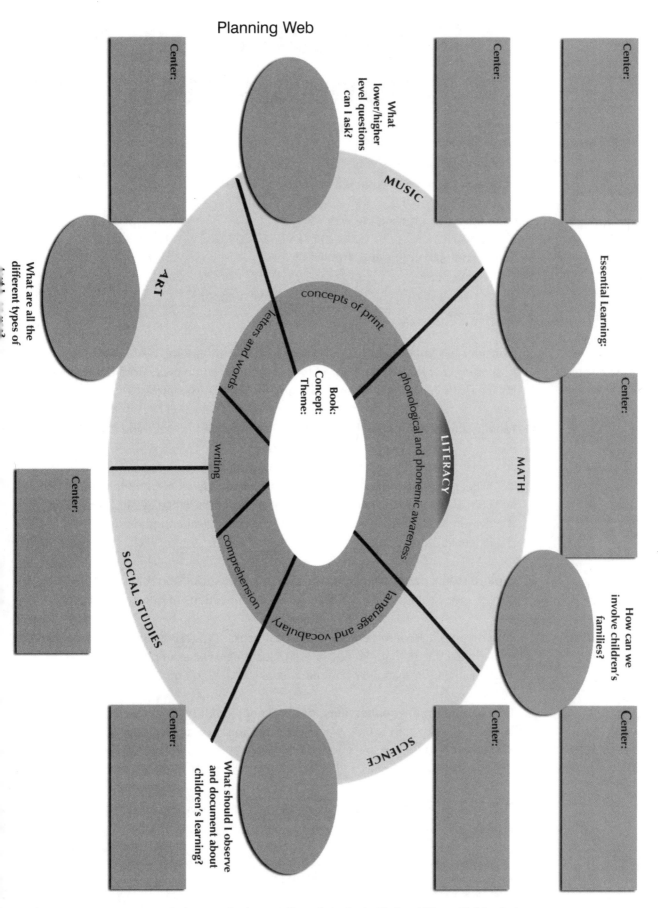

Steps for Using a Planning Web

Think of a planning web as your "teaching conscience." It triggers your thinking and helps you keep several things in mind simultaneously.

Here are the steps for using the web:

1. **Select your starting point.** It might be:
   - a good book,
   - a specific skill or concept within a subject area, or
   - a theme.

2. **Consider essential learning.** Ask yourself: "Why am I doing this? What is my purpose? What do I want children to learn so they come away from this experience having made meaningful connections and feeling competent?"

3. **Identify literacy opportunities.** Think about the different ways you can address literacy learning. Things to consider include:
   - What are the different types of text you can use?
   - What questions will you ask to extend children's language and thinking?
   - How will you help children learn concepts of print, language and vocabulary, comprehension (listening and reading), phonological and phonemic awareness, letters and words, and writing?

4. **Explore subject area connections** (math, science, social studies, art, music). If you started with a subject area concept, look for connections to other subjects.

5. **Enrich your classroom centers or interest areas.** What props or experiences can you add to centers that extend children's learning? (For example, blocks, manipulatives, dramatic play, listening, cooking, and so on.)

6. **Think about family connections.** Always keep in mind ways to include families. For example, invite a family member to read the story to a small group. If you started with a book, you might get a copy of the book in a second language spoken by children in your classroom and invite a parent to read it to the class.

7. **Plan for assessment.** Think about what you want to observe and document about children's learning and how you will do it.

The Essential
Literacy
WORKSHOP
BOOK

Extending Read-Alouds to Centers

Children enjoy hearing stories again and again. They feel proud as they begin to "own" the text in a favorite story. Ways they show ownership are by retelling the story, "pretend" reading the story, predicting accurately what will come next in the story, and describing the characters and setting in detail.

A beginning list of ways to extend read-alouds to literacy-focused centers includes:
- listening to the story on tape in the listening center;
- using flannel pieces and a flannel board to retell the story;
- drawing and writing about a favorite part of the story;
- using puppets to dramatize part of the story;
- using magnetic letters to recreate the interesting vocabulary words in the story;
- sequencing activities related to beginning, middle, and end; and
- rereading the book with a partner.

Read-alouds can extend to learning centers. For example:
- making a mural of the characters and setting of the book in the art center;
- making puppets in the art center;
- creating the story setting in dramatic play and dramatizing parts of the story;
- creating the story setting in the block area;
- exploring a concept from a book in the math or science center;
- making a recipe from a book in the cooking center;
- going outdoors for a walk to do or see something similar to what happened in the story; and
- making patterns in the math center based on the patterns in the book.

HANDOUT 10.6

Thinking About Content and Concepts

This chart is designed to help you think about subject area content, skills, and concepts. It should be modified to address your local curriculum standards.

Subject Area	Key Concepts and Skills (not a comprehensive list)
Literacy	Reading 　　Concepts of print 　　Phonological and phonemic awareness 　　Comprehension 　　Letters and words Speaking and Listening 　　Language development and vocabulary Writing
Science	Inquiry skills 　　Asking questions 　　Collecting and using data 　　Communicating information and ideas 　　Observing and gathering information Life Science 　　Physical characteristics 　　Basic needs 　　Growth, change, and life cycles 　　Habitats Physical Science 　　What things are made of 　　What happens to objects in different situations Earth and Space 　　Land and sky 　　Characteristics and patterns of change Science and Technology 　　How tools and inventions are used

Subject Area	Key Concepts and Skills (not a comprehensive list)

Math	Numbers, quantities, and counting
	Patterns
	Geometry
	    Shapes
	    Position
	Measurement
	    Ordering, comparing, and describing
	    Using non-standard and standard tools
	Collecting and organizing data with graphs
	Problem solving
	Communicating

Social Studies	Political science
	    Rules and routines
	    Interactions with others
	    Conflict resolution
	Culture
	    Similarities and differences
	    Families and how they live
	    Traditions
	Geography
	Economics
	    Work
	History

Art	Uses a variety of media for expression and representation Responds to creations and events
Music	Participation and expression Expresses appreciation for musical experiences

HANDOUT 10.7

Content and Concept Books

Math

Attributes and Patterns

The Button Box by Margarette S. Reid
Hannah's Collections by Marthe Jocelyn
Patterns by Ivan Bulloch
A String of Beads by Margarette S. Reid

Measurement

10 Minutes till Bedtime by Peggy Rathmann
All Shapes and Sizes by Shirley Hughes
The Biggest Boy by Kevin Henkes
Biggest, Strongest, Fastest by Steve Jenkins
Fire Engine Shapes by Bruce McMillan
Inch by Inch by Leo Lionni
Just a Little Bit by Ann Tompert
The Long and Short of It by Cheryl Nathan
The Shape of Things by Dayle Ann Dodds
Shapes, Shapes, Shapes by Tana Hoban
The Three Bears by Byron Barton
Twelve Snails to One Lizard: A Tale of Mischief and Measurement by Susan Hightower
What Shape? by Debbie MacKinnon
Who Sank the Boat? by Pamela Allen

Numbers and Counting

Anno's Counting Book by Mitsumasa Anno
Fish Eyes: A Book You Can Count On by Lois Ehlert
How Many, How Many, How Many by Rick Walton
Moja Means One: A Swahili Counting Book by Muriel L. Feelings
Off and Counting by Sally Noll
One Duck, Another Duck by Charlotte Pomerantz
One Hungry Monster: A Counting Book in Rhyme by Susan Heyboer O'Keefe
Some, More, Most by Judy Freudberg
Ten, Nine, Eight by Molly Bang
Trucks You Can Count On by Doug Magee
Up to Ten and Down Again by Lisa Campbell Ernst
Who's Counting? by Nancy Tafuri

The Essential
Literacy
WORKSHOP
BOOK

Position
Elephants Aloft by Kathi Appelt
Hurry Home, Spider by David Crossley
Inside Mouse, Outside Mouse by Lindsay Barrett George
Rosie's Walk by Pat Hutchins

Problem Solving
Albert's Alphabet by Leslie Tryon
Joseph Had a Little Overcoat by Simms Taback
Little Quack by Lauren Thompson
Lottie's New Beach Towel by Petra Mathers
Pepito the Brave by Scott Beck

Science

Colors
Brown Bear, Brown Bear, What Do You See? by Bill Martin, Jr.
Flower Garden by Eve Bunting
I Need a Lunch Box by Jeanette Caines
If You Want to Find Golden by Eileen Spinelli
Is It Red? Is It Yellow? Is It Blue?: An Adventure in Color by Tana Hoban
Mouse Paint by Ellen Stoll Walsh
Samuel Todd's Book of Great Colors by E. L. Konigsburg
The Very Hungry Caterpillar by Eric Carle
Who Said Red? by Mary Serfozo

Day and Night
How Many Stars in the Sky? Lenny Hort
The Napping House by Audrey Wood
Twilight Comes Twice by Ralph Fletcher
What the Sun Sees, What the Moon Sees by Nancy Tafuri
Why Is It Dark? by Chris Arvertis

Observing, Describing, and Using Senses
Bear's Busy Family by Stella Blackstone
Busy Bunnies' Five Senses by Teddy Slater
Forest Friends' Five Senses by Cristina Garelli
I Saw the Sea and the Sea Saw Me by Megan Montague Cash
It Looked Like Spilt Milk by Charles G. Shaw
Jonathan and His Mommy by Irene Smalls
Max Found Two Sticks by Brian Pinkney
My Five Senses by Aliki
Seven Blind Mice by Ed Young

The Essential Literacy WORKSHOP BOOK

HANDOUT 10.7
(continued)

Touch Will Tell by Marcia Brown
Walk with Your Eyes by Marcia Brown
Where Are You Going, Manyoni? by Catherine Stock

Opposites
Bathwater's Hot by Shirley Hughes
Dog In, Cat Out by Gillian Rubenstein
Dry or Wet? by Bruce McMillan
Earth, Sky, Wet, Dry: A Book of Nature Opposites by Durga Bernhard
Exactly the Opposite by Tana Hoban
A High, Low, Near, Far, Loud, Quiet Story by Nina Crews
Is It Dark? Is It Light? by Mary D. Lankford
Up the Steps, Down the Slide by Jonathan Allen
What Is Up When You Are Down? by David F. Marx

Things Change
Caps, Hats, Socks, and Mittens: A Book About the Four Seasons by Louise W. Borden
Change: Getting to Know About Ebb and Flow by Laura Greene
Pumpkin, Pumpkin by Jeanne Titherington
You'll Soon Grow into Them, Titch by Pat Hutchins

Social Studies

Community Living
Abuela by Arthur Dorros
Bunny Money by Rosemary Wells
Families by Ann Morris
I See a Sign by Lars Klove
Mei-Mei Loves the Morning by Margaret Tsubakiyama
My Steps by Sally Derby
Officer Buckle and Gloria by Peggy Rathmann
Red Light Stop, Green Light Go by Andrew Kulman

Feelings
Down the Road by Alice Schertle
Elizabeti's Doll by Stephanie Stuve-Bodeen
On Mother's Lap Ann Herbert Scott
Pablo's Tree by Pat Mora
Sheila Rae, the Brave by Kevin Henkes
Sometimes I'm Bombaloo by Rachel Vail

Friendship and Conflict Resolution

Best Friends by Miriam Cohen
Four Hens and a Rooster by Lena Landstrom
Jamaica and Brianna by Juanita Havill
Leonardo, the Terrible Monster by Mo Willems
The Little Red Hen: An Old Story by Margot Zemach
The Rainbow Fish by Marcus Pfister
That's What Friends Are For by Valeri Gorbachev
This Is Our House by Michael Rosen
Where Are You Going? To See My Friend! by Eric Carle and Kazuo Iwamura

Similarities and Differences

A Country Far Away by Nigel Gray
All Families Are Special by Norma Simon
Bein' with You This Way by W. Nikola-Lisa
Big Dog…Little Dog by P. D. Eastman
Cleversticks by Bernard Ashley
Crow Boy by Taro Yashima
Leo the Late Bloomer by Robert Kraus
Some Things Are Different, Some Things Are the Same by Marya Dantzer-Rosenthal
Two Little Trains by Margaret Wise Brown
What Daddies Do Best by Laura Joffe Numeroff
What Mommies Do Best by Laura Joffe Numeroff
Wilfrid Gordon McDonald Partridge by Mem Fox

Appendix A

Recommended Children's Literature to Support Literacy

Title	Author	Category
In the Small, Small Pond	Denise Fleming	Alliteration
In the Tall, Tall Grass	Denise Fleming	Alliteration
Miss Mary Mack	Mary Ann Hoberman	Alliteration
Mouse Mess	Linnea Riley	Alliteration
My First Nursery Rhymes	Bruce Whatley (illustrator)	Alliteration
My Very First Mother Goose	Iona Opie (editor)	Alliteration
Sam Sheep Can't Sleep	Phil Cox	Alliteration
Silly Sally	Audrey Wood	Alliteration
Alligators Al	Maurice Sendak	Alphabet
Alphabears: An ABC Book	Kathleen Hague	Alphabet
Alphabet Mystery	Audrey Wood	Alphabet
Alphabet Salad	Sarah L. Schuette	Alphabet
Alphabet Under Construction	Denise Fleming	Alphabet
Chicka Chicka Boom Boom	Bill Martin, John Archambault	Alphabet
Click, Clack, Quackity-Quack	Doreen Cronin	Alphabet
Eating the Alphabet	Lois Ehlert	Alphabet
Firefighters A to Z	Chris L. Demarest	Alphabet
I Stink!	Kate McMullan	Alphabet
Miss Bindergarten Gets Ready for Kindergarten	Joseph Slate	Alphabet
Now I Eat My ABC's	Pam Abrams	Alphabet
Pignic: An Alphabet Book in Rhyme	Anne Miranda	Alphabet
26 Letters and 99 Cents	Tana Hoban	Alphabet/Numbers
Apples and Pumpkins	Anne Rockwell	Alphabet/Numbers
Bread, Bread, Bread or any book by author	Ann Morris	Concepts
Exactly the Opposite	Tana Hoban	Concepts
Fish Eyes: A Book You Can Count On	Lois Ehlert	Concepts
Flower Garden	Eve Bunting	Concepts
Gilberto and the Wind	Marie Hall Ets	Concepts
I Know an Old Lady Who Swallowed a Fly	Simms Taback	Concepts

Title	Author	Category
Inch by Inch	Leo Lionni	Concepts
Leonardo, the Terrible Monster	Mo Willems	Concepts
Lunchtime for a Purple Snake	Harriet Ziefert	Concepts
M & M's Counting Book	Barbara Barbieri McGrath	Concepts
Mary Smith	Andrea U'Ren	Concepts
Mister Seahorse	Eric Carle	Concepts
My Five Senses	Aliki	Concepts or narrative
On Mother's Lap	Ann Herbert Scott	Concepts
Outside Inside	Kathleen Fain	Concepts
Pumpkin, Pumpkin	Jeanne Titherington	Concepts
Red Leaf, Yellow Leaf	Lois Ehlert	Concepts
Rosie's Walk	Pat Hutchins	Concepts
Sheila Rae, the Brave	Kevin Henkes	Concepts
Shhhhh! Everybody's Sleeping	Julie Markes	Concepts
Sometimes I'm Bombaloo	Rachel Vail	Concepts
That's What Friends Are For	Valeri Gorbachev	Concepts
You'll Soon Grow into Them, Titch	Pat Hutchins	Concepts
Ask Mr. Bear	Marjorie Flack	Cumulative pattern
Drat That Fat Cat!	Pat Thomson	Cumulative pattern
Go Away, Big Green Monster!	Ed Emberley	Cumulative pattern
Good Night, Gorilla	Peggy Rathmann	Cumulative pattern
It Could Always Be Worse	Margot Zemach	Cumulative pattern
Mother, Mother I Feel Sick Send for the Doctor Quick, Quick, Quick	Remy Charlip	Cumulative pattern
The Napping House	Audrey Wood	Cumulative pattern
The Rose in My Garden	Arnold Lobel	Cumulative pattern
The Very Quiet Cricket	Eric Carle	Cumulative pattern
This Is the House That Jack Built	Simms Taback	Cumulative pattern
Too Much Noise	Ann McGovern	Cumulative pattern
Are You My Mother?	P. D. Eastman	Cumulative pattern
Blueberries for Sal	Robert McCloskey	Easy to read
City Signs	Zoran Milich	Easy to read

Title	Author	Category
Don't Let the Pigeon Drive the Bus!	Mo Willems	Easy to read
Four Friends Together	Sue Heap	Easy to read
Goodnight Moon or any book by author	Margaret Wise Brown	Easy to read
It's Not Easy Being Big!	Stephanie St. Pierre	Easy to read
Little Quack	Lauren Thompson	Easy to read
More More More Said the Baby	Vera B. Williams	Easy to read
Mrs. Mooley	Jack Kent	Easy to read
The Very Hungry Caterpillar	Eric Carle	Easy to read
Pancakes, Pancakes!	Eric Carle	Easy to read
Pepito the Brave	Scott Beck	Easy to read
Ten, Nine, Eight	Molly Bang	Easy to read
The Pigeon Finds a Hot Dog!	Mo Willems	Easy to read
Truck Duck	Michael Rex	Easy to read
Yo! Yes?	Chris Raschka	Easy to read
A Chair for My Mother	Vera B. Williams	Narrative
Anansi and the Moss-Covered Rock	Eric A. Kimmel	Narrative
A Pocket Full of Kisses	Audrey Penn	Narrative
A-Tisket, A-Tasket	Ella Fitzgerald	Narrative
Bear Snores On	Karma Wilson	Narrative
Bear Wants More	Karma Wilson	Narrative
Black All Around!	Patricia Hubbell	Narrative
Click, Clack, Moo	Doreen Cronin	Narrative
Diary of a Worm	Doreen Cronin	Narrative
Go Away, Big Green Monster!	Ed Emberly	Narrative
Goldilocks and the Three Bears	James Marshall	Narrative
Hannah's Collections	Marthe Jocelyn	Narrative
Just Enough and Not Too Much	Kaethe Zemach	Narrative
Mary Smith	Andrea U'ren	Narrative
Moo Who?	Margie Palatini	Narrative
Mrs. Chicken and the Hungry Crocodile	Won-Ldy Paye, Margaret H. Lippert	Narrative
Mouse Paint	Ellen Stoll Walsh	Narrative
The Button Box	Margarette Reid	Narrative
The Carrot Seed	Ruth Krauss	Narrative
The Dog Who Cried Wolf	Keiko Kasza	Narrative
The Giant Hug	Sandra Horning	Narrative
The Grouchy Ladybug or any book by author	Eric Carle	Narrative
The Relatives Came	Cynthia Rylant	Narrative
The Three Billy Goats Gruff	Paul Galdone	Narrative
Little Blue and Little Yellow	Leo Lionni	Narrative
Stand Tall, Molly Lou Melon	Patty Lovell	Narrative
Stone Soup	Marcia Brown	Narrative
The Dot	Peter H. Reynolds	Narrative
The True Story of the Three Little Pigs	Jon Scieszka	Narrative
The Three Bears	Paul Galdone	Narrative

Title	Author	Category
Tops and Bottoms	Janet Stevens	Narrative
Whistle for Willie or any book by author	Ezra Jack Keats	Narrative
A, My Name Is Alice	Jane Bayer	Phonological
Art	Patrick McDonnell	Phonological
Big Pig on a Dig	Phil Cox	Phonological
Car Wash	Susan Steen, Sandra Steen	Phonological
Click, Clack, Moo	Doreen Cronin	Phonological
Roller Coaster	Marla Frazee	Phonological
The Flea's Sneeze	Lynn Downey	Phonological
The Magic Hat	Mem Fox	Phonological
The Stars Will Still Shine	Cynthia Rylant	Phonological
Toad Makes a Road	Phil Cox	Phonological
To Market, To Market	Anne Miranda	Phonological
Duck in the Truck	Jez Alborough	Phonological
Good-Night, Owl!	Pat Hutchins	Predictable
If You Give a Mouse a Cookie	Laura Joffe Numeroff	Predictable
Mother, Mother, I Want Another	Maria Polushkin Robbins	Predictable
Mrs. Wishy-Washy	Joy Cowley	Predictable
The Story of Little Babaji	Helen Bannerman	Predictable
The Wheels on the Bus	Maryann Kovalski	Predictable
The Gingerbread Boy	Paul Galdone	Predictable
Brown Bear, Brown Bear, What Do You See?	Bill Martin	Predictable
Caps for Sale	Esphyr Slobodkina	Repetition
Happy Birthday Moon	Frank Asch	Repetition
Joseph Had a Little Overcoat	Simms Taback	Repetition
Little Quack	Lauren Thompson	Repetition
Millions of Cats	Wanda Gag	Repetition
Miss Spider's Tea Party	Dave Kirk	Repetition
Over in the Meadow	John Langstaff	Repetition
The Doorbell Rang	Pat Hutchins	Repetition
The Mitten	an Brett	Repetition
The Three Little Pigs	Paul Galdone	Repetition
Tikki Tikki Tembo	Arlene Mosel	Repetition
We're Going on a Bear Hunt	Michael Rosen	Repetition
Who Took the Cookies from the Cookie Jar?	Bonnie Lass, Philemon Sturges	Repetition
A House Is a House for Me	Maryann Hoberman	Repetition
And Here's to You	David Elliott	Rhyme
A Pig Is Big	Douglas Florian	Rhyme
Barnyard Banter	Denise Fleming	Rhyme
Boom Chicka Rock	John Archambault	Rhyme
Cha-Cha Chimps	Julia Durango	Rhyme
Down By the Bay	Raffi	Rhyme

Title	Author	Category
Hey, Little Ant	Phillip Hoose, Hanna Hoose	Rhyme
Honey, I Love	Eloise Greenfield	Rhyme
I Ain't Gonna Paint No More!	Karen Beaumont	Rhyme
Is Your Mama a Llama?	Deborah Guarino	Rhyme
Itsy Bitsy Spider	Iza Trapani	Rhyme
Miss Polly Has a Dolly	Pamela Duncan Edwards	Rhyme
Mooses Come Walking	Arlo Guthrie	Rhyme
My Truck Is Stuck!	Kevin Lewis	Rhyme
Sheep in a Jeep	Nancy Shaw	Rhyme
The Cat in the Hat or any book by author	Dr. Seuss	Rhyme
The Day the Babies Crawled Away	Peggy Rathman	Rhyme
The Wind Blew	Pat Hutchins	Rhyme
Tortillitas Para Mama and Other Nursery Rhymes	Margot C. Griego	Rhyme
Wild About Books	Judy Sierra	Rhyme
An Egg Is Quiet	Diana Ashton	Vocabulary
Chicks and Salsa	Aaron Reynolds	Vocabulary
Dance	Bill T. Jones, Susan Kulkin	Vocabulary
Epossumondas	Colleen Salley	Vocabulary
Fancy Nancy	Jane O'Connor	Vocabulary
G Is for Goat	Patricia Polacco	Vocabulary
Giraffes Can't Dance	Giles Andreae, Guy Parker-Reese	Vocabulary
It Looked Like Spilt Milk	Charles G. Shaw	Vocabulary
Owen and Mzee: The True Story of a Remarkable Friendship	Isabella Hatkoff, Craig Hatkoff, Paula Kahumbu	Vocabulary
Paper Parade	Sarah Weeks	Vocabulary
Song of the Flowers	Takayo Noda	Vocabulary
Tar Beach	Faith Ringgold	Vocabulary
The Other Side	Jacqueline Woodson	Vocabulary
The Way I Feel	Janan Cain	Vocabulary
You and Me	Martine Kindermans	Vocabulary

The following extensive bibliography lists children's books about people who are culturally, linguistically, and/or ability diverse:
http://www.fpg.unc.edu/~pfi/pdfs/diversity_booklist.pdf

Recommended Children's Literature Books in Spanish

Title	Author
Buenas noches, luna (Good Night Moon)	Margaret Wise Brown
El conejito andarín (The Runaway Bunny)	Margaret Wise Brown
El gran granero rojo (The Big Red Barn)	Margaret Wise Brown
La oruga muy hambrienta (The Very Hungry Caterpillar)	Eric Carle
De la cabeza a los pies (From Head to Toe)	Eric Carle
Tren de carga (Freight Train)	Donald Crews
Perro Grande... Perro Pequeno (Big Dog... Little Dog)	P.D. Eastman
El canto de las palomas (Calling the Doves)	Juan Filipe Herrera
¿Me quieres, mamá? (Mama, Do You Love Me?)	Barbara M. Joosse
Un almuerzo con ponche (A Lunch with Punch)	Jo S. Kittinger
Oso pardo, oso pardo, ¿qué ves ahí? (Brown Bear, Brown Bear, What Do You See?)	Bill Martin Jr.
Oso polar, oso polar, ¿qué es ese ruido? (Polar Bear, Polar Bear, What Do You Hear?)	Bill Martin Jr.
Kathy lo hizo (Katie Did It)	Becky Bring McDaniel
Bessey la desordenada pasa una noche de cumpleanos (Messy Bessey and the Birthday Overnight)	Patricia McKissack, Fredrick McKissack
¡Detenlo a ese gato! (Stop That Cat!)	Cari Meister
Osos, osos por todas partes (Bears, Bears, Everywhere)	Rita Milios
Muchas veces yo (So Many Me's)	Barbara J. Neasi
Si llevas un ratón a la escuela (If You Take a Mouse to School)	Laura Numeroff
De colores and Other Latin-American Folk Songs for Children	José-Luis Orozco
Diez deditos/Ten Little Fingers and Other Play Rhymes	José-Luis Orozco
¡Oh, cuan lejos llegaras! (Oh, the Places You'll Go!)	Dr. Seuss
¡Como el grinch robo la Navidad! (How the Grinch Stole Christmas)	Dr. Seuss
Los 500 sombreros de Bartolome Cubbins (The 500 Hats of Bartholomew Cubbins)	Dr. Seuss
¡Horton Escucha a Quien! (Horton Hears a Who)	Dr. Seuss
El Lorax (The Lorax)	Dr. Seuss
El gato en el sombrero (The Cat in the Hat)	Dr. Seuss
Huevos verdes con jamón (Green Eggs and Ham)	Dr. Seuss
Un pez, dos peces, pez rojo, pez azul (One Fish, Two Fish, Red Fish, Blue Fish)	Dr. Suess
Un beso en mi mano (The Kissing Hand)	Audrey Penn
El cuento de Pedrito Conejo (The Story of Peter Rabbit)	Beatrix Potter
Margarita y Margaret (Margaret and Margarita)	Lynn Reiser

Title	Author
Tortillas and Lullabies/Tortillas y cancioncitas	Lynn Reiser
Doctor de Soto (Edicion En Espanol)	William Steig
Senor Felipe's Alphabet Adventure: El alfabeto espanol	Sharon Hawkins Vargo
Alexander y el dia terrible, horrible, espantoso,	Judith Viorst
horroroso (Alexander and the terrible....)	

Appendix B

Resources for Literacy and Language Development

Adams, M.J., Foorman, B.R., Lundberg, I., & Beeler, T. 1997. *Phonemic awareness in young children: A classroom curriculum.* Baltimore, MD: Paul H. Brookes Publishing.

Alvarado, C. 1996. Working with children whose home language is other than English: The teacher's role. *Childcare Information Exchange, 107,* 48-50.

Armbruster, B. B. & Osborn, J. H. 2001. *Reading instruction and assessment: Understand the IRA standards.* Boston: Allyn and Bacon.

Armington, D. 1997. *The living classroom: Writing, reading, and beyond.* Washington, DC: National Association for the Education of Young Children.

Bagley, M. T., & Foley, J. P. 1996. *Suppose the wolf were an octopus: K to 2.* Unionville, NY: Royal Fireworks Press.

Beaty, J. 1996. *Building bridges with multicultural picture books: For children 3-5.* Upper Saddle River, NJ: Prentice Hall.

Beavers, L., & D'Amico, J. 2005. *Children in immigrant families: U.S. and state-level findings from the 2000 Census. A KIDS COUNT/PRB Report on Census 2000.* Baltimore: The Annie E. Casey Foundation; Washington, DC: Population Reference Bureau.

Berk, L. E., & Winsler, A. 1995. *Scaffolding children's learning: Vygotsky and early childhood education.* Washington, DC: National Association for the Education of Young Children.

Blevins, W. 2004. *Phonemic awareness songs & rhymes.* New York: Scholastic.

Bowman, B. (Ed.). 2002. *Love to read: Essays in developing and enhancing early literacy skills of African American children.* Washington, DC: National Black Child Development Institute, Inc.

Bowman, B., Donovan, M. S., & Burns, M. S. 2000. *Eager to learn: Educating our preschoolers, executive summary.* Washington, DC: National Academy Press.

Bredekamp, S., & Copple, C. (Eds.). 1997. *Developmentally appropriate practice in early childhood programs (Rev. ed.).* Washington, DC: National Association for the Education of Young Children.

Burns, M. S., Griffin, P., & Snow, C. E. (Eds.). 1999. *Starting out right: A guide to promoting children's reading success.* Washington, DC: National Academy Press.

Campbell, R. (Ed.). 1998. *Facilitating preschool literacy.* Newark, DE: International Reading Association.

Clay, M. 2001. *Change over time in children's literacy development.* Portsmouth, NH: Heinemann.

Clay, M. 2000. *Concepts about print: What have children learned about the way we print language?* Portsmouth, NH: Heinemann.

Clyde, J. A., & Condon, M. W. F. 2005. Celebrating young learners at work: Valuing reading-like behavior. *Beyond the Journal, Young Children* 60 (2).

Copple, C. (Ed.). 2003. *A world of difference: Readings on teaching young children in a diverse society.* Washington, DC: National Association for the Education of Young Children.

Culturally and Linguistically Appropriate Services () provides additional resources on the subject of English language learners.

David, J., Onchonga, O., Drew, R., & Grass, R. 2005. Head Start embraces language diversity. *Young Children,* 60 (6), 40-43.

Delacre, L. 1992. *Arroz con leche: Popular songs and rhymes from Latin America.* New York: Scholastic.

Derman-Sparks, L., & Phillips, C. B. 1997. *Teaching/learning anti-racism: A developmental approach.* New York: Teachers College Press.

DeVries-Post, A., Scott, M., & Theberge, M. 2000. *Celebrating children's choices. 25 years of children's favorite books.* Newark, DE: International Reading Association.

Dragan, P. B. 2005. *A how-to guide for teaching English language learners in the classroom.* Portsmouth, NH: Heinemann.

Edwards, L.C., Bayless, K.M., & Ramsey, M.E. 2005. *Music: A way of life for the young child, fifth edition.* Upper Saddle River, NJ: Prentice Hall.

Elicker, J., & Mathur, S. 1997. What do they do all day? Comprehensive evaluation of a full-day kindergarten. *Early Childhood Research Quarterly,* 12 (4), 459-480.

Ericson, L., & Juliebo, M. F. 1998. *The phonological awareness handbook for kindergarten and primary teachers.* Newark, DE: International Reading Association.

Espinosa, L.M. & Burns, M.S. 2003. Early literacy for young children and English-language learners. In C. Howes (Ed.).*Teaching 4- to 8-year-olds: Literacy, Math, multiculturalism, and classroom community.* (pp. 47-69). Baltimore, MD: Paul H. Brookes Publishing.

Fox, M. 2001. *Reading magic: Why reading aloud to our children will change their lives forever.* Boston: Harcourt.

Garcia, E.E. 1993. The education of linguistically and culturally diverse children. In B. Spodek (Ed.). *Handbook of research on the education of young children.* (pp.372-384). New York: Macmillan/McGraw-Hill.

Gardner, H. 1983. *Frames of mind: The theory of multiple intelligences, second edition.* New York: Basic Books.

Genishi, C. 2002. Research in review. Young English language learners: Resourceful in the classroom. *Young Children* (57) 4, 66-70.

Glickman, C.D., Gordon, S.P., & Ross-Gordon, J.M. 1998. *Supervision of instruction: A developmental approach* (4th ed.). Needham, MA: Allyn and Bacon.

Goldstein, L.S. 1997. Between a rock and a hard place in the primary grades: The challenge of providing developmentally appropriate early childhood education in an elementary school setting. *Early Childhood Research Quarterly,* 12 (1), 3-27.

Gould, P., & Sullivan, J. 1999. *The inclusive early childhood curriculum: Easy ways to adapt learning centers for all children.* Beltsville, MD: Gryphon House.

Graves, D. 2003. *Writing: Teachers and children at work.* Portsmouth, NH: **Heinemann.**

Hakuta, K., & August, D. (Eds.). 1998. *Educating language-minority children.* Washington, DC: National Academy Press.

Hargrave, A.C., & Sénéchal, M. 2000. A book reading intervention with preschool children who have limited vocabularies: the benefits of regular reading and dialogic reading. *Early Childhood Research Quarterly,* 15 (1), 75-90.

Harding, N. 1996. Family Journals: The Bridge from School to Home and Back Again. *Young Children,* 51 (2), 27-30.

Hart, B. & Risley, T.R. 1999. *The social world of children learning to talk.* Baltimore, MD: Paul H. Brookes Publishing.

Heroman, C., & Jones, C. 2004. *Literacy: The creative curriculum approach*. Washington, DC: Teaching Strategies.

Hill-Clark, K., & Robinson, N. 2004. It's as easy as A-B-C and Do-Re-Mi: Music, rhythm, and rhyme enhance children's literacy skills. *Young Children,* 59 (5), 91-95.

Hohmann, M. 2002. *Fee, fie, phonemic awareness: 130 prereading activities for preschoolers*. Ypsilanti, MI: High/Scope Press.

Hong Xu, S., & Rutledge, A. L. 2003. Chicken starts with ch! Kindergartners learn through environmental print. *Young Children,* 58 (2), 44-51.

Howes, C. 2003. *Teaching 4- to 8-year olds: Literacy, math, multiculturalism, and classroom community*. Baltimore, MD: Paul H. Brookes Publishing.

Hull, K., Goldhaber, J., & Capone, A. 2002. *Opening doors: An introduction to inclusive early childhood education*. Boston, MA: Houghton Mifflin.

Jalongo, M. R. 2004. *Young children and picture books: Literature from infancy to six* (second edition). Washington, DC: National Association for the Education of Young Children.

Jalongo, M. R. 2003. *Early childhood language arts* (third edition). Boston: Pearson Educational Group, Inc.

Jalongo, M.R. 1996. Using recorded music with young children: A guide for nonmusicians. *Young Children* (51) 5, July, 1996.

Jenkins, E. 1993. *Ella Jenkins' this is rhythm*. Bethlehem, PA: Sing Out Publication.

Koralek, D. 2003. *Spotlight on young children and language*. Washington, DC: National Association for the Education of Young Children.

McCarrier, A., Pinnell, G. S., & Fountas, I. C. 2000. *Interactive writing: How language and literacy come together, K-2*. Portsmouth, NH: Heinemann.

McDonald, D.T. 2002. *Music in our lives: the early years, tenth edition*. Washington, DC: National Association for the Education of Young Children.

McGee, L. M., & Richgels, D. J. 2000. *Literacy's beginnings: Supporting young readers and writers* (third edition). Boston: Allyn and Bacon.

Morrow, L. M. 2002. *The literacy center: Contexts for reading and writing*. Portland, ME: Stenhouse Publishers.

Morrow, L. M. 2005. *Literacy development in the early years*. Boston: Allyn and Bacon.

NAEYC Position Statement: Responding to Linguistic and Cultural Diversity. 1996. Washington, DC: National Association for the Education of Young Children.

National Reading Panel. 2000. *Report of the National Reading Panel*. Washington, DC: National Institute Child Health and Development.

National Research Council, Burns, S. R., Griffin P., & Snow, C. (Eds.). 1999. *Starting out right: A guide to promoting children's reading success*. Washington, DC: National Academy Press.

Neugebauer, B. (Ed.) 1992. *Alike and different: Exploring our humanity with young children*. Washington, DC: National Association for the Education of Young Children.

Neuman, S. B., & Roskos, K. (Eds.). 1998. *Children achieving: Best practices in early literacy*. Newark, DE: International Reading Association.

Neuman, S. B., & Roskos, K. 2005. Viewpoint. Whatever happened to developmentally appropriate practice in early literacy. *Young Children,* (60) 4, 22-26.

Neuman, S. B., Copple, C., & Bredekamp, S. 2000. *Learning to read and write: Developmentally appropriate practices for young children*. Washington, DC: National Association for the Education of Young Children.

Ordonez-Jasis, R., & Ortiz, R. 2006. Reading their worlds: Working with diverse families to enhance children's early literacy development. *Young Children,* (61) 1, 42-48.

Owocki, G. 1999. *Literacy through play.* Portsmouth, NH: Heinemann.

Owocki, G. 2001. *Make way for literacy: Teaching the way young children learn.* Portsmouth, NH: Heinemann & Washington, DC: National Association for the Education of Young Children.

Owocki, G. 2005. *Time for literacy centers: How to organize and differentiate instruction.* Portsmouth, NJ: Heinemann.

Owocki, G., & Goodman, Y. 2002. *Kidwatching: Documenting children's literacy development.* Portsmouth, NH: Heinemann.

Ranweiler, L. 2004. *Preschool readers and writers: Early literacy strategies for teachers.* Ypsilanti, MI: High/Scope Press.

Rencken, E., Jones, E., & Evans, K. 2001. *The lively kindergarten: Emergent curriculum in action.* Washington, DC: National Association for the Education of Young Children.

Ringgenberg, S. 2003. Music as a teaching tool: Story songs. *Young Children* (58) 5.

Rockwell, R., Hoge, D. R., & Searcy, B. 1999. *Linking language: Simple language and literacy activities throughout the curriculum.* Beltsville, MD: Gryphon House.

Roskos, K. A., Christie, J. F., & Richgels, D. J. 2003. The essentials of early literacy instruction. *Young Children, 58* (2), 52-60.

Sandall, S., McLean, M., & Smith, B. 2000. *DEC Recommended practices in early intervention/ early childhood special education.* Arlington, VA: Council for Exceptional Children.

Schickedanz, J. A. 1999. *Much more than the ABCs: The early stages of reading and writing.* Washington DC: National Association for the Education of Young Children.

Schickedanz, J. A., & Casbergue, R. M. 2004. *Writing in preschool: Learning to orchestrate meaning and marks.* Newark, DE: International Reading Association.

Seefeldt, C., & Galper, A. 2001. *Active experiences for active children: Literacy emerges.* Upper Saddle River, NJ: Prentice-Hall.

Snow, C.E., Burns, M.S., & Griffin, P. (Eds.). 1998. *Preventing reading difficulties in young children.* Washington, DC: National Academy Press.

Soderman, A. K., Gregory, K. M., & O'Neill, L. T. 1999. *Scaffolding emergent literacy: A child-centered approach for preschool through grade 3.* Upper Saddle River, NJ: Prentice Hall.

Spodek, B. (Ed.). 1993. *Handbook of research on the education of young children.* New York: Macmillan/McGraw-Hill.

Strickland, D.S. 2006. Language and literacy in Kindergarten. In D. F. Gullo, (Ed.). *K today: Teaching and learning in the kindergarten year.* Washington, DC: National Association for the Education of Young Children.

Strickland, D. S., & Morrow, L. M. (Eds.). 2000. *Beginning reading and writing.* Newark, DE: International Reading Association.

Tabors, P. O. 1997. *One child, two languages.* Baltimore, MD: Paul H. Brookes Publishing.

Teaching Tolerance Project. 1997. *Starting small: Teaching tolerance in preschool and the early grades.* Montgomery, AL: Southern Poverty Law Center.

Wilson, C. 2000. *Telling a different story: Teaching and literacy in an urban preschool.* NY: Teachers College Press.

Yopp, H.K. & Yopp, R.H. 2003. *Oo-pples and Boo-noo-noos: Songs and activities for phonemic awareness.* New York: Harcourt.

Ziegler, E., Singer, D., & Bishop-Josef, S. 2004. *Children's play: The roots of reading.* Washington, DC: Zero to Three Press.

Appendix C

Resources for Training and Presenting Workshops

Alexander, N. P. 2000. *Early childhood workshops that work*. Beltsville, MD: Gryphon House.

Anton, T. 1997. *Wake 'em up!* Landover Hills, MD: Anchor.

Backer, L., & Deck, M. 1996. *The presenter's EZ graphics kit: A guide for the artistically challenged*. St. Louis, MO: Mosby.

Barlow, C. A., Blythe, J., & Edmonds, M. 1999. *A handbook of interactive exercises for groups*. Boston: Allyn & Bacon.

Bloom, P. J. 2000. *Workshop essentials*. Lake Forest, IL: New Horizons.

Bloom, P. J., Sheerer, M., & Britz, J. 1991. *Blueprint for action: Achieving center-based change through staff development*. Lake Forest, IL: New Horizons.

Carter, M., & Curtis, D. 1998. *The visionary director: A handbook for dreaming, organizing, and improvising in your center*. St. Paul, MN: Redleaf Press.

Carter, M., & Curtis, D. 1994. *Training teachers: A harvest of theory and practice*. St. Paul, MN: Redleaf Press.

Garmston, R. 1997. *The presenter's fieldbook: A practical guide*. Norwood, MA: Christopher-Gordon.

Jones, E. 1986. *Teaching adults. An active learning approach*. Washington, DC: National Association for the Education of Young Children.

Koehler, M. 1999. *Administrator's staff development activities kit*. The Center for Applied Research in Education. Paramus, NJ: Prentice Hall Direct.

Margolis, F. H., & Bell, C. R. 1984. *Managing the learning process*. Minneapolis: Lakewood Books.

Mill, C.R. 1980. *Activities for trainers: 50 useful designs*. San Diego: University Associates.

Newstrom, J., & Scannell, E. 1998. *The big book of presentation games*. NY: McGraw-Hill.

Scannel, E., & Newstrom, J. 1983. *More games trainers play*. NY: McGraw-Hill.

Scannell, E., & Newstrom, J. 1991. *Still more games trainers play*. NY: McGraw-Hill.

Sharp, P. 1993. *Sharing your good ideas: A workshop facilitator's handbook*. Portsmouth, NH: Heinemann.

Silberman, M. 1999. *101 ways to make trainings active*. San Francisco: Jossey-Bass/Pfeiffer.

Solem, L., & Pike, B. 1997. *Fifty creative training closures*. San Francisco: Jossey-Bass/Pfeiffer.

Weinstein, M., & Goodman, J. 1980. *Playfair*. San Luis Obispo, CA: Impact.

Williamson, B. 1993. *Playful activities for powerful presentations*. Duluth, MN: Whole Person Associates.

Selected Internet Resources for Trainers

http://www.columbia.edu/acis/bartleby/bartlett
http://www.famous-quotations.com
http://www.greenleafenterprises.com/quotes.php
http://humanresources.about.com/od/icebreakers/
http://www.inspirationpeak.com
http://www.motivateus.com
http://www.presentersresource.com
http://www.presentationresources.net
http://www.presentersuniversity.com
http://www.squarewheels.com
http://www.starlingtech.com/quotes
http://www.trainerswarehouse.com

Appendix D
Glossary of Literacy Terms

Alliteration—The repetition of the same letter or sound at the beginning of two or more words immediately following each other, or at short intervals. Examples: Fe, Fi, Fo, Fum and Miss Mary Mack.

Alphabetic principle—Knowing that words are made from letters.

Closed-ended questions—Questions that can be answered finitely by either "yes," "no," or one-word answers, or that have a right and wrong answer. These questions are restrictive and can be answered in a few words. Examples: How may/can I help you? Where have you looked already? How are you today? What color is the ball?

Complex sentences—A complex sentence contains an independent clause and a dependent clause. Examples: Mrs. Bergey, who is a teacher at Lakeview School, enjoys teaching writing. After we went to the store to buy sneakers, we stopped at the park.

Environmental print—Words found in the everyday surroundings of a child, such as food labels, road signs, store signs, and so on.

Grapheme—A letter or letters that make up an individual sound or sounds. Examples: *A*, *B*, *Th*, and *Sh*.

Guided reading—Reading instruction in small, flexible groups of students with similar instructional needs.

Higher-level question—A question that stimulates thinking and requires a more extensive or elaborate answer. Examples: What might happen if…? What do you think…? What are some ways we can…?

Interactive writing—The process in which a teacher shares a pen with a child to write down a child's spoken words, while making explicit decoding and print features and forms. In interactive writing, the teacher does not simply write the words the child or children say, she involves the children in the writing process by: stating specific conventions ("We need to leave a space between the words."); discussing letter formations ("The capital E has three lines off the big line."); stretching out the word so children can hear the sounds ("/c/ /a/ /t/"); and inviting the child to write a letter, letters, or a word that they can write ("Jordan, your name has the same /j/ sound as jump. Can you make the J for us?).

Morning message—A message written each day on a chart in the classroom about an event or an interesting question and used that day as the basis for discussion about its content as well as skills and concepts related to print and writing.

Onomatopoeia—A word whose sound suggests its sense. Examples: *buzz, hiss,* and *quack.*

Onset and rime—Onset is all the sounds of a word that come before the first vowel (examples: /str/ in the word straight, or /b/ in the word ball). The rime is the first vowel in a word and all the sounds that follow it (examples: /aight/ in straight or /all/ in ball).

314

■ ■

Open-ended questions—Questions that invite students to answer in more detail and are not restricted to one-word answers. An answer to an open-ended question gives us a window into what the child is thinking and feeling and encourages children to use language more fully. Examples: What else can you do with the playdough? What could you use to make the tower stand up? What do you think would happen if…?

Phoneme—Sounds made by individual letters and groupings of letters that make up a single sound. Examples: SH-E has two phonemes; P-I-G has three phonemes; B-A-TH has three phonemes; and WR-O-N-G has four phonemes.

Phonemic awareness—The ability to hear spoken words as a sequence of spoken sounds and the ability to identify and manipulate those sounds.

Phonics—The relationship between learning the alphabetic principles of language and the knowledge of letter-sound relationship.

Phonological awareness—The range from beginning awareness of basic speech sounds and rhythms to rhyme awareness and sound similarities and, at the highest level, to awareness of syllables or phonemes.

Print-rich environments—A setting in which different kinds of print are displayed that have meaning to the children. Signs, labeled centers, wall stories, word displays, labeled murals, bulletin boards, charts, and poems are just a few ways to display print. This does not mean putting labels on everything in sight, such as the door, the window, tables, and so on; nor does it mean making word walls that have no meaning to the children.

Reading—To speak aloud printed or written words.

Reading comprehension—To understand the meaning of written or printed characters, words, or sentences.

Rebus charts—A chart that has representations of words in the form of pictures or symbols.

Rhyme—Repetition of the ending sound in two or more words. Example: Hat-cat-sat.

Shared reading—An adult and child reading a book together using context and picture cues.

Syllable—A vowel, either by itself or with one or more consonants, that produces a single sound.

Word wall—A type of display that features interesting, challenging, related, and/or high frequency words that are usually organized alphabetically. These lists should be generated by the children and may relate to a particular topic. Example: If it starts to rain outside, the teacher may ask the children to think of all the words related to raining (*umbrella, raincoat, puddles,* and so on). This is not meant to be a drill wall, or words with no relevance to children, making it wallpapering.

Resources

Morrow, L.M. 2001. *Literacy development in the early years*. Boston: Allyn and Bacon.

Neuman, S. B., Copple, C., & Bredekamp, S. 2000. *Learning to read and write: Developmentally appropriate practices for young children*. Washington, DC: National Association for the Education of Young Children.

Ranweiler, L. 2004. *Preschool readers and writers. Early literacy strategies for teachers*. Ypsilanti, MI: High/Scope Press.

Appendix E

Glossary of Training Terms

Carousel Brainstorming

Carousel brainstorming is a variation on basic brainstorming that allows participants to move around. Use flip chart paper to create charts, each with a different question or topic written across the top. Hang the charts around the room with at least four or five feet between each chart. Have participants count off to form groups of four to seven people, depending on the number of charts and the number of people in your workshop. For example, if you have six charts, participants would count off by six. If you have 30 people in your workshop, each group will have five people.

Each group is assigned a different colored marker and begins at a different chart. Provide 3–4 minutes for each group to add ideas to their chart. Call time and have groups rotate clockwise to the next chart, holding on to their color marker. At the new chart, the group reads the previous group's ideas, indicates agreement with a check or puts a question mark if they disagree or do not understand. Then they add new ideas. The carousel process continues until all groups have added their ideas to each chart and are back to their original charts. Review the activity by addressing the question marks on each chart.

Gallery Walk

The gallery walk can be used to review an activity. After participants have completed an activity in which charts are created, ask the groups to post their charts around the room. Invite the participants to walk around and review charts to learn about what each group discussed. You can structure the gallery walk so participants work in groups of twos or threes, or alone. You might do a silent gallery walk in which all participants take their notebooks, walk around reading each chart, and jot down key insights to share with their table groups or with the group as a whole.

Name Tents

If participants do not know each other, name tents are an easy way to encourage people to learn each other's names. Give each participant an index card or a piece of construction paper. The participants fold the index cards or construction paper in half to form a tent on which they write their name on both sides. They then place this in front of them when they are seated at a table.

Parking Lot

The Parking Lot (also called a Bin or Issues or Questions) is a place to record ideas, questions, or future agenda items. This chart is especially useful in deferring a conversation to another time without losing track of the current agenda. At the same time, it ensures that the item will be addressed in the future. Participants should be encouraged to use the Parking Lot during breaks to note any questions or ideas for further discussion. This is effective for participants who are hesitant to raise questions in a public manner. It is important to address the parking lot items prior to the conclusion of the session.

Round-Robin Technique

Round robin simply means taking turns. You might use a round-robin technique so individuals or small groups each have a turn doing an activity. Or, you might use a round-robin technique to give each individual or small group a turn to share an idea.

Walk and Talk

The trainer provides a topic for a brief discussion and allocates an amount of time so participants, in groups of twos or threes, can go for a walk and discuss the topic. It gives people time to talk with someone new and to move around the room.

Appendix F

Sample Agendas with Shorter Time Frames

Each of the original workshops in this book is designed for a 3-hour format. The workshop agendas on the following pages are examples of how to use the information, agendas, and activities in the original workshops to create workshops with shorter time frames to meet your individual needs. This allows you to select the necessary depth based on need and time constraints and to combine topics based on the length of a session. In the agendas that follow, all references relate to the original workshops.

Agenda for 1½-Hour Workshop for

Workshop 1: Fostering Language Development

Date:
_____

Trainer:
_____

Contact Information:

Objectives

In this workshop, participants will:

- gain a deeper understanding of children's language development and its relationship to their thinking;
- learn more ways to encourage conversation and support children's vocabulary development;
- acquire strategies for developing children's listening and speaking skills throughout the day; and
- examine ways to promote children's language and thinking through good literature.

1. Opening Activity: Tuning into Children's Language and Thinking [20 minutes]

2. Welcome and Logistics [5 minutes]

3. Introducing the Topic: Fostering Language Development [35–40 minutes]

4. Activity: Interesting Words in Read-Aloud Books [15–20 minutes]

5. Discussion [5–10 minutes]

6. Closure [5–10 minutes]

Agenda for 1-Hour Workshop for

Workshop 2: Beyond Open and Closed Questions

Date:

Trainer:

Contact Information:

Objectives

In this workshop, participants will:

- focus on ways to extend language and encourage higher-level thinking; and
- acquire strategies for asking questions to support higher-level thinking.

1. Activity: Group Storytelling [10 minutes]

2. Presentation of Taxonomy and Activity: Six Major Cognitive Operations [45 minutes]

3. Closing book and statement with sugar packet [5 minutes]

Agenda for 1¼-Hour Workshop for

Workshop 3: Supporting English Language Learners

Date:

Trainer:

Contact Information:

Objectives

In this workshop, participants will:

■ gain a deeper understanding of the development of home language and acquisition of a second language;

■ acquire strategies for supporting home language development and English language learning; and

■ collect ideas for literacy materials, props, and ways to meet the needs of English language learners.

1. Opening Activity: Many Languages [15 minutes]

2. Welcome and Logistics [5 minutes]

3. Discussion [10 minutes]

4. Activity: Classroom Strategies [20–25 minutes]

5. Discussion [10–15 minutes]

6. Closure [10 minutes]

■ ■

Agenda for 1½-Hour Workshop for

Workshop 4: Phonological and Phonemic Awareness

Date:

Trainer:

Contact Information:

Objectives

In this workshop, participants will:

- gain understanding of phonological and phonemic awareness;
- acquire strategies for teaching phonological and phonemic awareness; and
- collect ideas for using chants, fingerplays, poetry, rhyming books, and songs to promote phonological and phonemic awareness.

1. Opening Activity: Name Play [10 minutes]

2. Welcome and Logistics [5 minutes]

3. Introducing the Topic: Phonological and Phonemic Awareness [20–30 minutes]

4. Activity: Promoting Phonological and Phonemic Awareness [20–25 minutes]

5. Discussion [10 minutes]

6. Closure [10 minutes]

Agenda for a 1½-Hour Workshop, Part One of a Two-Part Workshop for

Workshop 5: Creating Environments to Support Literacy

Date:

Trainer:

Contact Information:

Objectives
In this workshop, participants will:
- gain a deeper understanding of how to plan and set up preschool and kindergarten learning environments that support emergent literacy and foster active learning; and
- acquire strategies for creating developmentally appropriate print-rich environments that facilitate meaningful learning, support diversity, and promote literacy development.

1. Opening Activity: Focusing on the Literacy Environment [10 minutes]

2. Welcome and Logistics [5 minutes]

3. Introducing the Topic: Creating Environments to Support Literacy [40–45 minutes]

4. Activity: Print Has a Purpose [15–20 minutes]

5. Discussion [10–15 minutes]

Agenda for a 1½-Hour Workshop, Part Two of a Two-Part Workshop for

Workshop 5: Creating Environments to Support Literacy

Date: _____

Trainer: _____

Contact Information: _____

Objectives

In this workshop, participants will:

■ gain a deeper understanding of how to plan and set up preschool and kindergarten learning environments that support emergent literacy and foster active learning; and

■ collect ideas for literacy materials, props, and ideas to enhance learning centers.

1. Welcome and Logistics (5 minutes)

2. Activity: Infusing Literacy in Centers [20–25 minutes]

3. Discussion [10–15 minutes]

4. Activity: Dramatic Play Themes to Support Literacy [30–35 minutes]

5. Discussion [5–10 minutes]

6. Closure: Reflections [10 minutes]

Agenda for 1½-Hour Workshop for

Workshop 6: Supporting Children as Writers

Date: _____

Trainer: _____

Contact Information: _____

Objectives

In this workshop, participants will:

- gain understanding of how children develop as writers;
- identify strategies to promote writing throughout the day;
- explore techniques and materials to encourage children's writing in centers;
- learn that becoming a competent writer involves knowing and understanding the forms, function, and features of writing; and
- understand how writing can be integrated throughout the day and within the environment.

1. Opening Activity: Acrostic Poem [10–15 minutes]

2. Welcome and Logistics [5 minutes]

3. Introducing the Topic: Supporting Children's Writing [30 minutes]

4. Activity: Constructing Knowledge About Writing [30 minutes]

5. Mini-Lecture: Features of Writing

Agenda for 1½-Hour Workshop for

Workshop 7: Using Literacy Centers in Kindergarten

Date: _____

Trainer: _____

Contact Information: _____

Objectives

In this workshop, participants will:

- understand the importance of centers for young children;
- identify ways to promote literacy in centers during choice time and during your scheduled literacy/language arts period; and
- acquire practical tips for making centers successful in kindergarten classrooms.

1. Opening Activity: Pick a Prop [10 minutes]

2. Welcome and Logistics [5 minutes]

3. Introducing the Topic: Literacy Learning Centers in Kindergarten [15–20 minutes]

4. Activity: Literacy Centers Rotation [40 minutes]

5. Discussion [5-10 minutes]

6. Closure [10 minutes]

Agenda for 1½-Hour Workshop for

Workshop 8: Using Music to Support Literacy

Date:

Trainer:

Contact Information:

Objectives

In this workshop, participants will:

■ gain understanding of how music supports literacy learning;

■ acquire strategies for supporting literacy with musical activities throughout the day; and

■ learn how to support children's expressive and receptive language development by creating new words and themes for familiar songs.

1. Opening Activity: Music Is a Part of Our Lives [5 minutes]

2. Welcome and Logistics [5 minutes]

3. Introducing the Topic: Using Music to Support Literacy [20-30 minutes]

4. Activity: Creating Music Picture Books [25–30 minutes]

5. Discussion [5–10 minutes]

6. Closure [10 minutes]

Agenda for a 1½-Hour Workshop, Part One of a Two-Part Workshop for

Workshop 9: Literacy to Support Diversity and Inclusion

Date:

Trainer:

Contact Information:

Objectives

In this workshop, participants will:

- explore and share their ethnic and cultural backgrounds and family histories using children's books and other literacy materials;
- gain an understanding of how to incorporate families into the literacy curriculum;
- discuss how to support diversity with literacy experiences;
- learn about the range of special needs in children and the meaning of inclusion;
- acquire strategies to help children express, share, and celebrate their own uniqueness and commonalities; and
- analyze children's books for bias and stereotypes.

1. Opening Activity: Family Memories [20 minutes]

2. Welcome and Logistics [5 minutes]

3. Introducing the Topic: Diversity, Inclusion, and Their Links to Literacy [25-35 minutes]

4. Activity: Analyzing Books for Bias [25-35 minutes]

5. Discussion [10 minutes]

Agenda a 1½-Hour Workshop, Part Two of a Two-Part Workshop for

Workshop 9: Literacy to Support Diversity and Inclusion

Date: _____

Trainer: _____

Contact Information: _____

Objectives

In this workshop, participants will:

■ explore and share their ethnic and cultural backgrounds and family histories using children's books and other literacy materials;

■ gain an understanding of how to incorporate families into the literacy curriculum;

■ discuss how to support diversity with literacy experiences;

■ learn about the range of special needs in children and the meaning of inclusion;

■ acquire strategies to help children express, share, and celebrate their own uniqueness and commonalities; and

■ analyze children's books for bias and stereotypes.

1. Opening Activity: Brief Review of Part One of the Workshop [10-15 minutes]

2. Welcome and Logistics [5 minutes]

3. Activity: Family Questionnaire [35–45 minutes]

4. Discussion [10-15 minutes]

5. Closure: Reflections on Using Literacy to Support Diversity and Inclusion [10 minutes]

Agenda for 1½-Hour Workshop for

Workshop 10: Literacy Across the Curriculum

Date:

Trainer:

Contact Information:

O b j e c t i v e s

In this workshop, participants will:

- ■ learn ideas for teaching literacy while simultaneously addressing content across many subject areas;
- ■ use a planning web to support teaching literacy across the curriculum; and
- ■ develop practical lesson plans to use in their classrooms.

1. Opening Activity: Collections [15– 20 minutes]

2. Welcome and Logistics [3–5 minutes]

3. Introducing the Topic: Literacy Across the Curriculum [15–20 minutes]

4. Activity: Content or Concepts [30–35 minutes]

5. Discussion [5 minutes]

6. Closure [5 minutes]

Appendix G

Workshop 1

SLIDE 1

WELCOME TO TODAY'S WORKSHOP

Fostering Language Development

The Essential
Literacy
WORKSHOP
BOOK

WORKSHOP 1   Gryphon House grants permission for this PowerPoint presentation to be used by professionals using *The Essential Literacy Workshop Book*.

SLIDE 2

Fostering Language Development

■ **Learning language is a thinking process.**
  ◆ Children work at figuring out the rules of language.
  ◆ Appreciating how children are hypothesizing about language motivates them to keep learning language.

■ **Language development is the first step toward literacy.**
  ◆ Language development makes reading and writing possible.
  ◆ Children need vocabulary to comprehend written language.
  ◆ Knowing the patterns and sequences of language supports comprehension.

The Essential
Literacy
WORKSHOP
BOOK

WORKSHOP 1

How Children Acquire Language

- Language learning is innate for humans.
- The environment and interactions have a significant impact on children's language development.
- Children learn by "creating" language.
- Children learn language through play.
- It is important to encourage children to use and develop their native language.

The Essential
Literacy
WORKSHOP
BOOK

WORKSHOP 1

Using Fanciful Language

- **Step 1: Write a vignette (with your group)**
  - Write a two- to three-sentence vignette describing what a child is doing (and possibly saying) at the center or during the routine indicated on the back of your Vocabulary Assignment Sheet. Record it on an index card.
- **Step 2: Exchange vignettes**
  - Pass your group's vignette to another group.
  - Read and discuss the vignette you receive.
  - Review the vocabulary chart that relates to the center discussed in the vignette.
- **Step 3: Role-play a conversation between a teacher and a child**
  - With a partner, take turns role-playing a conversation based on your vignette. (One person is the teacher, the other is the child.)
  - The partner playing the role of the teacher should use new and fanciful vocabulary words from the chart in the conversation.
  - Switch roles.

The Essential
Literacy
WORKSHOP
BOOK

WORKSHOP 1

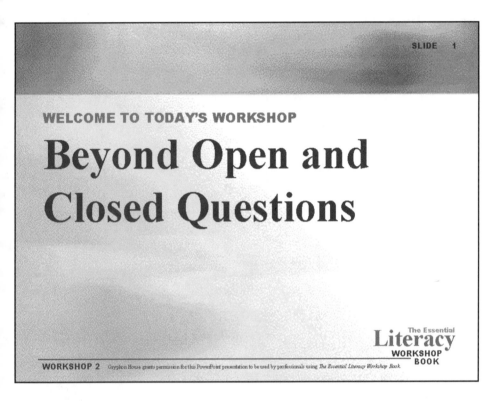

WELCOME TO TODAY'S WORKSHOP

Beyond Open and Closed Questions

SLIDE 1

Literacy
The Essential
WORKSHOP
BOOK

WORKSHOP 2 Gryphon House grants permission for this PowerPoint presentation to be used by professionals using *The Essential Literacy Workshop Book*.

SLIDE 2

How Teachers Talk to Children

- **Procedural**
  - Giving directions and managing behavior

- **Informational**
  - Stating facts and answering questions

- **Praise or reprimand**
  - Acknowledging children's actions

- **Questions**
  - Inviting children to talk
    - Closed questions
    - Open-ended questions

(Glickman, Gordon, & Ross-Gordon 1998)

Literacy
The Essential
WORKSHOP
BOOK

WORKSHOP 2

SLIDE 3

Bloom's Taxonomy of Educational Objectives

■ **Six Major Cognitive Operations**

■ **Lower-Level Thinking Processes**

L-1 Knowledge—Information gathering

These are questions that check the basic facts about people, places, or things.

L-2 Comprehension—Confirming

These are questions that check understanding and memory of facts.

(Bloom 1956)

The Essential
Literacy
WORKSHOP
BOOK

SLIDE 4

Bloom's Taxonomy of Educational Objectives

■ **Higher-Level Thinking Processes**

L-3 Application—Illuminating

Application questions test the ability to use knowledge in a practical, problem-solving manner.

L-4 Analysis—Pulling apart of pieces

These are questions that select, examine, and break apart information into its smaller, separate parts.

L-5 Synthesis—Creating

Synthesis questions utilize the basic information in a new, original, or unique way.

L-6 Evaluation—Judging, predicting

Evaluation questions determine the value of information, including making judgments about the information.

(Bloom 1956)

The Essential
Literacy
WORKSHOP
BOOK

SLIDE 5

Creative Questioning

- Ask open-ended questions.

- Ask children to use their senses.

- Ask children about changes.

- Ask questions with many answers.

- Ask "What would happen if…" questions.

- Ask "In how many different ways…" questions.

The Essential
Literacy
WORKSHOP
BOOK

WORKSHOP 2

SLIDE 1

WELCOME TO TODAY'S WORKSHOP

Supporting English Language Learners

Literacy
The Essential
WORKSHOP
BOOK

WORKSHOP 3   Gryphon House grants permission for this PowerPoint presentation to be used by professionals using *The Essential Literacy Workshop Book*.

SLIDE 2

Demographics

- Over the past two decades, the percentage of school-age children speaking a language other than English at home has nearly doubled.

- By the year 2010, more than 30% of all school-age children will come from U.S. homes in which the primary language is not English.

- 2005 Annie E. Casey Kids Count Data reported that 19% of U.S. children speak a language other than English at home.

The Annie E. Casey Foundation KIDS COUNT State-Level Data Online (2005).

Literacy
The Essential
WORKSHOP
BOOK

WORKSHOP 3

Demographics *(continued)*

- Over 300 languages are spoken by English language learners coming to school, including:

Spanish	Portuguese
Mandarin	Hindi
Urdu	Japanese
Arabic	Russian
Polish	French
Hungarian	Gujarati
Haitian Creole	Korean
Vietnamese	Tagalog

The Essential
Literacy
WORKSHOP
BOOK

WORKSHOP 3

Literacy Achievement

- 38% of 4th graders in the United States scored below proficient reading level in 2005. Following are data from specific states:

CA = 50%	NV = 48%	TX = 36%
IL = 38%	FL = 35%	NY = 31%

- Compare the above percentages with the number of school-age children who speak a language other than English at home.

CA = 43%	NV = 28%	TX = 31%
IL = 21%	FL = 24%	NY = 26%

The Annie E. Casey Foundation, KIDS COUNT State-Level Data Online www.kidscount.org

The Essential
Literacy
WORKSHOP
BOOK

WORKSHOP 3

SLIDE 5

Achievement Gap

Children who speak a non-English language at home

and children of Hispanic/Latino backgrounds

are at significantly greater risk

of reading difficulties and subsequent

academic underachievement.

(Snow, Burns, & Griffin 1998)

The Essential
Literacy
WORKSHOP
BOOK

WORKSHOP 3

SLIDE 6

Language as a Foundation for Learning to Read

"Excellent literacy instruction in multilingual settings may be possible only if children's home languages are taken into account in designing instruction."

—National Reading Council, 1998

"Oral and written language experiences should be regarded as an additive process, ensuring that children maintain their home language while also learning to speak and read in English."

—International Reading Association, 1998

The Essential
Literacy
WORKSHOP
BOOK

WORKSHOP 3

How Are These Children Being Taught?

Decades of research documents academic and social benefits from having strong home language and cultural foundation.
(Garcia 1993; Tabors 1997; Espinosa & Burns 2003; NAEYC 1996; Ordonez-Jasis & Ortiz 2006)

However, many programs throughout the United States that serve English language learners focus on English learning rather than on the maintenance of children's primary language. Attention to culture is often superficial and "touristy."

The Essential
Literacy
WORKSHOP
BOOK

WORKSHOP 3

Why Support a Home Language?

■ All children are cognitively, linguistically, and emotionally connected to the language of their homes.

■ Children are more likely to become readers and writers of English when they are already familiar with the vocabulary, grammar, and concepts (for example, colors, shapes, weather, time, family, and so on) in their primary language.

■ Experiences with their own language allow children to develop phonemic awareness and other oral language skills, which predict later reading success.

■ Many early literacy and other cognitive skills transfer from one language to another. Children literate in their first language will apply these skills to the second language.

The Essential
Literacy
WORKSHOP
BOOK

WORKSHOP 3

SLIDE 9

How Can We Support ELLs in Our Classrooms?

■ Approach learning and language from a linguistic as well as a multicultural perspective.

■ This perspective enables children to value and appreciate their cultural identity, to feel secure about their home language, and to respect the diversity of other children and adults.

Literacy
The Essential
WORKSHOP
BOOK

WORKSHOP 3

SLIDE 10

Bilingual Children

Children acquire language within a variety of cultural and linguistic settings and in the context of their homes and communities.

(Tabors 1997, Hart & Risley 1999)

Literacy
The Essential
WORKSHOP
BOOK

WORKSHOP 3

Language Development

English language learners:

* exhibit the same language milestones as children whose home language is English;
* may acquire vocabulary at a slower rate and have limited total vocabularies in each language; and
* have a combined vocabulary in both languages likely to equal or exceed that of the English language-only child.

All children develop language in direct relation to:

* the number and variety of words spoken to a child; and
* opportunities to use language to interact with adults and other children.

Literacy
The Essential
WORKSHOP
BOOK

WORKSHOP 3

Learning a Second Language: Developmental Sequence

There will be differences in the way children progress in learning a second language.

English language learners:

1. Use their home language.
2. Go through a nonverbal period.
3. Use individual words and phrases in a new language, and some children will switch between languages.
4. Begin to develop productive use of the second language.

(Tabors 1997)

Literacy
The Essential
WORKSHOP
BOOK

WORKSHOP 3

Where to Start

- Gather information about the cultural and linguistic backgrounds of the children in your classroom.

- Accomplish this through:
  - formal questionnaires;
  - informal discussions with family members;
  - telephone calls home; and
  - discussions with others (teachers, staff, community) from the same cultural and linguistic backgrounds.

- Reflect on your own culture, attitudes, and biases.

Literacy
The Essential
WORKSHOP
BOOK

WORKSHOP 3

Remember...

- Teacher expectations significantly influence the quality of children's learning opportunities.

- Teachers who have low expectations for children are not confident that they can teach those children, and as a result may attribute children's failures to lack of intellect and deficient home lives.

- Teachers with strong self-confidence and feelings of efficacy in their teaching abilities have high expectations for all children.

Literacy
The Essential
WORKSHOP
BOOK

WORKSHOP 3

SLIDE 15

Instruction begins when you, the teacher,

learn from the learner; put yourself in his place

so that you may understand... what he learns

and the way he understands it.

—Soren Kierkegaard (1813-1855)

The Essential
Literacy
WORKSHOP
BOOK

WORKSHOP 3

SLIDE 1

WELCOME TO TODAY'S WORKSHOP

Phonological Awareness and Phonemic Awareness

WORKSHOP 4   Gryphon House grants permission for this PowerPoint presentation to be used by professionals using *The Essential Literacy Workshop Book*.

Literacy The Essential
WORKSHOP BOOK

SLIDE 2

Name Play

Create alliterative phrases for your names.

Work together.

Use a marker to write the alliterative phrase for your name on your name tent.

Literacy The Essential
WORKSHOP BOOK

WORKSHOP 4

SLIDE 3

Phonological Awareness

Hearing the sounds in spoken language is a listening skill.

A child with phonological awareness can:

- identify and make oral rhymes:
  dip, sip, lip, glip
  mat, sat, cat, hat

- hear, identify, and play with the sounds in words:
  sun, sit, and song (all begin with the /s/ sound)
  bite, dot, and sit (all end with the /t/ sound)
  dust, dog, dig, and stop (ask which word doesn't fit and why)

- hear the syllables in words:
  Clap for each sound in your name ("Ra-shan").
  Snap for each sound in umbrella (um-brell-a).

The Essential
Literacy
WORKSHOP
BOOK

WORKSHOP 4

SLIDE 4

Phonological Awareness

To support children's development of phonological awareness:

■ use songs, rhyming games, nursery rhymes, and rhyming poetry;

■ play syllable clapping games;

■ play games with the sounds in words (for example, group objects by their beginning sounds, ask which word doesn't fit, and so on);

■ talk with children about words and sounds in everyday situations; and

■ choose read-aloud books that focus on sounds.

The Essential
Literacy
WORKSHOP
BOOK

WORKSHOP 4

Phonemic Awareness

Phonemic awareness is a more advanced phonological awareness skill.

A child with phonemic awareness can hear, identify, and manipulate individual sounds (phonemes) in spoken words, such as:

* "bug" has three sounds (/b/ /u/ and /g/);
* add the /l/ sound to "ate" to make the word "late"; and
* take away the /t/ sound from "train" to get the word "rain."

Phonemic awareness is an important step toward understanding the alphabetic principle: Words are composed of letters, and each letter in a printed word is connected to a spoken sound.

Phonemic awareness is associating the letter symbol with the sound it makes; it is different from phonics.

Literacy The Essential
WORKSHOP BOOK

WORKSHOP 4

Supporting Phonemic Awareness

To support children's development of phonemic awareness:
- use songs, chants, fingerplays, rhyming games, nursery rhymes, and rhyming poetry.

- play games that ask children to listen for beginning and ending sounds, such as
  * "If your name begins with the same sound as Ryan's, you may line up to go outside."
  * "Let's find all of the things in our classroom that begin with the same sound as 'soup'."

- play "What Is Left When We..."
  * "What is left when we take the /s/ sound away from 'smile'?"
  * "What is left when we take the /n/ sound away from 'moon'?"

- play games where children segment and blend the sounds in words. For example:
  * "The letters 'st' + 'op' make 'stop'. Without the 'st', it would be 'op'."

Literacy The Essential
WORKSHOP BOOK

WORKSHOP 4

Fuzzy Wuzzy (Traditional)
Fuzzy Wuzzy was a bear.
Fuzzy Wuzzy lost his hair.
Then Fuzzy Wuzzy wasn't fuzzy,
Was he?

Literacy
The Essential
WORKSHOP
BOOK

WORKSHOP 4

Poetry Activity

Choose a poem from one of your collections.

Write the poem on a chart so it supports what you want to teach children about the sounds of language and words.

Include a few picture clues to help children "read" the poem.

Develop a plan for different ways children can repeat recitations, using strategies from Handout 4.4 or other ideas.

Brainstorm different times of the day when you might chant the poem with children.

Prepare to present a creative recitation to the whole group.

Literacy
The Essential
WORKSHOP
BOOK

WORKSHOP 4

SLIDE 9

Phonological and Phonemic Awareness Games

Review and discuss the ideas for games on the handout.

Try each of the games and come up with additional ideas. Practice by alternating between playing the roles of teacher and children.

Think of ways to extend one or two games so children who are ready can begin to learn letter names and their corresponding sounds (phonics).

Prepare to share ideas for one game.

The Essential
Literacy
WORKSHOP
BOOK

WORKSHOP 4

SLIDE 1

WELCOME TO TODAY'S WORKSHOP

Creating Environments to Support Literacy

Literacy
The Essential
WORKSHOP
BOOK

WORKSHOP 5   Gryphon House grants permission for this PowerPoint presentation to be used by professionals using *The Essential Literacy Workshop Book.*

SLIDE 2

Good Environments Promote Literacy

Arrange classrooms so children can:

* Construct meaning through firsthand activities that support the use of language.
* Develop awareness of the purpose and function of print.
* Use language, speaking, listening, reading, and writing in connection with their interactions with the learning environment, materials, peers, and teachers.
* Use language to share information and opinions, to persuade others, and to solve problems.
* Talk to others about their ideas and questions, elaborate on experiences, and clarify their thinking.
* Feel successful as they learn new skills, vocabulary, and knowledge.

(Seefeldt & Galper 2001)

Literacy
The Essential
WORKSHOP
BOOK

WORKSHOP 5

A Good Learning Environment

A good learning environment
encourages children to feel successful
and builds self-confidence.

Literacy The Essential
WORKSHOP
BOOK

Developing a Literacy-Rich Play Environment

1. Infuse the learning environment to support literacy-rich play. The four major functions of written language:
   - environmental
   - occupational
   - informational
   - recreational

2. Establish a print-rich learning environment.
3. Establish at least one classroom literacy center.
4. Provide books and varied writing materials in many centers.
5. Introduce literacy props based on familiar experiences to centers.
6. Start a collection of literacy materials.

(Owocki 1999; Morrow 2002)

Literacy The Essential
WORKSHOP
BOOK

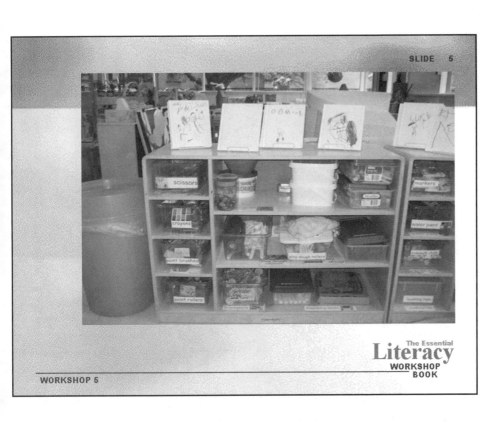

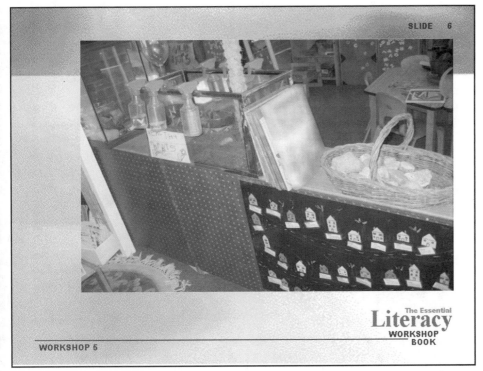

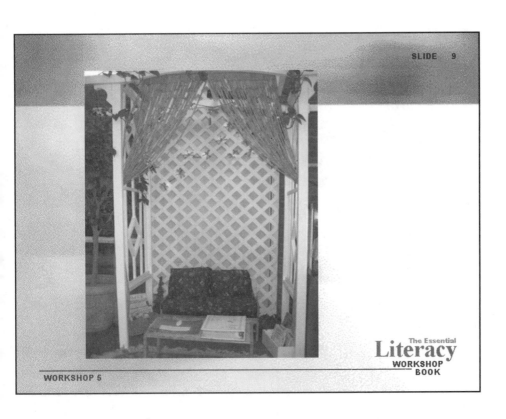

SLIDE 9

WORKSHOP 5

The Essential
Literacy
WORKSHOP
BOOK

SLIDE 10

WORKSHOP 5

The Essential
Literacy
WORKSHOP
BOOK

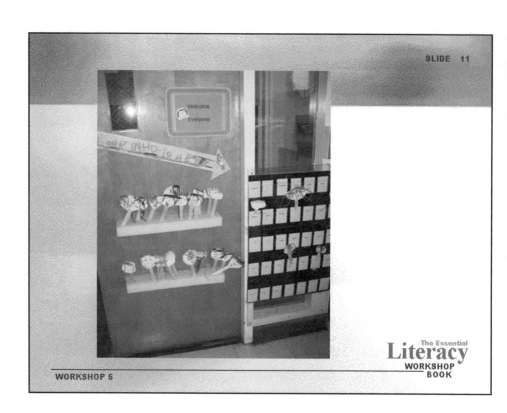

SLIDE 11

WORKSHOP 5

The Essential
Literacy
WORKSHOP
BOOK

SLIDE 12

Activity: Dramatic Play Themed Centers

Instructions

1. How will this theme be introduced?

2. How will you motivate children's interest in this theme and ensure that they have the necessary experience to support their play?

3. What materials will be added?

4. How will the theme be organized?

5. What roles are there for the children to play and how can you support children's literacy learning in this play center?

The Essential
Literacy
WORKSHOP
BOOK

WORKSHOP 5

SLIDE 13

Reflection

Good teachers continually self-evaluate and reflect on their role in facilitating literacy through active learning.

- Do the children in my class read and write during play?

- Are materials meaningful?

- Do I take time to capitalize on teachable moments?

- What functions does literacy serve in the children's play?

- Are the children exploring a variety of genres and forms of written language?

- Do the children have the materials they need to explore the features of print?

The Essential
Literacy
WORKSHOP
BOOK

WORKSHOP 5

SLIDE 1

WELCOME TO TODAY'S WORKSHOP

Supporting Children as Writers

The Essential
Literacy
WORKSHOP BOOK

WORKSHOP 6   Gryphon House grants permission for this PowerPoint presentation to be used by professionals using *The Essential Literacy Workshop Book*.

SLIDE 2

Children Want to Write

Children want to write.
They have been writing since
they could first grasp a tool
that makes a mark.
Before they came to your classroom,
they wrote on driveways, sidewalks, walls,
mirrors, cabinets, books, and paper
with crayons, markers, chalk, pens, pencils, or lipstick.
A child's scribbles, symbols, and lines
convey his or her sense of being.
"I did this. I was here. I am me."

The Essential
Literacy
WORKSHOP BOOK

WORKSHOP 6

SLIDE 3

Categories and Stages of Children's Writing

Marks and Scribbles

Scribble Writing

Letter-Like Forms and Individual Letters

Letter Strings and My Name

Invented Spelling

Conventional Forms

Literacy
The Essential
WORKSHOP
BOOK

WORKSHOP 6

SLIDE 4

Marks and Scribbles

At 17 months, Madison is beginning to make her mark on the world.

Literacy
The Essential
WORKSHOP
BOOK

WORKSHOP 6

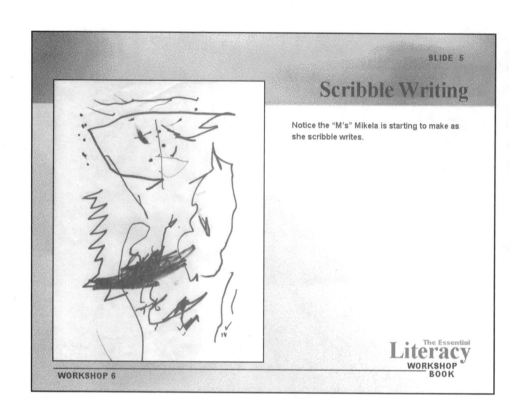

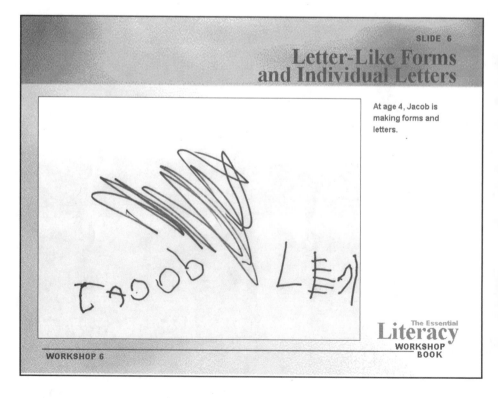

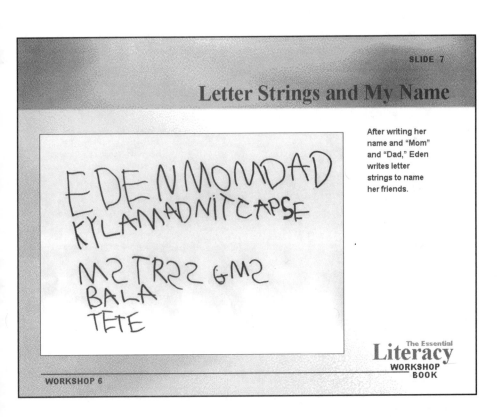

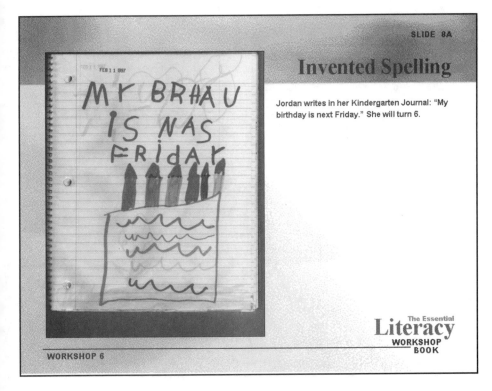

SLIDE 8B

Invented Spelling

Spelling progresses as children gain more letter sound recognition and sight words.

Dear Mrs. Forbes,
I am going to Florida and Rhode Island too. Jordan will see you and I might see you in school again. I got new shoes. They are black and they are sparkles.
Love, Alexa

The Essential
Literacy
WORKSHOP
BOOK

WORKSHOP 6

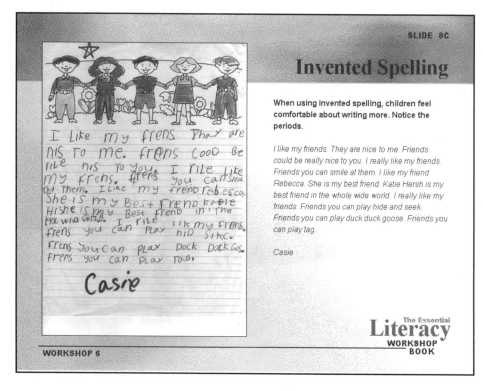

SLIDE 8C

Invented Spelling

When using invented spelling, children feel comfortable about writing more. Notice the periods.

I like my friends. They are nice to me. Friends could be really nice to you. I really like my friends. Friends you can smile at them. I like my friend Rebecca. She is my best friend. Katie Hersh is my best friend in the whole wide world. I really like my friends. Friends you can play hide and seek. Friends you can play duck duck goose. Friends you can play tag.

Casie

The Essential
Literacy
WORKSHOP
BOOK

WORKSHOP 6

Conventional Forms

Dear tooth Fariy,
How are you? I lost another molar! Today I went on a plane all by my self! I am staying at my aunts house. Well see you next time I loose a tooth. Bye Bye.

Love,
Alexa ♡

It is always helpful to use conventional spelling and form when writing a letter to the Tooth Fairy!

The Essential
Literacy
WORKSHOP BOOK

WORKSHOP 6

Why I Write

Brooke on Writing

Everybody has to write. You need to write so you can get along in the world. There's lots of things to write like stories, songs, poems, jokes, riddles, information, cards, letters, emails, text messages, journals, diaries, instructions, grocery lists, checks, signs, labels, or just a note to someone. You have to think about what you are writing, because writing is different for different things. If you are writing a sign or instructions or a grocery list, then you have to write what it is, but when you write a story or a poem, you write what you want to write. You get to use your imagination or to express feelings. Some things like lists or recipes don't have to be in complete sentences but when you write a story, you have to use sentences and paragraphs.

When I start to write a story, I think about what should I say first, how should I start off, and sometimes I think what would be the best way to start and end my story. I have always wanted to get stories out of my mind. I want to be an author because if I was an author then the things I write about to express me would be shown to the world. Writing is a very fun thing. You can write about an adventure that a Hamburger had or you could write about friendship. I love writing very much because it makes me be creative and think about my readers.

—Brooke Ramsier, age 11

The Essential
Literacy
WORKSHOP BOOK

WORKSHOP 6

Significant Features of Written Language

Letters and words convey meaning.

Objects can be represented by print.

What is said can be written. What is written is read the same way, always.

There is a right way to write.

Letters form words and are written in a line.

Letters make sounds.

Words have a beginning and an end; words together make sentences.

The Essential
Literacy
WORKSHOP
BOOK

WORKSHOP 6

Suggestions to Support Writing

- Provide a variety of useful writing and drawing materials in all centers.
- Anticipate various emergent forms of writing.
- Encourage children to write their own way.
- Invite children to write or dictate a story.
- Encourage children to write to one another.
- Accept children's additions to your writing.
- Display and send home samples of children's writings.
- Listen to children "read" their writing.
- Make encouraging and specific comments.
- Model the usefulness of writing.
- Make your writing strategies explicit.
- Notice environmental print.
- Encourage children to write.
- Provide opportunities and materials for book-making.
- Relate meaningful writing experiences to projects and themes.
- Create a Writing Center and vary the materials in it.
- Carefully observe children's writing. Knowing where children are in their thinking enables you to support them based on their current levels of development.

The Essential
Literacy
WORKSHOP
BOOK

WORKSHOP 6

SLIDE   1

WELCOME TO TODAY'S WORKSHOP

Using Literacy Centers in Kindergarten

Arrival Activity: Pick a Prop
- Select a prop from the prop table and take it with you to your table.
- Use the prop as a metaphor to finish this sentence:
  "My role as a teacher is like a ___(your prop)___ because ___(your explanation)___."

Literacy
The Essential
WORKSHOP
BOOK

WORKSHOP 7   Gryphon House grants permission for this PowerPoint presentation to be used by professionals using *The Essential Literacy Workshop Book.*

SLIDE   2

Literacy Learning in Kindergarten Centers

- **Why are centers important for young children?**
  - Center-based learning responds to how young children think and learn. Effective centers:
    - offer purposeful, hands-on, active learning;
    - engage children in thinking and problem-solving;
    - allow for decision-making and choice;
    - are open-ended and responsive to different levels of learners; and
    - allow children to work independently, collaboratively, and successfully.

- **Use learning centers and literacy-focused centers to promote literacy learning.**
  - Include a portion of each day for children to choose learning centers.
  - Use focused literacy centers during a literacy block so children can work independently while the teacher works with small groups.

Literacy
The Essential
WORKSHOP
BOOK

WORKSHOP 7

SLIDE 3

Tips for Successful Centers

- At the beginning of the year, have fewer centers and keep them simple until children learn the routines.
- Establish predictable times on the schedule for centers so children can anticipate when and for how long they can work.
- Teach children predictable routines for working in centers.
- Use morning circle time or meeting to teach routines.
- Think carefully about the materials you include in centers.
- Teach children the proper care and use of materials.
- Teach children procedures for getting, cleaning up, and storing materials.
- Label materials in storage bins with words and pictures so they are easy for children to take from and return to shelves.

Literacy
The Essential
WORKSHOP
BOOK

WORKSHOP 7

SLIDE 4

Tips for Successful Centers *(continued)*

- Establish a clear system for making choices and moving through centers and teach it to children.
- Use a planning board or choice chart for children to choose centers.
- Establish procedures for children and teachers to keep track of children's choices.
- Vary the materials in centers to keep children interested.
- Observe children at work; if a center is not working well, talk with children and encourage them to help determine necessary changes.
- Ensure that there is room in each center for three to five children, depending on the center.
- Use a checklist or other record-keeping method for centers so you can keep track of where children go.

Literacy
The Essential
WORKSHOP
BOOK

WORKSHOP 7

SLIDE 5

Discussion: Literacy Centers Rotation

As you describe your center activity to others in your group, discuss the following questions:

■ What were some qualities of the center activities that you found valuable?

■ What were some of the specific decisions and choices you made to accomplish tasks at the centers?

■ How did the activities in each center address the diverse skill levels of learners?

The Essential
Literacy
WORKSHOP
BOOK

WORKSHOP 7

SLIDE 6

Extending Literacy Centers

Collaborate with others at your table.

Choose one center from the previous activity to focus on first.

Identify two or three ways you can extend or adapt the activity.

Keep in mind:
■ the standards addressed by the activity;
■ decisions and choices children can make;
■ different levels of learners; and
■ demonstrating the activity to children so that they can work independently.

If you have time, reflect on a second center.

The Essential
Literacy
WORKSHOP
BOOK

WORKSHOP 7

365

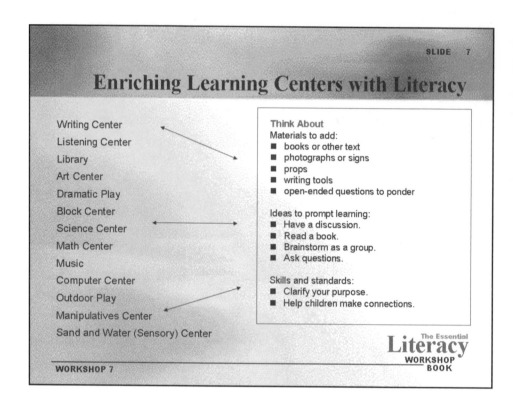

SLIDE 1

WELCOME TO TODAY'S WORKSHOP

Using Music to Support Literacy

Please add your ideas
to the three charts
posted around the room.

The Essential
Literacy
WORKSHOP
BOOK

WORKSHOP 8   Gryphon House grants permission for this PowerPoint presentation to be used by professionals using *The Essential Literacy Workshop Book*.

SLIDE 2

Musical Intelligence

Of the eight multiple intelligences
described in his book, *Frames of Mind,*
Howard Gardner said that
the EARLIEST to emerge in children is
Musical Intelligence.

(Gardner 1983)

The Essential
Literacy
WORKSHOP
BOOK

WORKSHOP 8

Inventing Music

All children should have opportunities to invent music and lyrics in order to develop their vocabularies by:

* singing songs from a variety of genres and cultures;
* singing familiar and new songs; and
* making up their own songs.

Early experiences "playing" with musical lyrics supports children's comfort with creating:

* poetry;
* prose;
* rhymes; and
* rhythms.

The Essential
Literacy
WORKSHOP
BOOK

WORKSHOP 8

Responding to Music

All children should have opportunities to respond to music in order to develop their listening skills, vocabulary, and phonological awareness as they focus on the rhythms, words, and melodies they hear:

* using their bodies (clapping, dancing);
* using rhythm instruments (including commercially made instruments and those made by teachers and children);
* using props (scarves, puppets, and so on); and
* using words ("This song makes me feel _____.").

The Essential
Literacy
WORKSHOP
BOOK

WORKSHOP 8

SLIDE 5

Listen to and Enjoy Music

All children should have opportunities to listen to and enjoy music that helps them relax, laugh, and, at the same time, attend.

■ Example of relaxing music

■ Example of music that supports laughter

■ Example of music that helps children pay attention

WORKSHOP 8

SLIDE 6

Directions for Activity:
Creating Music Picture Books

■ Read your group's assignment.
■ Sing the first verse of your tune to make sure everyone is familiar with it.
■ Create new lyrics to the song; the lyrics must connect to your assigned theme.
■ Each person must write a verse and create a page for your group's book.
■ Use pictures, words, and symbols for your page.
■ After your pages are completed, assemble your book.
■ Decide on a title.
■ Make a cover.

WORKSHOP 8

SLIDE 1

WELCOME TO TODAY'S WORKSHOP

Literacy to Support Diversity and Inclusion

Literacy
The Essential
WORKSHOP
BOOK

WORKSHOP 9   Gryphon House grants permission for this PowerPoint presentation to be used by professionals using *The Essential Literacy Workshop Book*.

SLIDE 2

Who Do We Include in a Definition of Diversity?

- Children from various cultural backgrounds

- Children who are English language learners (non-English speaking or of limited English proficiency)

- Children with learning differences (gifted, learning disabled, ADHD, and so on)

- Children who are at risk

- Children who have physical impairments (visual, hearing, mobility, communication and language disorders)

Literacy
The Essential
WORKSHOP
BOOK

WORKSHOP 9

SLIDE   3

What Is Inclusion?

Inclusion is the right of all children, no matter their diverse abilities, to participate actively in regular classroom settings with typically developing children.

It involves:
- bringing support services to children wherever possible rather than taking them out of the classroom;

- the belief that this experience is beneficial for typically developing children and their families, as well as for children with special needs and their families; and

- legal mandates that include ADA, IDEA, and IFSPs or IEPs.

The Essential
Literacy
WORKSHOP
BOOK

WORKSHOP 9

SLIDE   4

Linking Diversity, Inclusion, and Literacy

- Every child is a unique individual.

- Identifying each child's special needs is the teacher's first step in supporting diversity.

- When we respect children's diverse backgrounds and abilities, we support their self-image.

- Meaningful conversations and activities involving children's identity, home, and family are critical components in supporting literacy skills.

The Essential
Literacy
WORKSHOP
BOOK

WORKSHOP 9

SLIDE 5

Guidelines for Selecting Diversity/Inclusion Books for Classroom Libraries

- Children can get to know and love characters who are different than they are. They have an opportunity to get to know children and families they would not ordinarily meet.

- Some books should include characters who reflect the individuals in the classroom population.

- Books should be free of bias and stereotyping.

- Make sure to include books about children with special needs.

Literacy
The Essential
WORKSHOP
BOOK

WORKSHOP 9

SLIDE 6

Analyzing Children's Books for Bias

1. Analyze the illustrations.

2. Analyze the story line.

3. Look at the lifestyles.

4. Weigh the relationships among people.

5. Note the heroes.

6. Consider the effects on a child's self-image.

7. Consider the author's and illustrator's background and perspective.

8. Look at the copyright date.

Literacy
The Essential
WORKSHOP
BOOK

WORKSHOP 9

We Must...

We must. . .

■ recognize that all children are linguistically and emotionally tied to the language and culture of their homes;

■ understand that children demonstrate their knowledge and capabilities in many different ways;

■ involve families in their children's literacy development;

■ learn about children's home and family life; and

■ incorporate diverse languages and perspectives into our classroom literacy environment as we create and support opportunities for reading, writing, listening, speaking, and viewing.

The Essential
Literacy
WORKSHOP
BOOK

WORKSHOP 9

Instructions for Activity:
Linking Family Puppet and Literacy

1. Identify one person in the group to be the scribe.
2. The scribe makes three columns on the chart paper.
3. In column one, list the name of each person's family puppet.
4. In column two, next to each family puppet's name, identify a book, song, or poem that relates to the puppet. (You do not have to identify the author if you use a book.)
5. In column three, identify a center where children might play with the puppet.
6. Each group completes one chart.
7. When finished, hang your charts on the wall.

Example:

Name of puppet	Book/Poem/Song	Center
Uncle Bob, construction worker	*Freight Train* by Donald Crews or *Changes, Changes* by Pat Hutchins	Block Center or woodworking table

The Essential
Literacy
WORKSHOP
BOOK

WORKSHOP 9

SLIDE 1

WELCOME TO TODAY'S WORKSHOP

Literacy Across the Curriculum

The Essential
Literacy
WORKSHOP
BOOK

WORKSHOP 10 Gryphon House grants permission for this PowerPoint presentation to be used by professionals using *The Essential Literacy Workshop Book*.

SLIDE 2

Collection Directions

1. Dump your collection in the middle of the table.

2. Play with your collection!

3. Write down the different words your group uses to describe the objects in your collection.

The Essential
Literacy
WORKSHOP
BOOK

WORKSHOP 10

SLIDE 3

Two Minutes–Two People

Our collection was:

Two ways we used our collection were:

Skills and concepts we explored while playing included:

The Essential
Literacy
WORKSHOP
BOOK

WORKSHOP 10

SLIDE 4

Literacy Across the Curriculum

■ Help children become experts.

■ Think about essential learning.

■ Use literacy experiences to help children make meaningful connections.

   ♦ Start with a book and extend it to other subjects.

   ♦ Start with a subject-related content or concept and connect it to literacy.

   ♦ Start with a theme and make literacy connections and subject area connections.

The Essential
Literacy
WORKSHOP
BOOK

WORKSHOP 10

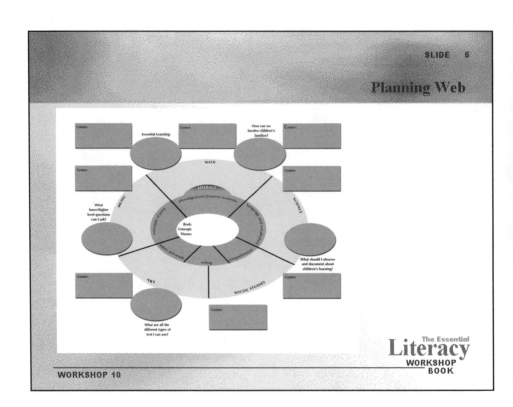

SLIDE 5

Planning Web

WORKSHOP 10

The Essential
Literacy
WORKSHOP
BOOK

SLIDE 6

Responding to the Book

Discuss two questions.

1. What are some of the ways children might respond to this story?

2. What is the essential learning that children can take away from this story and what are some experiences that extend the story?

WORKSHOP 10

The Essential
Literacy
WORKSHOP
BOOK

Activity: Content/Concept Planning

- Look at your subject-specific content assignment.
- Brainstorm ways you might help children make connections to this content.
- Review the books related to the concept.
- What is the essential learning you want children to acquire related to the content?
- Which books can be most helpful?
- What other literacy connections can you make?
  - What vocabulary opportunities are there?
  - What open-ended questions can you ask?
  - What writing experiences could connect?
  - Do you have ideas for centers?
  - How will you observe and document children's learning?

Everyone in the group should keep track of ideas generated.
- Prepare to share the following:
  - your concept
  - ideas for essential learning
  - 1–2 books you selected
  - a center connection

The Essential
Literacy
WORKSHOP
BOOK

WORKSHOP 10

Theme Brainstorming

Brainstorm ideas for your section of the web.

You will have a few minutes at each chart.

When the timer rings, rotate clockwise to the next chart.

When you come to a new chart, review it and:
- Put a checkmark (√) if you agree with the idea
- Put a question mark (?) if you disagree or have a question
- Add new ideas

When you return to your original chart:
- Note how it has changed
- Prepare to address question marks

The Essential
Literacy
WORKSHOP
BOOK

WORKSHOP 10

377

Children's Books Index

The Essential Literacy Workshop Book

Index